Ritual Masks

Ritual Masks

Deceptions and Revelations

BY

Henry Pernet

Translated by Laura Grillo

Wipf & Stock
PUBLISHERS
Eugene, Oregon

Wipf and Stock Publishers
199 W 8th Ave, Suite 3
Eugene, OR 97401

Ritual Masks
Deceptions and Revelations
By Pernet, Henry
Copyright©1992 by Pernet, Henry
ISBN: 1-59752-585-5
Publication date 3/1/2006
Previously published by University of South Carolina Press, 1992

Contents

Illustrations	vii
Series Editor's Preface	ix
Introduction	1

Part One:
Everywhere and in All Times?
The Universality of the Mask — 7
   Chapter 1: Geography of the Ritual Mask — 9
   Chapter 2: The Age of the Ritual Mask — 23

Part Two:
From the Dead to Cosmos:
What Does the Ritual Mask Represent? — 43
   Chapter 3: Spirit, Event, and World System — 45
   Chapter 4: The Mask, the Dead, and Its Model — 81
   Chapter 5: Mask, Psychoanalysis, and Ambivalence Toward the Dead — 103

Part Three:
The Mask, Its Wearer, and Women — 115
   Chapter 6: The Ritual Mask and Its Wearer — 117
   Chapter 7: The Mask and Women — 136

Conclusion — 159

Bibliography — 167

Index — 195

Illustrations

1. Dancer wearing ornaments and paint — 14
2. The "horned God" or "scorcerer" of Trois-Frères — 25
3. Coitus scene from T-in Lalan — 30
4. Figure of Inahouanrhat — 33
5. Mask of Nahal Hemar — 39
6. Three dancers wearing *sirige* masks — 50
7. *Amma ta* mask — 52
8. *Imina na* mask — 54
9. *Kanaga* mask — 61
10. *Ijele* mask — 65
11. Neo-caledonian mask — 67
12. Mask representing a bear and its *inua* — 73
13. Kwakiutl deer-human mask — 75
14. Baining remodeled skull, New Britain — 83
15. *Jipae* mask — 88
16. *Hevehe* mask — 92
17. Mask of the Mende female society, *sande* — 148

Series Editor's Preface

AMONG THE more intriguing aspects of the study of comparative religions has been the exoticism perceived in cultures that are radically "other" than our own. Perhaps no phenomenon has expressed this sense of otherness better than the ritual mask and its uses. In *Ritual Masks: Deceptions and Revelations*, originally published in French as *Mirages du masque* (Geneva, 1988), Henry Pernet examines closely actual masks and their contexts and uses, in light of which he tests major trends in Western interpretation of them. The author's findings, based on a very extensive analysis of the literature in a variety of languages, are that several of the widely accepted and perpetuated theories of masking are groundless, or at least very limited in application. The author's main conclusions are easily summarized: the mask is not universal, it has not existed in all times, it does not represent principally spirits or the dead, and the mask is not generally used to enable its wearer to "become" what is represented.

In this stimulating essay, which proceeds with remorseless logic and empirical insistence, Pernet does more than expose fallacies and faulty data upon which influential theories have been grounded. He also raises the troubling question of whether Western theories of masking have not reinforced long-lasting assumptions about the "division of the field of study of anthropology and history of religions between primitives and civilized, societies with and without writing." Although the author does not provide a new general theory of ritual masks—he does not think such a task is possible at this time—he does offer a splendidly abrasive critique and clears away much useless prior theorizing on the subject. Further, Henry Pernet's essay is far from being a totally negative statement, for he provides many points and leads—based mostly on African, Native American and Melanesian data—for an improved approach to the ritual mask in comparative research.

Frederick Mathewson Denny

Ritual Masks

Introduction

"The mask is universal; its origin goes back to the dawn of time. It represents a spirit and its wearer becomes the spirit it represents. The mask terrorizes women who flee from it because they believe they are truly dealing with a spirit." These are all familiar affirmations from the literature devoted to masks. Together or independently, these phrases have been repeated so many times that they are now taken to be self-evident. They make up a common core of preconceived ideas on the ritual mask, some dating back several centuries, and belong to our imaginary universe.

Indeed, from at least as early as the sixteenth century, travelers, missionaries, and topographers left descriptions of masking societies which cannot be dismissed. Still, the study of masks did not really begin until the nineteenth century. It was in this period that the first interpretations and general theories on popular European traditions were developing, especially following the work of the Grimm brothers (Jacob, 1785–1863; Wilhelm, 1786–1859) for whom folktales revealed vestiges of beliefs and myths referring to former pagan gods. A short time later, Wilhelm Mannhardt (1831–1880) became interested in the popular religion of his time, especially in that which was observable in rural areas; he gathered numerous documents and brought to light the predominance of a belief in fertility spirits and in the existence of a correspondence between plant life and human life. Under his influence, many masked festivals came to be thought to incorporate ancient beliefs relating to fertility. The masks that played a part in them were therefore interpreted as representing the demons of the plant world.

In the same period, Edward B. Tylor (1832–1917) established the basis for anthropology as a science of man and his culture. It is not his theory of animism that is of interest here but the fact that he was describing the evolution of civilization from the time of the first men—which, in his view, the contemporary "primitives" represented to a very great extent—up to civilized man. To this end, he made use of the comparative method to organize an impressive volume of facts and documents according to his evolutionist perspective. He similarly analyzed the process in which elements belonging to an older stage of evolution survive in later stages where, according to him, they no longer function correctly.

Thus as early as the last quarter of the nineteenth century one finds the different factors that will constitute the essence of the approach to the problem of masks, as much for the study of folklore as for anthropology, until World War II. The first factor is the evolutionist point of view, through which one reconstructs the history of Western society by classifying all known societies according to the degree of civilization they have attained. From this viewpoint, the peoples without writing studied by ethnology enable us to "relive" the stages that Western society underwent thousands of years ago. Also in evidence by this time is the notion of "survival," according to which vestiges of older customs that resisted evolution survived beyond the time in which these customs had their true meaning. A third factor, the intensive use of the comparative method, helped to uncover the original meaning of a custom and to reconstitute the past stages of the evolution of a society under investigation by underscoring what anthropology reports about more "primitive" peoples.

Before the end of the nineteenth century, specialists already had a significant volume of comparative material on masks. In 1883, Adolf Bastian wrote a general study on the role of masks; in 1886, Richard Andree reorganized and summarized documents from the world over and from different ages, making a wide range of material readily accessible by organizing it into categories which would be constantly taken up thereafter. Finally, in 1898, Leo Frobenius published a long article that associated the mask with secret societies whose purpose was to represent the spirits of the dead. At the source of this complex, there was, according to him, a reaction of men against matriarchy, which would explain the fact that women are for the most part excluded from all masking rituals. These theses would influence anthropological and folkloristic studies of the mask for several decades to come.

In a famous article published in 1932–33, Karl Meuli formulated a general theory of primitive masks which he then used to shed light on European traditions. This interpretation comprised a synthesis of theories founded on evolutionism, the notion of survivals, and the comparative method, to which his thesis added the contribution of psychoanalysis. It played an important role in the history of the study of masks holding influence within as well as outside the circle of specialists. (I will return to this several times within the book.) Meuli's article was published, however, at a time when ethnology was gradually abandoning the great theories of the beginning of the century in favor of concentrating attention on localized research, investigated in greater depth and conducted according to more rigorous methods. A similar change in approach took hold a short time later, beginning in the 1940s, in the study of popular traditions.

In both of these cases, the development called into question both the attitude of the researcher in confrontation with the traditions approached and the interpretations accepted up to that time. A consequence of the theory of survivals, for example, was that culture had not been studied as a contemporary phenomenon with its own coherence, but rather as an assemblage whose diverse elements could be interpreted relatively independently from their relation to one another. Critics of the theory nevertheless pointed out that no custom could possibly be a pure survival: since it had survived, it would have also preserved a function in the society in which it is observed. From that time on, studies increasingly would consider each custom as part of a contemporary system, the analysis of which would necessarily bring to light the function that each of its constitutive elements fulfilled. One no longer compared isolated elements but rather, aimed at drawing parallels between systems of relations. Finally, the problem of the continuity of cultures and cultural traits was raised on new grounds, reintroducing the historic dimension into research in place of the notion of survival which, actually, negated history.

The peoples studied by ethnology were thereby reincorporated into their long history, a connection that general theories about "primitives" had tended to obscure. For folklore, taking the historic dimension into consideration tended to make what had previously been considered to be very ancient appear more recent. Thus one notes, for example, that certain Swiss masks whose grimacing expression and monstrous faces were believed to be a measure of their archaism, in fact only dated to the nineteenth century and that their appearance could be traced to the vogue for the exotic that had marked that century and by the knowledge of "primitive" customs, mostly diffused by the missionaries' gazettes, which it incited (Chappaz-Wirthner 1974:85–86). This does not mean that these traditions are not grounded in an extension of more ancient customs, but it does force one to take into account the play of influences and continual changes that touch traditions through the course of history. From then on, ethnologists as well as folklorists would situate their research within its concrete historic context.

But the great theories of the past did not disappear. On the contrary, they gained a certain autonomy in comparison to the contemporary ethnological research and survived for two principal reasons. First, they reflected the imaginary universe of the Westerner, which did not evolve at the same pace as ethnology. This lag favored the survival of outdated conceptions among the public. Second, given the very nature of the evolution within ethnology, no universal explanation of the mask surfaced to replace the theories of the past; therefore, whenever an author needed to express generalities about masks, the simplest solution lay in reiterating the theories of the beginning of the century, with some small and occasional modifications. Examples of this phenomenon abound in books on art, in exposition catalogs, and in popularized works,[1] but also in the work of scholars who, not being specialists and encountering the ritual mask in a study devoted to another

---

1. In its first draft, the bibliography of this book included more than 1,500 references; it would have been completely out of proportion to the text of this book. Therefore I have had to reduce it to two-thirds its original size and, as a result, forego listing the hundreds of works which, although consulted for the preparation of the text, are not directly cited. Permit me to thank here the numerous libraries without the aid of which I would never have been able to gather the documentation necessary for the preparation of this book; I owe particular recognition to the librarians of the Bibliotheque Cantonale et Universitaire of Lausanne and to the Joseph Regenstein Library of the University of Chicago.

INTRODUCTION   5

problem, took up the former theories without verifying whether or not they were well founded.²

In these circumstances, it seemed to me useful to write not the umpteenth book on the mask, but a readily accessible essay on some of the most widely circulated ideas of the literature on masks, precisely those I have cited at the beginning of this introduction. I propose to put them to the test by returning to the available ethnological documentation and by avoiding both jargon and great theoretical flights in favor of a very simple method: each of these affirmations, presented as a general rule, will be confronted with data from a certain number of societies with masking traditions. Briefly, I will juxtapose the particular cases with the general theory which, by definition, should be able to give an account of them. This method has the advantage of enabling the reader who is not a specialist to draw his or her own conclusions while becoming familiar with a certain number of traditions. But it must be clear from the outset that I do not pretend to develop, from the mosaic of facts and documents that will be presented, a new general theory destined to replace those in question; this would be methodologically unacceptable. Nevertheless, this discussion will enable me to underscore the problems that are posed, to formulate a few hypotheses, and to trace various avenues of reflection that will offer the reader an orientation in the vast field of the ritual mask.³

I will not cover this field in its entirety, however. For the most part, the general rules that will be examined were formulated from studies of the masks of African, Melanesian, and American socie-

---

2. The ethnologists themselves can be victims of this facility. At the end of the 1970s for example, I had occasion to hear a specialist of the region of the Sepik (New Guinea) introduce his exposition with a summary of Meuli's theory, then present the masks of Sepik as exceptions to the rule . . . without determining at the outset whether the theory really had the value of a general rule.

3. It has been about twenty years since I first began to take an interest in ritual masks. I have therefore, through the years, benefited from remarks, suggestions and criticisms of my professors and of fellow students at Chicago, of participants in various conferences or colloquia where I presented certain aspects of my research, of readers of journals or books in which preliminary versions of my reflections were published (Pernet 1969, 1979, 1981, 1982a, 1982b, 1985, 1987), in short, of all those with whom I have spoken about masks. Given the impossibility of naming them all, I am anxious to assure them here of my profound gratitude.

ties.[4] I will therefore confront them with documents from these same three regions, those very traditions that served as a basis for the elaboration of the theories in question. In so doing, I will forgo dealing with European masks (or those of European origin) or Asian masks.

While, in the narrow and usual sense of the word, the mask is a false face behind which one hides in order to disguise oneself (Montandon 1934:723), in the following pages, I shall hold in principle to a definition that is a bit wider, which considers that an object is a mask when it covers all or part of the face to disguise the wearer or to conceal his identity. Nevertheless, it will be apparent as early as the first chapter that the very definition of the mask raises an important problem.

The masks that interest us here are called "ritual" masks. Perhaps it would be useful to recall here that, in the common usage of the term, a rite is an act that is repeated and whose efficacy is, at least in part, of an extra-empirical order (Cazeneuve 1957b:4). In general, these are religious rites, religion being, from this perspective, "an institution consisting of culturally patterned interaction with culturally postulated superhuman beings" (Spiro 1966:96). I must state explicitly that I make no pretense of settling in these few lines the problem of the definitions of rite and religion or of thus minimizing questions to which whole libraries have been devoted. It is simply a matter of indicating to the reader the perspective in which I shall use these terms.

And now, let us turn to the consideration of masks.

---

4. Such societies used to be called "primitive," but are more often referred to now as societies "without writing." This dichotomy "societies with/societies without writing" is the legacy of the division of the world between the "civilized" and the "savage." This is just as difficult to justify and is perhaps the first of such inherited ideas it would be well to denounce here. All the same, just as the theories that I examine were constituted on the basis of documents coming from this set of societies, I shall undertake my verification from these same people, which I designate in toto by the expression "societies without writing." I ask the reader to see in this only a shorthand for what would otherwise be expressed by a much longer and more precise formulation, that is, "societies which the authors whose theories I am testing grouped under the rubric of 'primitive societies' and 'societies without writing.'"

Part One

Everywhere and In All Times? The Universality of the Mask

CHAPTER 1

Geography of the Ritual Mask

"IN EVERY age and in every region of the world, human societies have used the mask." This affirmation appears so often at the beginning of works treating the ritual mask that it deserves only a brief glance before the reader moves on to the central subject of the author. And yet, in a few words, this sentence dismisses questions that should be kept present in our minds at all cost, even if for the time being no satisfactory response to them can be offered. I shall come back to the phrase "in every age" in the next chapter; but what is meant by "in every region of the world"? If it is simply an affirmation that one finds masks on the five continents (Europe, Asia, Africa, America and Oceania), this is certainly true. All the same, given the diversity of the societies found on each of these continents, a declaration of such a general nature does not teach us very much. On the other hand, if it is an affirmation of the presence of the mask in every culture, this is certainly false, at least if one holds to the first definition of the mask: an object with which one covers all or part of the face in order to disguise or conceal one's identity.

Indeed, although the mask, in the sense just defined, is very widespread, it can still not be considered universal. Even in the regions that are traditionally held to be the privileged domain of the mask, substantial areas often exist where the mask is not used. For example, in Africa masks are essentially present only in an arc from Senegal in the northwest to Zambia, Angola, and as far south as the Kalahari, with offshoots to the area east of Lake Nyasa. In the New World, the intensive use of the mask is more frequent in the western heights of the two Americas than in the other regions. In Oceania, finally, the mask is practically absent from Polynesia, while it is extremely widespread in Melanesia where nevertheless one observes numerous exceptions.[1]

There is no existing inventory of societies with and without

---

1. See Bleakley 1978:4; Cranstone 1961:32; Krickeberg 1932:56–57; Lommel 1970:11–48; Palavecino 1954:39 and map p. 7; Teilhet 1979; Wissler 1946:27–30. Cf. Lévi-Strauss 1960a:21.

masks. Such a list would be extremely difficult to devise since it would have to take into account changes intervening throughout history: certain societies originally using masks later abandoned the institution while others that had not had a masking tradition adopted one. Therefore, at this point it is best to begin with the simple observation that there are gaps in the distribution of masking as an institution, and I shall focus on the position that the literature dealing with masks adopts in light of these gaps. One can, generally speaking, identify three typical approaches: (1) purely and simply ignoring the question, (2) filling in the gaps, and finally (3) more rarely, seeking an explanation for the particular distribution of the mask.

It is the first attitude, for example, that has been chosen by a substantial number of works which attempt to treat a given society or a particular aspect of the mask and only approach the general problem by way of introduction. Such works rely on global studies that are relatively old or that continually repeat the generalities others before them have expressed, without precise references. In so doing, they reinforce for the public the impression that the mask is universal and do not seem to perceive the necessity of focusing on its geographic distribution to achieve a deeper knowledge of the phenomenon. They therefore pass over the central question by ignoring it, concentrating the whole of their attention instead on the particular problem of interest to them.

The second category includes especially the many works that propose that there is a continuity between masks, paintings (on the head or body), tattoos, and even scarifications. To understand such a position, one must begin with the problem raised by the very definition of the term "mask," a problem that reappears several more times in this book and is of great importance in understanding certain general ideas circulating about the ritual mask.

Even though everyone assumes he or she knows what a mask is, one has only to open a dictionary to realize that this word in fact applies to a great number of objects and covers a very wide range of meanings. This diversity of meaning arises repeatedly in history and ethnology where the authors use the term "mask" in sometimes very different senses. In the narrow and usual meaning of the word, the mask is a false face with which one hides the features in order to disguise oneself (Montandon 1934:723). Nevertheless, the mask also refers to ornaments that crown the head but do not cover it, to the elements of costumes worn in front of the face (veils, visors), and to entire or partial disguises of the body or face. Also designated by this term are all representations of a face, whether or not they are worn on the face or on the head of a dancer. This therefore includes mannequins, effigies, features that have been molded, sculpted or applied to buildings or vessels, hanging masks, finger masks, pocket masks, etc. Finally, as mentioned above, the definition is extended to paintings, tattooing, and scarification. Consequently, a disturbing confusion prevails in the literature, leading one scholar to determine that the word "mask" identifies no coherent class of institutions of any use to social anthropologists (Jedrej 1980:220).

In the following pages, I shall hold in principle to the definition that an object is a mask when it covers all or part of the face in order to disguise the wearer or dissimulate his identity.[2] This definition includes, for example, cases in which a sculpted element is placed on the head of the wearer and whose face is then hidden by a piece of fabric or a fringe of fibers. I shall thereby avoid considering a priori this "object with which one covers the face" as the most significant element of an entire ensemble consisting of the mask, the wearer, the costume, the accessories, music, song, and dance. In that respect, the reader should free him or herself from the fascination that masks which have "faces" hold over the imagination. This requires a considerable effort since the interest that Western artists brought to the mask when they discovered "primitive" art was directed almost exclusively at the face; in the same way, museum collections and the numerous works that have made masks known to the public essentially consist of "faces" and thereby contribute to reinforcing this limited interest in the face of a mask. In fact, as Sieber noted, "the presentation of an isolated mask in a museum constitutes a gross misrepresentation, not only of the social values inherent to the complex comprised of mask, costume, dance, music and other related traits, but of the aesthetic component of the mask in its original context."[3] This remark applies particularly well to a mask such as the Otobo of the Kalabari

---

2. It is not important here to distinguish types of masks according to the manner in which they are worn (in front of the face, on the crown of the head, as helmets, etc.) or the proportion of the head or body of the wearer that they cover.

3. Sieber 1962:9; as well as Meyer and Parkinson 1895:2–3.

(Niger delta), which is painted as carefully as other masks but which is then entirely hidden by palm fronds.[4]

The almost exclusive interest in the face caused the many masks that have no "face" but simply a hood, a cone covered with leaves or a fringe of fibers falling in front of the face of the wearer, to be relegated to a secondary level of importance. This fascination also has contributed to the relatively limited interest shown in the costume of the mask, too quickly and too often considered as a simple adjunct to the mask whose main purpose is to disguise the wearer. It risks causing one to underestimate the importance of other elements of the complex of the mask as well. For example, among the Dan (Liberia and Ivory Coast), it is the headdress, not the "face," that gives an indication at first glance of the type of mask with which one is dealing. Consequently, when the Dan wish to change a mask from one category to another, they begin by modifying the headdress: if they wished to transform the *kaogle* mask whose behavior is aggressive, gay, and mocking to the *guna-gle* mask, they would slowly and progressively change the headdress by adding some feathers to make it more impressive. The mask will behave in a more controlled manner; it will not dance as rapidly. Finally to complete the metamorphosis, the face will be changed in turn and the mask will be recognized as another type of character.[5] Similarly, certain bobo masks (Burkina Faso) are rigorously identical in appearance and only the colors, notably the color of the tunic and some ornamental details—small feathers, appendages made of esparto placed on the skull-cap—enable one to distinguish among them (Le Moal 1980:180). Recall as well that in ancient Egypt, the masks designated for priests were composed of only the heads of animals since the priests who held the role of anthropomorphic divinities had no need of masks: the headdresses and the specific emblems of the gods that they represented were sufficient for them to be recognized (Sainte Fare Garnot 1960:61). Sometimes, the mask is in fact nothing more than a great structure of raffia carried by several bearers and having only the briefest outline of a face (Peek 1983:38). In other cases, where the mask does include a face, its meaning can be conveyed in the superstructure that serves as its base more than in

---

4. Horton 1965:21 and pl. 49–50.
5. E. Fischer 1980:86–87; cf. Adams 1987:42–43; Goonatilleka 1976:10–16, 21 n.2.

the face itself (Bédouin 1967:115). Finally, among the Sénoufo (Ivory Coast, Mali, Burkina Faso), in "the character that is created by the combination of the human animator, the costume, the associated ornamentation, the accompanying music, song and dance, the mask is only an accessory, often interchangeable" (Bochet 1965:644).

The face is therefore not necessarily the place where the meaning of the mask is concentrated. That being so, it is apparent that when examining an ensemble encompassing all the elements of the mask (costume, headdress, dance, etc.), it would be difficult to decide that one is not dealing with a mask simply because the face of the dancer is painted instead of hidden by a worn hood, a false face, or a fringe (fig. 1). Therefore, it is not surprising that numerous authors see a continuity between painting and masks. This position is further sustained by a number of other similarities: painting, like masks, is a temporary adornment; both appear on particular occasions (initiation, marriage, death, lifting of interdictions); the functions of the painting seem comparable to those filled elsewhere by the mask (representation, identification, disguise). This relation between painting and masks can then be seen from two principal perspectives: on the one hand, one can see in them a genetic or chronological relation. Advocates of such a position consider paintings either as a primitive form of the mask,[6] or as a survival, a derivative or a substitute for the mask.[7] On the other hand, one might just as readily affirm the existence of a mere functional relationship between the two adornments without establishing a true genetic link between them. This, of course, does not explain why certain peoples have masks and others do not.[8]

By including various forms of adornments, one also raises new problems. Thus, when Lévi-Strauss declares that "if one includes face paint and tattoos in the definition of the mask, it would be found in all societies,"[9] he introduces a new question. In fact, generally speaking, tattooing tends to identify an individual, to

---

6. Bastian 1883:336; Hartmann 1967:12; MacGowan and Rosse 1924:3; Montandon 1934, 728; Nevermann 1933:159; Niessen 1960:274; cf. Koehler 1833:1–2.
7. Adande 1955:24; Christinger and Borgeaud 1963:23
8. Ebeling 1984:10; Eliade 1968:143; Grimes 1975:508; Lommel 1970:75; Lot-Falck 1975:41; Mauss 1938:272; Millot 1963:233–36; Paulme 1956:10–11; Segy 1953:99; Shalleck 1973:x.
9. Lévi-Strauss 1961:12, cf. Buraud 1948:145.

1. Dancer wearing ornaments and paint: Yemal, New Guinea. From Gardi and Bühler 1958:137.

situate him in his social context or to protect him from evil forces. By definition it is indelible.[10] Hence it is difficult to see how masking and painting, which are temporary, could be classified in the same category as tattooing, which aims at permanence. In fact, Lévi-Strauss distinguishes elsewhere between the mask (as including tattoos and painting) and "the mask per se," and speaks of "masking cultures," which seems to imply that the mask, at least the mask "properly speaking," is not present in all cultures.[11]

The third of the general categories defined above includes the works that, in light of the geographic gaps observed in the distribution of the mask, attempt to find a historic or systematic explanation for them, if not both. Three examples demonstrate both the difficulty of the problem and the different types of hypotheses proposed. A prime example is found in the works of members of the historicocultural school of Vienna, which tried to explain the geography of the mask by the relation it would have had with those societies called "matriarchal." According to this school, at some prior epoch women played a preponderant role in society, and men created secret societies in order to resist women's attempts to dominate them; masks were then the aggressive means utilized to conquer and ensure power over women. While this theory, to which I shall return in chapter 7, can no longer be accepted today, it is nevertheless worth pointing out that it is one of the all too rare examples in which the distribution of the mask is treated as a problem to which a solution that is at once historic and sociocultural must be found.

Ilse Schneider-Lengyel (1934:35) adopts a negative approach and proposes another type of interpretation: according to her, the essential and also the simplest of reasons for the gaps in the geographic distribution of the mask is probably due a lack of desire on the part of peoples without masks to express themselves through the plastic arts; rather, they devised other means and possibilities for formulating and expressing their beliefs. This hypothesis raises yet other questions, of course: Why is it that certain people have the need to express themselves "plastically" while others do not? Do peoples without masks and those with masks express similar beliefs by different means? Do they express different beliefs that require different means? Ilse Schneider's theory addresses the

---

10. Joshi 1976:45; Mauss 1967:99; cf. Maertens 1978:19–20.
11. Lévi-Strauss 1973–74, 1:288, 291. Discussion in Teilhet 1979:198–99.

opinion offered about the Vanuatu by Speiser (1923:431), who suggested that in those cultures where sculpture, that is to say statuary, is lacking, masks are equally absent. This remark unfortunately cannot be considered universally valid and even Speiser himself identified cases where one finds statues and not masks, and others where masks are present but not statues (1946:44). Moreover, in certain regions of Africa, it is the absence of statuettes that was explained by the presence of the mask (Vandenhoute 1948:3). In addition, Ilse Schneider is mistaken when she affirms that the mask is absent, for religious reasons, from Islamicized regions.[12] If it is possible that certain masks were abandoned following the conversion of their wearers to Islam (Leiris 1933:51), Stevens (1973) showed clearly that the establishment of Islam in a given region does not necessarily result in the elimination of the art of the mask. To the contrary, the Zara of southwest Burkina Faso created masks specifically to represent the djinns (Bravmann 1977:46). Furthermore, this is not an isolated case.[13] The explanation advanced by Schneider is therefore insufficient. This author must nevertheless be credited with noting the existence of gaps in the geography of the mask and with trying to propose an explanation for them, thus opening up the discussion instead of closing it with a declaration of universality.

Considering, on the one hand, that the religion of cultivators is dominated by the belief in the power of the dead and that, on the other hand, masks represent precisely the spirits of the dead, Meuli (1946:9–10) concluded that masks are characteristic of peoples who are cultivators. Two major objections nevertheless can be leveled against his hypothesis. First of all, even a rapid survey of the principal regions in which masking is found reveals that, contrary to the opinion of Meuli and of many other authors, most masks do not personify the dead (see chapter 3). Second, the explanation of Meuli only very imperfectly recognizes the presence of masks among hunters, especially in Asia and in America.[14] The hypothesis therefore cannot be sustained either, but one must not consequently fall into the obverse error and affirm, against all evi-

---

12. I. Schneider 1934:35; cf. Glotz 1975:4–5.
13. Bravmann 1974; J. Girard 1965; Mark 1983:9, 17; Rabaté 1967. Cf. Green 1987:69; Monts 1984.
14. The presence of the mask among hunting peoples served as a basis for the theory that the ritual mask was derived from a mask for camouflage used for hunting. See chapter 2.

dence, that "nomads seem to be more attracted by the mask than more sedentary societies, which would imply a relation to space" (Duvignaud 1980:8). It is to the credit of Meuli that he, like Schneider and the members of the historicocultural school of Vienna, saw the gaps in the geographical distribution of the mask and utilized his immense knowledge to attempt to bring about an explanation. His interpretation was perhaps the last of the great generalizations on the mask; it continues to exert a definite influence on contemporary works.[15]

It should be said that from the time they were forced to abandon the grand general theories of the nineteenth century and the beginning of the twentieth century specialists no longer showed much interest in the study of the geography of the mask. They were often satisfied with the vague and unverifiable affirmation that the ritual mask was too widely spread for anyone to be able to identify a center of diffusion.[16] Some even suggested that this wide distribution kept them from seeking the origin of the institution of the mask in a particular society under study,[17] a position that stems from either one of two postulations: First, that the diffusion is so ancient it would be vain to attempt to retrace it (see chapter 2); or second, that the fundamental conceptions that are at the origin of the mask are present in essence in all humans and as a consequence masks can develop in various places independently.[18] But in the second case what would be the origin of such a development? Historical or socioeconomic factors which are as yet to be determined? Chance and the arbitrary? One can see that this proposition does not in any way explain why certain populations use masks and others do not. Furthermore, it closes the discussion instead of opening it, which is particularly unproductive. It seems

---

15. In a general note relating to the word "mask," Burkert (1985:103, 388 n.42) gives seven references, of which three are to Meuli (1932–33, 1943, 1975), one to I. Schneider 1934 and one to Klingbeil 1935 (following a typographical error, the last two were combined in one single title). For his part, the folklorist Glotz (1980:89) declares that Meuli's hypothesis is the one that attracts him the most. Cf. Chappaz-Wirthner 1974:79; Gilbert, Guillemaut and Bourges 1980:7; Kuhn 1954:7; Röllin 1987:66. Chapter 5 of this book will be entirely devoted to the discussion of one aspect of Meuli's theory.

16. Bédouin 1967:8; Laufer 1959:906; Mead 1946:280; Montandon 1934:727.

17. For Fenton the fact that the use of the mask was so widespread across the world permitted him to assume that the custom of wearing False-Faces among the Iroquois sprang from their own culture (Fenton 1937:220). Later, he was forced to refine his position (see Fenton 1941:416; Hendry 1964:362–64).

18. Karutz 1901:361; cf. Gregor 1936:9–10.

much more positive to leave a problem open rather than hiding it behind a totally unverifiable "solution." About this latter approach Kroeber, already, had raised the point some time before that "the assumption of independent origin, where conviction is not pretty definitely forced by the facts in hand, has about it something similar to the assumption of spontaneous generation by the older zoologists. He contends that an examination in detail from the point of view of a working hypothesis of connection is normally preferable because it provides at least an explanation that can be tested and corrected, whereas the assumption of spontaneously independent origin generally amounts to falling back on a principle so vague that its effect is the checking of further enquiry of a historical nature."[19]

All too conscious of the errors of the past, ethnology had a tendency to adopt a rather chilly attitude: by treating each culture studied as wholly *sui generis*, a unique and more or less successful adaptation to a particular environment—a sort of island—ethnology often rejected any comparison that was not within a narrow range and regional in scope. The overly exclusive valorization of fieldwork resulted in a corresponding limitation of the historical and geographical horizon of many ethnologists and deprived us of more general works which would have enabled us to better understand today the institution of the ritual mask and its particular geographic distribution.[20]

There is, however, no doubt that certain problems can be truly grasped only from an extremely wide perspective. For example, one of the mythic themes most often linked to the mask is that of its discovery by a woman: it is a woman who found the mask and, for a time, it was women who possessed masks. This theme is itself part of a much more comprehensive whole that portrays women as the first owners of a number of sacred objects and rituals (see chapter 7). Consequently, when an ethnologist encounters this theme in a given society, it is normal and necessary that he describe how that tradition is explained by the members of the society in question. However, if he confines himself to this level,

---

19. Citing Ratzel in Koppers 1930:686. Cf. Lévi-Strauss 1973–74:1, 272–73. One will find various theories on the origin of the mask in Bastian 1883:336–38; Dall 1884:74–76; Gregor 1936:9–10; Villeminot and Villeminot 1966:264–65; see also chapters 2 and 7 of this book.
20. See Douglas 1970:76; Ingold 1985:384; Jedrej 1986:71; Lévi-Strauss 1979:145–46; F. Poole 1986, with an important bibliography.

his interpretation will remain extremely impoverished (for example, Errington 1974:119–21). By contrast, if the ethnologist were to put this particular case in relation to a wider whole, he would be in a position to explain the similarities and the differences, to formulate and to verify new hypotheses, to discern the originality of the society that he was studying.[21]

The same can be applied to informants' testimonies that were interpreted as revealing the existence of a ritual complex that notably included the mask, the myth of its discovery and subsequent loss by a woman to the benefit of men, the bull-roarer as the "voice of the mask," a sickness causing infertility or death as a consequence of women's transgressing prohibitions associated with the mask.[22] Such a configuration presents the following choices: (a) one can take as a point of departure the idea that there once existed, in Africa as well as in Melanesia and in America, conditions of such a comparable nature that they concurred in the formation of an ensemble of strikingly similar rituals; (b) one can surmise that a fundamental or structural link exists between the different elements of this hypothetical complex and that the latter could be rediscovered independently in various regions of the world; (c) finally, one can admit the working hypothesis of the diffusion of all or part of this cultural complex. Whatever the choice, it is nevertheless imperative to proceed with the historical and comparative study of societies where such a complex has been observed.

The bases for such a study are still greatly wanting. By contrast, on the local or regional level, interesting research has already been done that shows that by determining the evolution of trade networks, changes in political and socioeconomic conditions, and in examining the myth, the materials, the style of a mask, one can determine its origin, and even reconstitute its history.[23] These studies are often the products of art historians, and there are good

---

21. Cf. Ph. Borgeaud 1986:68–69; G. Lewis 1980:4.
22. See Speiser 1944 and chapter 7 of this book.
23. For example Borgatti 1979a on the incorporation around 1920–30 of masks representing women and the property of women but worn by men among the Edo of Nigeria; Drewal and Drewal 1983 on the origin and diffusion of the Gelede masquerade of the Yoruba of Nigeria and of Benin; Jedrej 1986 on the common origin of Dan and Mende masks; Schweeger-Hefel 1976 on the origin of certain masks of northern Burkina Faso. Also Green 1987; Poynor 1987; Roy 1987. On the diffusion of the Gorgon in China and in Oceania, see especially Dohrenwend 1975; Fraser 1966.

reasons for this: first, for societies where managing oral traditions often presents serious difficulties, art supplies invaluable evidence for a reconstruction of social and cultural history; second, the very evolution of the history of art predisposes art historians to ask questions that interest us here. In fact, for a long time, African art (for example) was considered to be "primitive," implying, among other things, that it was simpler than European art. It was presented as if there were a characteristic style for each ethnic group; one gave the impression of an art blindly obeying strict conventions, an art created by anonymous artisans whose status as artists was therefore cast into doubt. But in light of research that has intensified since the sixties, this impression has been completely dispelled. The aesthetic consciousness of Africans was recognized, and the link between art and the ethnic group shown to be more supple than had been supposed. This provoked new reflections on the notion of style, especially the consideration of the influence of certain individuals, of centers of production and the channels of exchange and commerce. The art historian was naturally led to study comparatively those styles (of masks, for example) found to exist in several ethnic groups, and in studying their various expressions, ask questions about the history of their development and their diffusion.[24]

Lévi-Strauss too insisted on this necessary step in going beyond the bounds of ethnicity, underscoring that before the colonial era, those peoples studied by ethnology lived in a more close-knit fashion: "with some rare exceptions, nothing that went on in one's home was lost on his neighbors, and the means by which each explained himself and represented the universe to himself was elaborated through an uninterrupted and vehement dialogue." Relying on the comparative study of traditions of the northwest coast of North America, he proposed a law of transformation of masks that can be summarized as follows: the plastic characteristics of masks bearing the same message are reversed in moving from a population to its neighbor; by contrast, when the plastic elements remain unchanged, it is then the messages that are inverted. This theory, in this precise form, has not yet been the object of detailed verification in other regions in which masks are found. Nevertheless, it has the merit of drawing attention to the

---

24. On this, see the excellent summary and bibliography of McNaughton 1987.

role that the "conscious or unconscious desire to affirm oneself as different, to choose among all the same options that the art of neighboring peoples rejected" can play in the interpretation of differences between masks of two peoples, and even in the explanation of either the presence or absence of masks.[25] L. Turner (1983:37) provides an example in which this desire to affirm oneself as different may have played a role in the rejection of the mask. Toward the end of the 1930s, the anthropologist Frank G. Speck tried to introduce the mask to the Naskapi (New Quebec and Labrador). But even though, at his request, the Naskapi made many a mask, they never integrated them into their system of belief. One of the reasons advanced attributed this refusal to the relationship that the Naskapi had with their neighbors, the Inuit, who did have masks. Because Inuit ate raw flesh, the Naskapi regarded them as akin to animals, to unnatural beings. There was, therefore, little chance that the Naskapi would adopt the mask and the accompanying ritual structure while, in their minds, these elements were characteristic of the Inuit.

Future historical and comparative studies will be able to ground themselves on progressively more precise bases thanks to the multiplication of archeological excavations in regions inhabited by masking societies. For West Africa, for example, the data accumulate at such a rapid rate that the syntheses formulated in 1980 were dated by 1983 (McIntosh and McIntosh 1983:216). It is, of course, hardly likely that these investigations will lead to the discovery of very old masks: the materials generally used do not keep well. Nevertheless, detailed information brought to bear on history and prehistory will lead to a better understanding of the background of masking and furnish elements which are indispensable to general studies so that they can be undertaken without risk of falling into the errors of the diffusionists.

But we are not yet at that point. In a recent work on African masks, Cole deplored our current ignorance and underscored one of the many unsolved mysteries in the history of African arts: that

---

25. Lévi-Strauss 1979:123, 144, 145. This preoccupation with identity is not only played out among neighboring ethnic groups but also between families belonging to the same ethic group, just as the rules of morphological differentiation between bobo masks show: in light of these rules, if the family with rights over a mask gives it up to another family, it must transform it in such a way that the original and its new version cannot be confused (Le Moal 1980:210).

certain African cultures make masks an important dimension of their religious and social life while others do not.²⁶ This remark is equally valid for other continents, and in general scholars are reduced to observing that, "there are often closely neighboring peoples belonging to the same race, sharing the same material conditions of life, where one makes use of masks, and the other does not."²⁷ One can only hope that this situation will encourage scholars to reconsider, using current methods of ethnographic, historical and archeological analysis, the problem raised by the geography of the ritual mask. For to renounce understanding why masks are present in certain societies and absent in others is, at the same time, to abandon all hope of understanding an extremely important aspect of this institution and, in the end, of the institution of masking itself.

Given the current state of our knowledge, one fact remains nevertheless indisputable: if one holds to a traditional definition of the mask, it is necessary to conclude that, contrary to what has often been written, the use of the mask, though widespread, is not universal. It is only when makeup, painting, and tattoos are included in the definition of the mask that the mask can be considered to be present in every society. Nevertheless, such an extension of the definition must be based on a systematic comparative study of these various forms of adornments, which yet remains to be done. Therefore, the affirmation of any so-called universality of the mask based on its assimilation to other forms of adornments only conceals a series of problems whose resolution is necessary to the very comprehension of the phenomenon.

---

26. Cole 1985:19, 106 n.4.
27. Bédouin 1967:8. See a tentative, geographically limited, explanation through a link with certain dominant traits of social organization in Siegmann 1980. For his part, Duvignaud affirms "that there are profound differences in the mores and beliefs, between societies having masks and societies without masks"; unfortunately, he does not describe what they are and adds, "We have very little on that" (Duvignaud 1980:8).

CHAPTER 2

The Age of the Ritual Mask

"IN EVERY age and in every region of the world . . . " The second part of this affirmation raises a certain number of problems, as described in chapter 1. But what of the first, asserting that masks exist "in every age"?

For most authors, the ritual use of the mask goes back to the "dawn of time," to the Paleolithic period. There is nothing astonishing in this since various European prehistoric paintings and engravings were considered, from the time of their discovery, to represent masked beings. At the time, this interpretation seemed all the more natural in that, independent of all documented proof, most scholars started from the premise that Paleolithic hunters used masks. In fact, the evolutionist theories that had enjoyed currency since the middle of the nineteenth century presented the contemporary "primitives" studied by cultural anthropology and ethnology as accurate representations of what prehistoric primitive societies had been. Since the "primitives" used the mask, one could therefore expect to find them in their prehistoric counterparts. Thus, for Breuil, "it is not the existence of masks of the upper quaternary that should surprise us, but on the contrary, it is that these peoples should have lacked manifestations so universally widespread among all those of the same social stage, and which those of a more advanced evolutionary stage almost always preserved in one form or another" (1914:421).

Furthermore, this expectation was reinforced by the fact that one of the most widespread theories explained the invention of the mask as a necessity of hunting, in which the hunter had the idea of disguising himself as an animal in order to draw near to his prey. Once this technique was corroborated by ethnographic documents from various contemporary "primitive" societies, one supposed that it must have been found among the "ancient" primitives as well.[1] As a consequence, a number of figures have

---

1. See Cartaihac and Breuil 1906, in particular, pages 164, 196–97, 225 and 242. Cf. Barnett 1966:267–68; Birket-Smith 1929:71, 162, 255–56, 334–35; J. G. D. Clark 1954:170; Reinbacker 1956:149–50.

been interpreted as representing hunting masks. However, since this explanation did not enable one to understand the most complex figures and did not integrate well with magic or religious theories put forward about Paleolithic art, the hypothesis was completed with the suggestion that hunters had moved from a purely utilitarian disguise to a ritual disguise that gave rise to masked dances of a magical character.[2]

It was around 1897, with reference to the drawings of Gourdan and of Mas d'Azil, that Piette first put forward the idea that certain Paleolithic drawings could be explained as a disguise (Breuil 1914:420). This hypothesis was further developed by Cartailhac and Breuil in 1906 and, from 1912 on, it was widely accepted by a number of specialists that several figures in the caverns are representations of men wearing sacred masks.[3] Consequently, the figures of Paleolithic mobiliary or wall art that seemed to present human and animal characteristics at the same time are frequently interpreted as masked figures. The most famous of these figures is without contest the representation of the "sorcerer" on the wall of the Trois-Frères cave discovered in Ariège during the First World War (fig. 2).

This figure is etched and painted on a vault that dominates the part of the cave called "sanctuary," and is above the most remarkable panels of animals. This character of the middle Magdalenian period (about 12,000 B.C.E.) "presents itself as a stooped man, with big round eyes of a night bird (or of a lion, or a 'ghost'), dressed with deer antlers, with the ears and shoulders of a reindeer or a stag. The lower part of his back has a horse's tail under which hangs a sex organ with a more human appearance, but which is placed like that of a feline."[4]

---

2. Le Quellec 1985:379; Maringer 1960:145.
3. Capitan, cited in Deonna (1914:107); cf. Breuil 1914:422. Capitan founds his certainty on the discovery at the Madeleine (Dordogne) of a shingle on which are engraved, according to him, a "man" and a "woman." It seemed most clear to him that the male figure wore a mask on his face. This opinion was still shared by Lantier (1961, fig. 43). By contrast, Leroi-Gourhan (1982:51) rejects this interpretation and replaces this figure in the development of an idealization or a stylization of the face; I shall return to this later.
4. Leroi-Gourhan (1975b:97). Reservations were sometimes expressed about the reading of this figure established by Breuil (Bédouin 1967:99; Reed 1976:137, n.1; Ucko and Rosenfeld 1967:204). To the extent that these reservations are based on the examination of photographs, it is fitting to recall that the "sorcerer" is entirely engraved but that its paint is unequally spread on it; it is therefore comprehensible that certain traits, in particular those that Breuil

2. The "horned God" or "sorcerer" of Trois-Frères. From Bégouën and Breuil 1958, pl. XX.

Initially, this figure had been interpreted as representing a dancing sorcerer. After further reflection, Breuil concluded that it was not a sorcerer but a god, a representation of what one today calls the master of animals, "the Spirit governing the multiplication of game and hunting expeditions" (Breuil 1952:176). But the name of "sorcerer" had already stuck to this figure and was never replaced by that of the "horned god" in the literature. It should be noted that for Breuil, the figure of this god was "decked out with the same symbols of magical power (mask) as his human ministers" (Bégouën and Breuil 1958:54). It was therefore a masked god. Yet, various authors, and Breuil himself, in reference to other figures, thought that the semi-human characters moreover represented composite, symbolic or mythic, beings.[5] According to Breuil, these two interpretations were not so far apart from one another: "As for the other idea of 'spiritual' or imaginary beings, it is not, in my opinion, so different from that of masks, since such conceptions seem to me a consequence of the use of disguises and the product of imaginations nourished by their spectacle; this is incontestable in current savage ethnography, and the antiquities of ancient Greece, Egypt or America, so rich in complex representations, can be explained (if one sets aside the inferior and vulgar art in favor of taking into account only true art) by the multiple reflections of masquerades, centuries-old customs whose origins plunge as far back as the Paleolithic age."[6]

Breuil relies particularly on Stow's hypothesis explaining the evolution from hunting disguise to the composite being: "The masked characters must represent primitive heros of the race who

---

called invisible except when viewed up close, do not appear in a photo (Breuil 1952:170, 176; Bégouën and Breuil 1958:86, pl. XIX and XX). Even if Breuil's sketches were faulty on certain points, there remain a sufficient number of other figures of composite beings in mobiliary or wall art for the problem to remain. See Leroi-Gourhan 1982:51–52; cf. Lumley 1985:176–78; Maringer 1960:145.

5. These two interpretations later remained in competition. Thus Frobenius considered that the "sorcerer" is typically the representation of a masked man (1932:42) while Narr holds that same idea as hardly likely and tends toward the therio-anthropomorphic representation, a superior being (1961:136); cf. Campbell 1960:308–11; Lévy-Bruhl 1963b:148–54; Maringer 1960:149–50; Marshack 1972:260, 272–74. For Höfler, this "masked figure" provides one of the first examples of the importance of the tail in animal disguises (1934:1, 62 and note 221). As for Züchner, he thinks he can distinguish among the various figures of "sorcerers," those that represent costumed men and those that show anthropo-zoomorphic beings (1972:132). On the interpretation of the sorcerer as representing a shaman, see Leroi-Gourhan 1977.

6. Breuil 1914:421; cf. Fenton 1941:406–407.

were renowned for the fantastic feats of their hunt, thanks to their capacity to make use of their disguises; but these more or less mythic persons were more or less confused with their disguises which became an integral part of their character, and this, according to the same author [Stow], in time would have led to semianimal gods like those of the Egyptians" (Cartailhac and Breuil 1906:197). Thus, while it is tempting to think, like Thiele (1985:436), for example, that the mask was created precisely to represent or to dramatize a composite mythical being, Breuil, following Stow, reverses this relationship and presents the mythic figure as resulting from the observation of the disguise used by the hunter, that is to say, as presupposing the hunting mask. This hypothesis, like many others, is absolutely undemonstrable on the basis of the available sources.

Toward the middle of the 1950s, the study of the meaning of Paleolithic rock art took a new turn. In order to explain the Paleolithic figures, one had evoked the peoples of northern Asia, as well as the Eskimos, the Indians of North and South America, the rock art and rock engravings of North Africa, the Bushmen of South Africa and the Australian tribes.[7] Nevertheless, Laming-Emperaire (1962:138) notes, "the addition of analogies between the heterogeneous facts does not constitute proof. The fact that the most competent in turn suggest totemism, hunting magic, sacred dances, masked sorcerers, gods, spirits, etc. shows the insufficiency of method." This kind of makeshift comparativism had pretty well paralyzed the scientific imagination, which tends to invent the means to advance evidence and control facts (Leroi-Gourhan 1964:4). Therefore in a first move, the scholars suspended the use of ethnographic parallels and then, in a second move, established very strict rules for their utilization (Leroi-Gourhan 1975a:54–55). Attempts were also made to draw up an inventory of what can be known: the systematic analysis of the relationship that the figures of wall art had with each other and with their position in the sites reveals a coherent but complex situation, which had been eclipsed by isolating the figures from their

---

7. Among the sources of comparatist interpretation, one must not neglect either "the influence (unconscious in the minds of the authors) of masked and horned figures of the rites of winter and Carnaval, common throughout Europe and somewhat reminiscent of the demoniac imagery of the last centuries" (Leroi-Gourhan 1977:23). Cf. Frobenius 1932:45.

context and in interpreting them through analogy with the traditions of peoples studied by ethnology.[8]

The example of animalized profiles, which were often interpreted as masks of animals worn by humans, is particularly instructive along these lines. Grouping together all the known human profiles, one notes that there is an almost imperceptible transition from the normal profile to that of the head of an animal. This change is especially brought about by the exaggeration in the straightening of the nose: the bridge of the nose is made longer and appears almost horizontal, which brings the lower part of the face into exaggerated protrusion, such that finally the whole face lengthens into a muzzle. This transformation only appears in male figures, while the transition in the female figures follows other canons. The profound reasons for this stylization escape us, but the idea of the mask is certainly not the most likely hypothesis.[9] Moreover, it seems that there are, besides "sorcerers" and other similar representations, composite animal figures that would be very difficult to interpret as masked beings.[10] Hence, would it not be wiser to observe, as did Laming-Emperaire, that although one often spoke of prehistoric masks, beginning with representations of humans with animal heads painted or etched on the walls of Paleolithic caves, it is more likely that these are representations of mythic or supernatural beings? "Maybe it is necessary to see in these very ancient figures the origin of sacred masks of many existing primitive groups, but the very existence of Paleolithic masks is still uncertain" (Laming-Emperaire 1964). If the study is limited to the documents themselves, it is prudent to speak only of "com-

---

8. A parallel change is observable in the field of excavations which evolved from the first searches for "souvenirs," to vertical cuts that aimed at establishing a chronology, then to horizontal searches tending to analyze complexes and to bring into view regional economic structures, etc. One will find a recent discussion of various hypotheses on paleolithic art, particularly that of "art for art," in Halverson 1987.

9. Leroi-Gourhan 1975b:292, 295; Leroi-Gourhan 1982:51.

10. For example, the female reindeer with the head of a bison in Trois-Frères which "preceded" a semi-human being (Breuil 1952:176 and fig. 129 and 139; Bégouën and Breuil 1958:58–59, fig. 61, 62, and 63; cf. Leroi-Gourhan 1975b:97). Maringer interprets this scene as a magic rite in which the semi-human being as well as the animals are the human hunters disguised, with this rite aiming, according to him, at forcing the animals to submit to the will of the hunter (1960:143–44). About this same scene, Lucas advances the idea of a sodomic behavior with the animals (1962:43–44). As is often the case in matters of wall art, it is difficult to decide if it is in fact truly a "scene" and to demarcate the elements that would compose it.

posite figures." It is in no case possible to affirm, as too many authors have done, that the documents "prove" the existence of ritual masks in Paleolithic times. They do not prove anything of the kind.

The difficulties of interpretation just sketched out are not particular to European Paleolithic documents. One finds them true for rock art in general, including the famous Saharan frescoes that are also regularly cited for demonstrating the great antiquity of the ritual mask. Is this justified? First, it is necessary to consider the engravings that most often achieve an extraordinary realism. Besides large animals, they also portray figures with human bodies and animal heads. In a number of cases, there appear heads of canids and almost certainly of jackals, but one can also recognize heads of antelopes, birds and even cats. Scholars have of course been tempted to see in these figures the image of men wearing hunting masks but, as Camps states,

> the men with zoomorphic heads of Hoggar and of Tassili n'Ajjer, to my knowledge more often have the heads of predators than the heads of herbivores or birds. With a preference for heads of felines and canids, I do not think that such masks can facilitate the approach to game. . . . All these figures are very realistic, the details of dress are sometimes indicated with a very great precision, bracelets, necklaces, belts are distinctly recognizable. . . . In spite of these precisions, no trait separates the mask from the head or the neck, no element for attachment is indicated, the head, neck and shoulders are in perfect continuity. . . . These animal heads are an integral part of the human bodies. If the mask can be explained in hunting scenes for technical or magical reasons, it is less understandable why the male characters are still masked in other occasions, such as for example, in the scenes of coitus of T-in Lalan, in Acacus, published by Mori. . . . I propose to see in these male figures with animal heads divine beings such as those which pharaonic Egypt kept in living memory for millennia. The scenes of T-in Lalan, according to this hypothesis, could be considered as representations of hierogamies [fig. 3].[11]

---

11. Camps 1975:325–26; cf. Camps 1974:257–58; Mori 1965:70–72, 88–89. It should be noted that "Egypt owes much to neolithic civilizations of Saharan

3. Coitus scene from T-in Lalan. From Mori 1965:70.

This analysis of Camps clearly presents the dilemma of masked man versus mythic being and seems to apply equally to a great extent to the paintings. Discovered in 1909 by Cortier, the cave paintings of Tassili were brought to the public by the Lhote missions. The works were grouped according to affinities within sets, whose characteristics were not clearly defined. (Are the criteria stylistic unities or distinct chronological ages?) Furthermore the distribution and description vary according to the author. Thus there is, for example, the "period" (or the phase, style,

---

Africa which were much older" (Camps in Anati 1975:439; cf. Lhote 1976:40–41). On the engravings of men with heads of jackals or cat from Fezzan (Libya), see Graziosi 1970; Le Quellec 1985:375–76. One also finds men with animal heads in cave paintings in southern Africa. Lewis-Williams (1982; 1985; 1986) interprets them in a shamanic context, as illustrating the trance or the voyage out of the body. According to him, they represent therianthropes and not masked men. The discussion that follows his 1982 article nevertheless gives a good idea of the problems that the interpretation of wall art documents raise. It should also be noted that the oldest painted fragments found in east Africa were dated between 17,000 and 24,000 years B.C.E.; they represent animals. The majority of documents of this region are much more recent, however (Lewis-Williams 1983:26–37).

school, group) of men with rounded heads or period of the antelopes, the phase of cattle herders or period of cattle, the period of the goat and sheep, the phase of the chariot or period of horse breeders and, finally the period of the camel or tifinar period.[12]

Several painted figures were interpreted as representations of masks or masked individuals, starting with the early stage of the style of rounded heads which shows "small characters painted in purplish-blue ocher, having a subschematic body and a round, always abnormally large head. Sometimes, the crown of the head is bare, but often it bears horns or other appendages that resemble feathers" (Lhote 1958:224–25). Making abundant use of ethnographic parallels with a number of African populations, Bernolles suggests that these are indeed masks. Following Bernolles, it is in the "round mask" that the true identity of the "rounded heads" must be seen, since, according to him, the latter have no basis in anthropological reality.[13] Muzzolini (1984:328), however, sees in them a voluntary refusal to make the details of the face precise; he does not know whether to attribute this refusal to an artistic convention or to a religious interdiction.

Just as with Paleolithic art, the authors are not in agreement on what a mask is or is not. Thus, the central figure of a fresco of Sefar is a "great god" for Lhote and Camps, but a woman ("mistress of dance") dressed in a horned hood-mask for Bernolles, and a great masked figure for Lajoux.[14] It is hard to imagine what would suggest an interpretation favoring the mask. In contrast, the three stylized faces of Sefar are unanimously called "masks." All the same, it is not a question of a "realistic" representation of

---

12. See especially Camps 1974:258–61; Lajoux 1977:32–34; Le Quellec 1985:366–69; Lhote 1958:223–39; McIntosh and McIntosh 1985:312; Striedter 1983:5–12. Based on the resemblances between Peul traditions and the figures of the period of cattle herders, Hampaté Ba and Dieterlen (1966) proposed a certain number of hypotheses which I will not detail here but which should be considered with the utmost caution (see Camps 1974:245; Vansina 1984:108). On a possible affiliation with Yoruba traditions, see Lawal 1975.

13. Bernolles 1966:96ff., 112. A frequent tendency in the interpretation of prehistoric documents is that when the head is proportionately more voluminous than the other dimensions of the individual would logically suggest, the mask appears as a likely explanation. By contrast, when the head is reduced to its most simple expression, or even disappears completely, one speaks more readily of stylization or convention. See Striedter 1983, 7; cf. Lajoux 1977, 158.

14. Lhote 1958:136–37, pl.2 and 50; Camps 1974:259; Bernolles 1966:175–79; Lajoux 1977:41, cf. p.52.

masks, recognizable as such, and this is probably why Lhote speaks of "stylized Negro masks." Perhaps it would have been more prudent to take one step further or back, here too, and to recognize that nothing definitively enables one to say that they are anything other than "stylized faces."[15]

My intention here is neither to demonstrate that no mask is represented in the Saharan documents, nor merely to abandon myself to the gratuitous pleasure of pitting specialists against one another. What does seem useful to emphasize, however, is that the meaning of the documents is far from being evident and that, in the interpretation provided, the prejudices or convictions of the interpreter often weigh more heavily than the document itself, causing frequent disagreement among researchers. Thus, caution is appropriate.

Among the documents which studies of the ritual mask invoke with the greatest insistence is the figure of Aouanrhet (Inahouanrhat). It is a figure treated in brick-red ocher, with a body covered with a white checkering, and with legs spread (fig. 4). For Lhote, the mask worn by this figure is of the same style as a Senoufo initiation mask. This parallel has been disputed by Bernolles, who proposed other styles and speaks of "bull disguise." Muzzolini does not exclude that it might be a stylization of a human face. Lajoux compares this figure with another discovered at Matalen-Amazar: the similarity is striking but the second figure is at least as enigmatic as the first, especially concerning its "costume" and its "attributes."[16] Its interpretation is not simple and although it is understandable that at first glance one would think of a masked man, it nevertheless remains true that nothing prevents one from seeing in it a mythic figure just as easily. Moreover, this latter interpretation might better explain the fact that, in the zone where these paintings are found, each site contains only one representation of "masks."

This observation by Lajoux (1977:173) gives us an idea of the

---

15. Lajoux 1977:54; Lhote 1958:258, pl. 52 and 53; cf. Cole 1985:15. Lommel believes that these "masks" bear a marked resemblance to the *kifwebe* masks of the Songe (Songye) of Zaire; apart from the existence of parallel polychromatic lines covering the face in both cases, it is hard to see from whence such a resemblance would come (1970:11–12, 49, pl. 26 and 27; cf. Merriam 1978). See other, hardly more convincing parallels in Bernolles 1966:139–41.

16. See Bernolles 1966:130–39; Lajoux 1977:58–59; Leiris and Delange 1967:255; Lhote 1958:89–90, 254; Muzzolini 1984:354, 358.

4. Figure of Inahouanrhat. From Lajoux 1977:58.

importance that a detailed inventory of the totality of cave figures of the Sahara and North Africa could have. Such a study is actually underway at the Frobenius Institute at Frankfurt am Main. It aims at devising a system enabling a certain number of data to be manipulated by computer. In the first work to appear, Striedter presents the theoretical (= semiotic) basis of the research and explains how different information is coded. Unfortunately, after having underscored that the authors of the paintings follow certain conventions, that there are various codes, that the meaning of a sign is determined by cultural convention, and that nobody can adequately interpret a sign if the code from which the sign originates is not available, Striedter uses as distinctive characteristics notions which are already, in themselves, interpretive, and not merely descriptive.[17] Such is the case in treating the idea of the "mask" (1983:178–81, 213): the part of the code that defines twenty types of masks actually groups figures for which this name was contested. The first of these types seems furthermore not to be a "mask" or a "face" at all, but rather a headdress, described as such by Camps (1974:335–36, 339; fig. 99); type 14 refers to a figure published by Graziosi as a "man with an animal head" (Bernolles, 1966:100, pl. XXIII/3a); type 16 corresponds to the "man with big ears" which, according to Perret (1936:57, 53, pl. VI/2), resembles the silhouette of an Egyptian divinity. It is regrettable that this inventory is not constructed on the basis of more neutral categories.[18]

In granting that representations of ritual masks were present in documents of the Sahara, is it therefore necessary to return to the "dawn of time"? This raises the problem of the chronology of these cave works about which there is no consensus. For Mori, the first engravings would have preceded the paintings by several thousand years; they would date back to the upper pleistocene (20,000–8000 B.C.E.) and to the beginning of the Holocene period. The basis for this "long" chronology is however still rather fragile. For Camps, by contrast, the etchings of great naturalistic style and the paintings in the style of the rounded heads are contemporary

---

17. Striedter 1983:6, 45, 47, 51, 52.
18. Cf. Vansina 1984:106–8. It is also regrettable that the code does not allow one to situate the topography of rock art with greater precision: Is the figure found at the back of a shelter, under an exterior flagstone, on a preeminent part, in a hollow? Leroi-Gourhan showed the importance that such consideration of location presented for the European paleolithic period.

to one another; they are placed in the period between the seventh and the beginning of the fifth millennium B.C.E. In more recent works, Muzzolini proposes to establish an even shorter chronology that would date the first engravings to the "Neolithic Humide period" (about 4500 B.C.E.); the anteriority of the paintings of rounded heads seems possible to him but not certain.[19] Since those figures most likely representing masks belong to the final phase of the style of rounded heads, it is possible to affirm that these documents therefore do not place masks as far back as the dawn of time, but only to the Neolithic period. At best they can be attributed to the beginning of the neolithization of that part of the world, but more likely during an ulterior phase, given that the present state of our knowledge makes any precision impossible.[20]

Space does not permit me to provide an analysis of all these other documents that were believed to prove the existence of ritual masks in diverse places in the world and at different epochs of the Stone age. I shall content myself with mentioning again a few select cases which will suffice to clarify my point of view.

In Star Carr (Yorkshire), at an excavation site dating to the beginning of the Mesolithic period, twenty-one stag "trophies" were uncovered, unfortunately in very bad condition, but which nevertheless appeared to have been worked in a particularly interesting way: the beams as well as the brow tine were reduced and

---

19. See Camps 1975:324; Le Quellec 1985:369–72; McIntosh and McIntosh 1983:229; Mori 1974; Muzzolini 1984:300ff; Ronneseth 1986.

20. The neolithization is signaled here by the abundance of pottery (Camps 1974, 217). Nevertheless, the use of terminology derived from European and Near Eastern prehistory with regards to Africa can be a source of confusion. The term "neolithic," for example, includes two principal definitions: (a) a technological definition referring to assemblages with pottery and ground stone and (b) an economic definition that includes food-producing societies, but, often, only sedentary societies practicing stockherding and agriculture. Certain authors combine the two by considering the technological innovation of pottery as tangible evidence of an economic change related to food production (in the Middle-East, cultivated gramineous plants appear at the end of the eighth millennium and vases in terracotta are modeled from the seventh millennium). This does not seem to be the case in the zone that concerns us here. The most recent excavations show that the use of pottery in the Saharan sites (from the eighth-seventh millennium) precedes the first domesticated plants by 5,000 years (in the absence of all documents prior to 2000 B.C.E. to the west of Lake Chad). The term "neolithic" must therefore be used with care. It is also not impossible that, at least in a portion of West Africa, pastoralism preceded agriculture by several thousand years, whereas traditionally it is considered to derive from agricultural systems. See McIntosh and McIntosh 1983:219, 238; cf. Williams and Faure 1980:451, 565; Ingold 1985:386; Mellaart 1971:15–17.

the remaining part hollowed out in such a way that it seemed to make the whole lighter without depriving it of its essential characteristics. Only the part of the skull bearing the antlers remained intact. In the best preserved specimens, the skull was perforated as if to allow thin straps to pass through it. Several hypotheses were proposed: these "frontlets" could be simply trophies, or could have served as headdresses (for hunting or rituals) accompanied by masks or not. Given the poor state of the pieces, which moreover bore marks of transformations and previous damage, it is hardly possible to determine their exact use without excessively resorting to ethnographic parallels.[21]

In 1954, in the south of Constantine (Algeria), at a level corresponding to the Upper Capsian period (7000 to 4500 B.C.E.), G. Laplace discovered a human skull that had been worked in a most exceptional manner: the back portion had been carefully removed, two holes pierced in the dome of the skull, and most significantly, a missing tooth replaced after death by an artificial one carved from a piece of bone. The hypothesis of the mask was of course proposed by certain authors, but after scrupulous examination, Vallois showed that this skull (probably that of a young woman) was intended to be hung and not worn as a mask.[22] As for the (ritual?) reasons for this preparation, it is not possible to determine. Had this skull been remodeled with resin, wax, or clay? Vallois does not discuss it and only mentions traces of ocher and the presence of two *unio* shells at the eyeholes. By contrast, Camps (1974:176) suggests that such was the case by referring to the plastered skulls found in Jericho and Tell Ramad, dating near to the period of the Capsian skull. Since these skulls were presented as the first evidence of the existence of the mask in the Mediterranean area, it is worth speaking of them briefly.[23]

In Jericho, at a level corresponding to the prepottery Neolithic B period (approximately 7600 to 6000 B.C.E.), twelve skulls were found that had been remodeled plastically with plaster of Paris; five of them also showed traces of having been painted at some time (K. Kenyon 1981:36). Why were these skulls prepared in such a manner? Various conjectures were made, and the hypothesis of the "mask" (with the skull being worn on top of the head, for

---

21. J. G. D. Clark 1954:168–72; Vlček and Kukla 1959:519–26.
22. Vallois 1971. On skull-masks, see below, chapter 4.
23. R. Zorzi in Juárez Frias and Pérez Rodrígez 1981:7.

THE AGE OF THE RITUAL MASK   37

example) is neither the only nor the most likely one.[24] Nevertheless, since the technique of remodeling skulls was also used by populations without writing in making masks, funerary mannequins or effigies, the Jericho skulls inevitably had to solicit speculations, among others, as to the Near-Eastern origin of certain Melanesian traditions. For Lommel, for example, "the masks of the South Sea peoples, particularly the Melanesians, which derive from the remodeled ancestor skull, drew their original inspiration from the Middle East, as the discoveries in Jericho dating from c. 5000 B.C. seem to indicate."[25] However, it has not been established either that the masks of the South Pacific did in fact derive from the remodeled skull, or, on the other hand, that the remodeled skulls of the Pacific had their origins in the Near East. The available documents do not allow for the verification of these speculations.

In 1962, a soft limestone mask probably coming from the region of Hebron was discovered. The Bedouin who found it during and illicit excavation had sold it, along with pottery deemed to have come from the same source, to a Catholic priest. As the exact conditions of the discovery were unknown, it was supposed that the mask dated to the same epoch as the pottery, that is to say, to the middle of the Bronze age, around 1600 B.C.E. (Winzinger 1964). A discovery made in 1983 enabled the question to be raised again based on new evidence: in a cave at Nahal Hemar, fragments from several stone masks were exhumed which were possible to date to the pre-pottery Neolithic B period, therefore to the same epoch as the molded, remodeled skulls, and more particularly to the seventh millennium B.C.E.[26] One of the pieces was par-

---

24. See for example K. Kenyon 1979:35–36; 1981:78. Remodeled skulls were also found at Beisamoun Ain Ghazal (near Amman) and Tell Ramad (on the plateau of Damas). See Cauvin 1985:172c; Lechevallier and Perrot 1973:107–8; Simmons and Rollefson 1985. Contenson (1967:20–21) put forward the hypothesis that at Tell Ramad small earthenware statuettes may have served to support the remodeled skulls, on the model of the neo-Guinean *korvar*. On the *korvar*, see Bühler 1969:50–51; Guiart 1963:306–10; Van Baaren 1968.

25. Lommel 1970:220; cf. 58. It should be noted that the skulls probably date to the seventh and eighth millennium, not the fifth as was supposed first of all by K. Kenyon (1972:93) followed by Lommel. For the latter, "it is possible that the custom of remodeling ancestor skulls originated in the Middle East and spread to Oceania. There is no evidence that it ever reached Africa" (1970:218). However, see the parallels established by Camps (1974:176) with the skull of Faïd Souar which were discussed above.

26. See Bar-Yosef 1985. According to one of the archaeologists responsible

tially reconstituted (fig. 5): it was a limestone mask with rounded eyes; the nose is missing, the mouth is small and the teeth (four upper and four lower) are indicated by incisions. Red and green painted bands radiate from the center of the face. Eighteen irregularly spaced holes are pierced on the edge of the mask and traces of asphalt can be discerned here and there.[27] It seems hardly likely that stone masks were placed on the face by a wearer during ceremonies (Bar-Yosef 1985:14). They could be funerary masks, or the facial portion of an effigy, or "masks" that were suspended on poles. These hypotheses had already been put forward about the so-called Hebron mask (Winzinger 1964:153) and nothing at the moment would suggest favoring one or the other. All the same these stone masks are the first sure and dated evidence attesting to the existence of "masks" (although the exact meaning of the word cannot be specified) in the seventh millennium B.C.E. However, without more information, it is not possible to conclude from this that in the same epoch there would have existed masks worn in ceremonies by living human beings. The first evidence to that effect seems to come from Egypt where "the most ancient representation of a masked figure appears, in all certainty, on a fragment of the side of the funerary temple of the king Sahourê in the fifth dynasty, around 2500 B.C.E.; the same mask is found on a fragment in bas-relief of a mastaba from the end of the Ancient Empire, as well as in the tomb of Kherouef during the eighteenth dynasty (around 1390 B.C.E.). This mask reproduces the feline features of the god Bès."[28]

The plastic art of ancient Europe was also employed to demonstrate the antiquity of the mask. Thus, Marija Gimbutas discovered an abundance of masks in Europe from the sixth millennium before our era. Unfortunately, some of the criteria that she used to bolster her interpretation are too subjective to be accepted without question. For example, she states, the heads of the figurines "appear unfamiliar, even ugly, presenting an uncomfortably non-

---

for the find, there were fragments of three or four masks (Alon 1985).

27. According to Bar-Yosef, the holes and the asphalt could have served to attach hair to the mask. Also uncovered at Nahal Hemar were exceptional skulls: they are coated with asphalt and have a net pattern on the top and back of the skull. Small, painted human figurines and fragments of a clay statue similar to those found in Jericho and in Ain Ghazal were also discovered (Bar-Yosef 1985:13–14).

28. Barguet 1960:64–65; cf. Vercoutter 1964:593.

The Age of the Ritual Mask

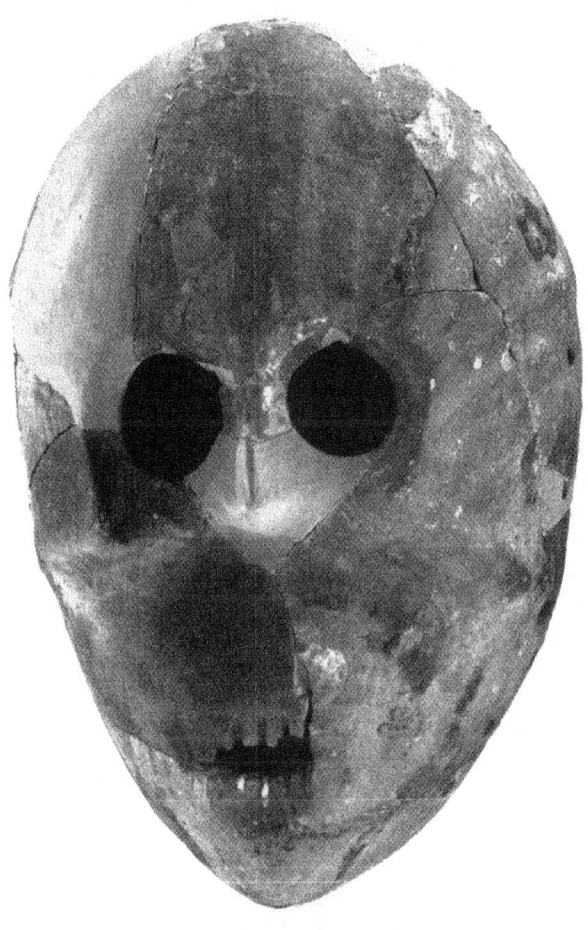

5. Mask of Nahal Hemar. From Bar-Yosef 1985:1.

human visage suggestive of a mask" or "the truncated lower part of the face ending in a sharp triangle shows it to be a mask."[29] The greater number of these "masks" that she thus discloses in her

---

29. Gimbutas 1982:57–58. See the reservations formulated by Guilaine 1985:48.

evidence seem to us rather to be the result of stylization. This explanation is at the same time simpler and closer to the evidence than interpretations such as "bird-masked woman holding a bird-masked baby" (p. 143, pl. 132) or "goddess, holding a baby, both wearing bear masks" (p. 194, p. 193) or again, "human-headed (masked) bull" (p. 225). Other "masks" seem able to be explained by the technique used for molding the face. Perhaps it is also in this manner that it would be appropriate to understand the only truly troubling example, in my opinion, appearing in the book by Gimbutas (p.58, pl. 27); but since only a photograph of this head is provided, without detailed discussion of the case, doubt remains as to its interpretation. It must be admitted, in that respect, that the sheer abundance of "masks" does more a disservice than it serves the purpose of this author who arrives at the surprising conclusion that figurines with unmasked heads and human facial features comprise the rarest category of Neolithic and Chalcolithic sculptures (p.43; cf. p. 54).

In one of her comparisons, Gimbutas maintains that "animal-headed demons walking upright, as depicted on Mycenaean frescos and gems, must be humans wearing masks" (1982:66). However, in examining the source cited by the author (Mylonas 1966, fig. 126), it is apparent that the beings represented are without human characteristics: neither their hands nor their feet look human, and their legs are articulated like those of animals. One could possibly be led to think of fantastic animals, but nothing authorizes the interpretation of "humans wearing masks." Mylonas himself speaks of "genii" or "demons" (1966:148, 162, 166–68). Once again, the conviction of the interpreter seems to have been weighed more heavily than the evidence itself. It is unfortunately not always possible to judge so clearly between competing interpretations. Thus, for example, in a seal found at Susa, Hole sees a masked human being carrying out ceremonies where Amiet leans rather in favor of its interpretation as a master-genie of the animals.[30] Another example is that of a cylindrical seal of Ugarit, on which some see representations of priests wearing

---

30. Hole 1982:320. Amiet 1972:36, 37, 50, 82. Hole believes that his interpretation is strengthened by the fact that the figure wears a medallion hung over the chest and that copper disks were found in the cemetery. Nevertheless it is difficult to see why the Susans would not have been able to represent a mythic being wearing this same disk. Compare as well the interpretations of Barnett 1966 and Amiet 1979; cf. Mellaart 1971:167.

horned animal masks for the execution of sacrifices; however, in its published form, it seems just as easy to view the figures as composite beings.[31] The only conclusion that one can draw with any assurance is that the documents are not as convincing as many would have liked to believe.

The question of the antiquity of the ritual mask brings us back to a point about method, extremely well expressed by Eliade: it would be absurd to "mistake the appearance of a belief with the date at which it is witnessed for the first time" (1976–83, 1:17). Applied to the mask, this rule means that one should not be satisfied with determining the age of the oldest mask known and considering that age as indicating the date of the appearance of the ritual mask. It is nevertheless important to remember that once one leaves the domain of dating museum pieces or archaeological documents, speculative elements, if not prejudices, naturally intervene. The brief examination above of certain evidence presented as proving the existence of the mask should have demonstrated this. An element of speculation appears just as frequently when masks are placed on a "chronological" scale established not according to the age of the mask, but its type. Most sources explicitly or implicitly used such a theory, the most widespread proposing that, at the outset, all masks were ritual masks and that they later evolved to produce spectacle masks, war masks, etc.[32] Bédouin expresses this very clearly when he writes:

> Although they testify to very ancient cultural complexes, the most 'ancient' of the masks of Oceania and Africa that we know do not date earlier than the nineteenth century. With the exception of funerary masks and rare wooden masks that can be dated to the pre-Columbian epoch, those of Indians and Eskimos are just as recent. By contrast, Japanese theater masks whose existence dates back several centuries (we have examples from the eighth century) belong to a much more

---

31. Schaeffer 1939:64, pl. X/2. The interpretation of Schaeffer is accepted by Eliade 1976–83:1, 430. See also at Tepe Yahyā, human figures with supernatural attributes from Lamberg-Karlovsky and Lamberg-Karlovsky 1972:178.

32. For example: Glotz 1978:31; Maesen 1961:31; Montandon 1934:726. The authors in question are not necessarily in agreement as to the number, nature, and succession of the various types, but they agree as to the precedence of the ritual mask over the spectacle mask.

'modern' artistic tradition than the former, if one admits that the theater is an intellectualized form of ritual dance and of sacred drama.[33]

There are two main reasons for the absence of ancient masks coming from contemporary societies: First, the materials used are generally perishable and fragile (wood, fiber, fabric, and even spider web as in Vanuatu); second, the fact that in numerous cases the mask is ritually destroyed after its use. It is quite possible that these same reasons are equally valid for prehistoric societies, but one cannot seize on this pretext to interpret the absence of documents. There is a link here between the problem of the geographical distribution and that of the antiquity of the mask. Indeed, once scholars gain a better understanding of why the mask is present in certain contemporary societies and not in others, it will perhaps be easier to identify, in pre- or protohistoric societies, those that are likely to have had ritual masks.[34] For, just as the mask is not universal today, nothing allows us to believe that it was so at any given moment in prehistory or in history.

At the end of this brief survey, it is possible to observe that the presence of the ritual mask in Paleolithic times remains doubtful but that with the Neolithic period, the probability of the existence of ritual masks increases, especially in the Near East, in Africa and in Europe. However, it remains impossible to fix a precise date or place for the appearance or appearances of this institution.

---

33. Bédouin 1967:98. According to Noma (1957:3, 6), the masks used in the Gigaku dance-drama are not only the first historic masks used in Japan but are among the oldest surviving examples of masks in the entire world. According to this author, 31 Gigaku masks from the seventh century from the temple Horyu-ji; 164 eighth-century masks are preserved in the Shoso-in and 28 more of the same period at Todai-ji, making a total of 223 masks from the seventh and eighth century still in existence. For Kleinschmidt (1966:7), this total is at least 247.

34. Regarding the mortuary masks from Mycenae, Mylonas suggests that placing masks in the graves of men was an intrusive element, an innovation imported from Egypt along with other elements and whose abandonment after its novelty wore off was rather natural, particularly because it had no place in the traditions of the people (1966:132–33; cf. Picard 1948:288–89). Already in those days the discovery of the mask—in this case, the mortuary mask—did not suffice to guarantee its lasting adoption.

Part Two

From the Dead to Cosmos: What Does the Ritual Mask Represent?

CHAPTER 3

Spirit, Event, and World System

IN CONSULTING general works on masks, or the generalities given in introductions to museum catalogs or to studies devoted to one or several particular masks, it is apparent that after universality, whose limits were described above, the idea that is most frequently reasserted is that ritual masks represent spirits. This idea is not always formulated so categorically; some authors prefer to add the qualification that "most" masks represent spirits. But what is remarkable is that those who express reservations in the presentation of the rule are then hardly interested in masks that are not among "most" and do not represent spirits. Two conclusions can be drawn from this lack of interest: either the restriction serves more as an oratory precaution than as an intention to distinguish clearly between several types of masks, each answering to a determined function or meaning; or these authors believe that ritual masks can be interpreted globally from those that do represent spirits. A certain number of authors take a further step and affirm that the spirits thus represented, or most of them, are those of the dead.[1]

What is striking about this approach is its statistical character, which probably betrays the exaggerated influence, in the Western imaginary universe, of the mask as a museum piece. In fact, many societies having masks also possess statuary; however, if they choose to represent a spirit by a mask worn by a dancer rather than by a statue, they probably aim at doing more than simply representing the spirit. Selecting examples from those regions most often drawn upon for the elaboration of theories about masks (Africa, Melanesia, America), I hope to verify that by fixing attention on the mask's representation of a spirit we risk missing something more important. I shall also keep in mind the thesis that masks represent the spirits of the dead, and will verify if such is indeed the case. No attempt will be made to present here the

---

1. The frequent confusion between the notions of spirits, the dead, and ancestors is examined in chapter 5.

whole of the symbolic, psychological, social, and political meanings of ritual masks; rather, working from the hypothesis that masks represent spirits, I shall limit myself to sketching the complements or the correctives that the societies in question will suggest. In order to give an idea of the complexity that the study of masks can involve, I shall begin by examining five Dogon masks in a relatively detailed manner, and only later move on to briefer remarks on some other traditions.

The Dogon inhabit a territory situated at the border of Mali and Burkina Faso, in the bend of the Niger River.[2] Their population is estimated at 250,000. They are cultivators, and agriculture is the basis of their economy. The core of their society is the extended family grouped under the authority of a patriarch. In the administration of the village, authority is exercised by a council of elders; the supreme authority is the Hogon, senior member of his age class and religious head of a region. The line is patrilineal and residence is patrilocal.[3]

In certain regions of the cliff and the plateau, every circumcised man becomes a member of a masking society (*ava* or *wa*) which is the male association in charge of, among others, the cult offered to he who experienced the first death, the mythic ancestor Dyongou Sérou, represented by the "great mask" or "great wood" (*mina na*). The mask is the collective property of the village.[4] The circumcised male must sculpt (or have sculpted) and then wear the mask of his choice in order to dance at funerals and above all

---

2. Dogon (singular Dogo) is the name that they give themselves; they were called Tombo by the Bambara, Kibisi by the Mossi and Habé by the Peul. This latter term was adopted for a while by the French administration, which accounts for its use by certain authors. For the greater part of these preliminary remarks, I follow Griaule and Dieterlen 1965:13–58; one will find a recent general presentation on the Dogon in Beaudoin 1984. See also *African Arts* vol. 21, no 4, (August 1988), which is devoted to Dogon art.

3. Calame-Griaule 1968:135. Nevertheless, according to certain informants, the ideal marriage partner would be the daughter of the maternal uncle, which led Griaule and Dieterlen to conclude that "this fact and other customs lead one to believe in the presence of a kinship system through women where the maternal uncle plays a great role" (1965:28; cf. Griaule 1954; Dieterlen 1956). Michel-Jones (1978:19) nevertheless contests that this theoretically preferential marriage is realized in practice.

4. Contrary to what DeMott thought (1982:82), the *ava* cannot be considered a "secret society." On the many meanings of the term *ava*, see Calame-Griaule 1965:439; Griaule 1963:62–63, 69–70, 189–90, 263–65; Dieterlen 1956:113, 133–34; Leiris 1941; Tait 1950:193–94.

during the rites of the ceremony marking the end of the period of mourning or *ama*.[5] These rites are addressed to the spiritual elements of the deceased whom they are to accompany, to bring, or to lead until the funerary pottery is deposited in the family altar, the latter act acknowledging that the deceased has now attained the rank of ancestor. The masks also intervene in various other practices, the principal ones consisting of rites for fertility and protection against certain dangers: rites regarding the fecundity of women, rain, and protection against sorcerers. Masks are also used as markers of prohibitions in order to protect harvests or cultures against theft or plunder (Griaule 1963:763–71).

The Dogons established a hierarchy of teaching levels for the instruction of initiates. Their knowledge is organized on a scale of four degrees which are, in order of increasing importance, "the word from the front" (*giri so*), "the word from the side" (*benne so*), "the word from behind" (*bolo so*) and the "clear word" (*so dayi*) (Griaule 1952:27). The Dogon first answered ethnographers' questions from the perspective of the first level of knowledge. It was only in 1946 that they decided to initiate French anthropologist Marcel Griaule to their highest degrees of knowledge and assigned one of their most competent elders, Ogotemmêli, the task of beginning his instruction.[6] In the discussion that follows, I shall refer schematically to two principal traditions contained in the sources: the first, a tradition that, following Calame-Griaule (1956:406), I call "popular," which corresponds for the most part with the evidence and ideas contained in the publications of the pre-Ogotemmêlian period (that is to say works that precede the research of 1947); and the second, a tradition that, in keeping with Michel-Jones (1978:16, 18), I call "learned," and one that is present in the dialogues with Ogotemmêli and the publications that followed them.

The works resulting from the Griaule missions raised various criticisms which are important for understanding documents concerning Dogon masks as well as those of other societies. The principal criticism of Griaule and his collaborators is that they identified "the scientific explanation with the metalanguage that

---

5. The wearing of certain masks carries the payment of a fee for the right, for example 200 cowries to wear the *kanaga* mask (Paulme 1940:250). Cf. Borgatti 1979b:4–5.
6. Griaule and Dieterlen 1965:54–55; Griaule 1966:4.

Dogon society uses in reference to itself and to which a few initiates are privy," and that they accepted the information furnished by the latter without criticism.⁷ Thus one could suspect that the coherence and harmony with which the Dogon society is credited reveals less its intrinsic properties than the cognitive coherence of the informants or the ideological schemas that the observers brought to the situation.⁸ Moreover, the studies in question generally are based on the principle that, since everything is prefigured in the myth, the myth explains everything and conditions everything; the studies, therefore, often betray a lack of attention to real practices or confuse dominant discourse and actual practice.⁹ Equally, they neglect elements that belong to the popular level of belief, elements about which we are much better informed by the first works than by the more recent ones.[10]

It is important, therefore, to keep in mind that texts reporting Dogon traditions can be marked in a more or less appreciable way by particular methodological choices. But it would be vain to believe that studies undertaken elsewhere by other teams, and to which one cannot extend the same criticisms, necessarily present a better image of masking traditions. Many remain fragmentary and are incapable of explaining the details of the masks or costumes, the rhythms or the steps of dance that are particular to them. Along these lines, the degree of acculturation attained by the societies under investigation is sometimes invoked. This is often a good reason, certainly, but the informant might just as well have chosen simply to leave the ethnologist in the dark. It should not be forgotten that it was only after fifteen years of contact that the Dogon consented to reveal their "learned" tradition to Griaule. Therefore, it is easy to imagine that due to a lack of interest in cosmology, a lack of time, or as a consequence of a less favorable

---

7. Michel-Jones 1978:21, 23; cf. Douglas 1975:139. According to Griaule, nevertheless, the "learned" tradition is not the exclusive domain of some specialists alone: the number of instructed Dogon represents about 30% of the total population, that is 15 to 20% for men and about 13% for women (Griaule 1952:33–34). I shall not attempt here to decide upon what role must be granted to the exegesis proposed—or hidden—by local informants, in the explanation of their tradition. One will find in Wagner 1984 a summary of the virulent debate which took place, on the same theme, regarding Melanesian traditions.

8. Fortes and Dieterlen 1965:10; Michel-Jones 1978:15–16; Schwimmer 1981:238; cf. Augé 1987:15; Elisofon and Fagg 1978:29; Hart 1985:248–49.

9. Michel-Jones 1978:15–16, 20, 32.

10. Calame-Griaule 1965:406–7. This work is an exception in the amount of information that it provides about the daily life of the Dogon.

Spirit, Event, and World System 49

relationship with their hosts, many ethnologists did not have the luck that Griaule had and therefore were not admitted to the highest levels of knowledge of the peoples they studied. Schweeger-Hefel (1970:108), for example, is perfectly conscious of this possibility and points out that what she may have learned of the probably extensive learned knowledge of the Nyonyosi corresponds to only the lowest levels of initiation, equivalent to what the average inhabitant of Sarma knows.

In the inventory of Dogon masks established by Griaule, one finds mammals, birds, reptiles, lizards, Dogon and foreign figures, as well as objects.[11] I shall turn, first of all, to the masks that are least likely to represent spirits, those in the category of things, in order to establish whether they should be considered of secondary importance, as simple exceptions to the rule of the spirit-mask, or whether they impart some basic understanding of Dogon masks in particular and expand our knowledge of ritual masks in general.

Take, for example, the *sirige* mask—translated as "two-storied house" in Griaule's inventory—which consists of a rectangular face topped by a very tall sculpted mast sometimes measuring more than five meters in height and whose summit is generally tapered to a point (fig. 6).[12] According to some of Griaule's sources, the *sirige* was a recent and profane mask, a simple sculpture inspired by the sight of a "two-storied house"; the vast movements traced by its mast were intended to show the strength of the jaw and the nape of the neck of the wearer to best advantage.[13] However, another informant told a myth that traced the *sirige* back to the Andoumboulou.[14] This reference seemed to indicate that the

---

11. Griaule 1963:399–401, 850–52. As for Dieterlen (1960:49–50), she distinguished four principal categories of masks: masks of initiation, representational masks and property of "societies," masks associated with agricultural activities, and masks worn exclusively during public ceremonies. I do not use these categories here since, on the one hand, they can overlap, and on the other, they are not concerned as much with the meaning of masks as with knowing who owns them, when they appear and to what extent they are secret, which is not my central interest here.

12. Griaule 1963:587–96; Griaule and Dieterlen 1965:169, 223, 438–49.

13. Griaule 1963:587. The storied house (*ginna*), lineage house, is the first built when a village is founded. "It is called 'family house' because it must shelter the set of collective altars that concern this family. That means that this dwelling is above all a temple" (Dieterlen 1965:53; cf. Griaule 1966:85–95).

14. Griaule 1963:594. The Dogon call the people that lived in the cliffs when they came to inhabit them the Tellem. According to a Dogon myth, the Andoumboulou, men small in stature and of a reddish skin pigmentation, preceded the Tellem and taught them to build their dwellings in the hollows of

6. Three dancers wearing *sirige* masks. From Beaudoin 1984:113.

sirige was considered to be older and more important than they wanted to admit. Later, the "learned" version brought to light a much more complex vision of the mask, in which there are four variants of the *sirige*.[15] The first evokes the work of Amma, supreme god; the movement of the mask wearer swirling around himself recalls the swirling motion of Amma in creating the world. The second variation recalls the complicated journeys of Ogo, the fomenter of disorder.[16] The third and fourth variations represent aspects of the descent and the impact of the ark.[17] Since the architecture of the two-storied house (*ginna*) also recalls both the ark and its descent, the link between the mask and the house therefore no longer proceeds only in such a way that one would represent the other: both refer equally to the same series of primordial events.

A similar remark can be made about the mask *amma ta* or "Amma's door" (fig. 7): at first, Griaule learned that this mask represented a sculpted granary door (1963:596). Later, he discovered that it also recalled the initial opening of Amma's clavicles, an important phase in Dogon cosmology. Furthermore, the term *amma ta* is "a euphemism meant to hide from non-initiates the

---

the cliff peaks; they also taught the Dogon their dances and the art of making masks. But there remains a certain confusion among the Dogon as to the real or mythic peoples that preceded them. The encounter with the Andoumboulou is sometimes presented as having taken place in Mandé, that is to say, before the migration of the Dogon to their actual habitat (Griaule 1963:59–60); some informants nevertheless affirm that the myths about these small people were taught to the inhabitants of the region of Sanga by those (Tellem) who occupied the country before them (Griaule 1963:55, n.1). The type of beliefs that the Dogon hold with regard to the Andoumboulou correspond to a tradition commonly shared by many African peoples and which some authors considered to be based on historic facts: Cornevin 1960:127–28; Delafosse 1922:11–12. On the Tellem and the archaeological discoveries made in the actual habitat of the Dogon, see Bedaux 1977; Huizinga 1968.

15. See Griaule and Dieterlen 1965:169, 438–39.

16. Griaule and Dieterlen 1965:175ff. Amma, supreme god, put the seeds of future beings in an original placenta which would later become the earth; one of these beings, Ogo, entered the world prematurely and began to sow disorder. Changed into a fox as his punishment, he is in perpetual conflict with his twin Nommo, sacrificed in the sky and resurrected for the reorganization of creation. Calame-Griaule 1968:136; Dieterlen 1978:176–77; Griaule and Dieterlen 1965:24–26.

17. The "learned" tradition includes several descriptions of descents of arks from the sky to the earth: three descents by Ogo and one by the Nommo in an ark filled with all that Amma had created and protected from the action of Ogo. It is to this latter descent that allusion is made here. See Griaule and Dieterlen 1965:417ff.

7. *Amma ta* mask. From Griaule 1963:599.

true name of the mask, *amma talu,* 'egg of Amma,' " another notion of capital importance in Dogon cosmology.[18]

The *sirige* and the *amma ta* masks demonstrate that the masks that are the least likely to represent spirits nevertheless have a capital significance since they recall cosmogonic events of the greatest magnitude. They also reveal a second extremely important fact: the same mask can be read at different levels (*sirige* = two-storied house, *sirige* = events to which the two-storied house also refers) without the various possible readings being contradictory or exclusive. It is precisely this which is a characteristic of Dogon traditions: figures, objects, events insert themselves in a network of very dense correspondences that must be taken into account in its entirety each time one attempts to grasp the meaning of one aspect or element of these traditions.

Let us turn now to those masks deemed to represent living beings or "spirits." To do this, it is indispensable that one first know that the Dogon distinguish the spiritual elements or "souls" (*kikinu* = breath) from the vital force (*nyama*), conceived as a fluid that circulates with the blood.[19] The *nyama* is an impersonal, unconscious energy, distributed among animals, vegetables, supernatural beings, and things of nature; it tends to sustain in their being the supports to which it is allocated. This vital force is divisible and transmissible, susceptible to qualitative and quantitative variations, sensitive to all impurity with which it is imbued and which it immediately communicates to its support. It is considered dangerous as soon as it is liberated from its usual support.

The "great mask" or "great wood" (*imina na*) is frequently cited in the literature. It is even sometimes considered as an archetype of the Dogon mask or the ritual mask, which is particularly paradoxical since the question arises as to whether or not it is in fact a mask at all. Indeed, the great wood is not a false face worn by a dancer, nor a disguise, and in fact, it is not danced.[20] It is actually a sculpted mast, painted with black and red triangles and

---

18. Griaule and Dieterlen 1965:165–66, 183.
19. The variations between popular and learned traditions are marked principally by matters relating to the spirits: we moved from two to eight, divided into two groups of two couples of twin spirits each. See, on the one hand, Dieterlen 1941:73ff.; Griaule 1962:161ff.; and on the other hand, Calame-Griaule 1965:32–48; Griaule and Dieterlen 1965:36–40, 373–75.
20. The information according to which certain great masks would have been worn in the past is hardly convincing. See Griaule 1963:238, n.3; Dieterlen 1960:49; cf. De Bilde 1979:25.

8. *Imina na* mask. From Griaule 1933:8.

whose appearance is suggestive of a snake (fig. 8).²¹ This mast is brought out on various occasions, but never in the manner of a traditional mask. This is why certain specialists consider the *imina na* to be more an ancestral effigy than a mask.²² Whatever the final decision on this point, it remains all the same that "the wooden snake is by far the most important object in the institution of masks" (Griaule 1963:230). For this reason and because of the interest it solicits among many authors, it is fitting to examine it in detail. Before doing so, it is necessary to examine the principal mythic events that led to its creation.²³

In the beginning, the world did not include death; at an advanced age, each being transformed itself into a snake or a genie. One day, just when the oldest man, Dyongou Sérou, had transformed himself into a snake, he encountered some young people who had appropriated Andoumboulou masks without his permission and were wearing them without consulting him. At this sight, the old man-snake hurled the most violent reproaches in the

---

21. Griaule 1963:178–79, 229–52.
22. Krieger and Kutscher 1960:11; Leiris and Delange 1967:132, 434; Paulme 1940:516. In many respects, the great wood functions as an altar as well. It is not the only one to do so, as will become apparent in chapter 6.
23. See Griaule 1963:61–66. We give here the report of events which unfolded among human beings. As for the similar events which took place beforehand among the Andoumboulou, see Griaule 1963:55–59.

Spirit, Event, and World System

Dogon language, but because he had used the language of men when he had already taken the form of an animal belonging to the world of the Yéban genies, he became impure, and as a result, he could no longer live among the genies. His new state, furthermore, kept him from returning to the world of men. He died then and there.[24] The men wrapped his body in red fibers. Unfortunately, there was a pregnant woman in the village who was dressed in fibers of the same color. This circumstance had serious consequences, causing her to bear a child that was red, like the fibers, and spotted, like the snake. When consulted, diviners informed the parents that the soul (*kikinu say*) and the vital force (*nyama*) of the snake had been liberated by its death. A support was needed to embody this force and this soul needed food that a representative (*nani*) chosen from among the living would provide it. Thus, the men sculpted a great mask to resemble the snake exactly, so that it would serve as the support for its *nyama*.[25] They also designated two companions for the child marked by the dead snake; they became the first initiates (*olubaru*).

This summary corresponds to the mythic events related by the popular tradition. As for the learned tradition,[26] the violation of prohibitions committed by Dyongou Sérou deprived him of one of his spiritual elements necessary for life. After his death, his transgression was forgiven; his brothers carved a great wood in his image where his spiritual elements then were gathered together in their entirety.

Ever since, every sixty years an itinerant ceremony called *sigui* is celebrated, though it does not extend over the whole of Dogon country. It commemorates, on the one hand, the revelation of the spoken word to men, and on the other hand, the story of the appearance of death among men. It is on the occasion of *sigui* that the great wood is carved. According to the theory in which masks represent the spirits of the dead, the explanation for the carving of the mask would appear relatively simple: with the

---

24. It is to be noted that this first creature to die had the form of a snake. The first human death occurs later in the person of Lébé. See Griaule 1963:70; Ganay 1937.

25. "The word *imina* can be applied to all masks. It is broken down into *mina*, a mandigo term meaning "catcher," and *i*, in place of *ya*, from *yama* or *nyama*. This name corresponds exactly to the function of the mask, which is to fix the *nyama*" (Griaule 1963:66, n.1). See also below what the learned tradition says.

26. See Dieterlen 1971:5–6; cf. Dieterlen 1956:119; Griaule 1966:158–65.

wood of the great mask having aged, it would be necessary to carve a new one, to renew the support for the spiritual elements of the first deceased, ever present in the world of men. Similarly, new initiates are necessary for the cult of the ancestor. The *sigui* then provides for a double renewal—a renewal of the wood and of initiates (Griaule 1966:165). However, such a materialistic view can explain the carving of only one great wood, since there is only one Dyongou Sérou. But in the example reported by Dieterlen, each of the four villages of Lower Sanga (Sanga-du-Bas) carved its own effigy and the four great woods appeared together during the ritual (Dieterlen 1971:9). It is therefore necessary to transcend this too narrow vision.

During the *sigui* ceremonies, certain dignitaries are the representatives, the living witnesses, of the mythic ancestors. These mythic ancestors are present because the events with which they were associated are commemorated. From this point of view, there is no fundamental difference between the great wood and the "woman of the sigui," for example.[27] Why is it then that Dyongou Sérou is the only one to be represented by an effigy? Why is there no dignitary serving as his witness? Or furthermore, why are not all mythic ancestors represented by effigies? The answer seems to be obvious and essential: Dyongou Sérou is represented—symbolically, adds Dieterlen (1971:4) —by the great wood because his breach of prohibition provoked a series of events (the first appearance of death, first carving of a great wood, first celebration of sigui) which are to be commemorated: the purpose is therefore not simply to represent him, but to recall the primordial events in which he was involved. Hence the importance attached not only to the presence of the great wood, but to all phases of its preparation (carving, painting, etc.). The particular importance of the great wood then derives from the mythic events that it recalls, which brings us closer to what was noted above about the *sirige* and the *amma ta*.

As for the other masks representing characters or animals, the most widespread justification given by the Dogon can be summarized as follows: such a being was killed, and in order to keep safe

---

27. From the religious point of view, the *yasigine*, "woman of the sigui," represents Yasigui, Ogo's twin (see note 16, chap. 3). She also takes part in funeral ceremonies where she plays the role of the mythic ancestor. Griaule and Dieterlen 1965:35; Dieterlen 1956:117–20, 128–29; Dieterlen 1978:181. See also chapter 7.

Spirit, Event, and World System   57

from the ill effects of his *nyama* now deprived of its support, men sculpted or made a mask to represent that being (Griaule 1963:419-587). The following, for example, is the narrative of events that led to the carving of the first animal mask. The excerpt here includes only a few aspects which are important to the discussion:[28] A man killed a *gomtogo*.[29] Having cut off its head, he embedded the skull in his hunter's altar. The powerful *nyama* of the victim was held in check by the *nyama* of the altar as well as that of the hunter.[30] When the latter died, however, the *nyama* of the altar alone was not strong enough to keep the dangerous force from becoming harmful. It attacked the son of the hunter who then fell ill. On the advice of diviners, a wooden mask was carved in the image of the animal. After a sacrifice, the head of the child was touched with the mask, which forced the *nyama* of the animal to leave him. Then a drawing of the mask was made on the wall of the shelter and put in contact with the mask so that, by a second transfer, the *nyama* moved from the mask to the rock painting. Thus rid of the *nyama* that had caused the sickness, the hunter's son was able to put the mask on his face since it had also been rid of any dangerous spiritual element; during the *dama* that followed the death of his father, he joined the other maskers. By his dance, the son thanked his father who in life had done all that was in his power to keep the *nyama* of the slain animal within his altar. But his action had another aim: it was hoped that it would contribute to the work of the other maskers, who had climbed on the mortuary terrace to force the soul of the dead to leave the village.

This narrative is very important as it includes several fundamental conceptions. First of all, the mask permits the transfer of the disturbing *nyama* from the sick child to the rock painting. At the moment when the mask is worn by the dancer, it is empty of any dangerous spiritual element, which means that it no longer supports the *nyama* of the animal that it is representing. Therefore, although it is obvious that the mask represents a "departed" being (the *gomtogo*), nothing suggests that the mask itself incorporates or represents the spirit of this being, nor that by a sort of sleight of hand, it represents the spirit of a deceased

---

28. This refers of course to the popular tradition found in Griaule 1963:74-77; see also the variation in Griaule 1963:422-23.
29. This animal is not clearly identified. Griaule 1963:419.
30. "An altar is a reservoir of *nyama* fed by the sacrifices and whose power is used for specific ends" Griaule 1963:75, n.4.

human being.[31] Finally, this text introduces the idea that the dance on the terrace of the dead man's house aims at inciting the soul of the dead to leave the village.

Nevertheless, this narrative does not solve all the problems. Although it demonstrates that the mask is empty of any dangerous spiritual element when it is worn, there is no doubt that the Dogon think that the mask is charged with a potentially dangerous *nyama*: "When a woman breaks a prohibition regarding masks (characters or accessories), she can be attacked by the *nyama* of the fibers"; in order to heal her, the myth of the discovery of masks by a woman is recited, and "passing the appropriate bark over the body of the patient, the officiant gathers into them the dangerous substance and finally brings all of it to an anthill" (Griaule 1963:269, 775–76). Therefore, there is some *nyama* in the mask and the costume, in particular in the accessory essential to the costume, the skirt of red fibers. The dyeing of these red fibers is one of the most important operations of the ritual marking the end of the period of mourning (*dama*): "red is the most beautiful of colors and also that which is most charged with religious meaning. It reminds one of blood; it recalls the color of the mythic fibers that Amma gave to the world. For all these reasons, it is considered to contain a powerful *nyama*" (Griaule 1963:353). This *nyama* is not dangerous only for women: the day before the operation, the men who are going to take charge of the dyeing purify themselves and make an offering so that the *nyama* does not affect them.

What then are these mythic fibers that the mask's costume recalls? According to one myth which has many variations, Amma gave a string of fibers to his wife, the Earth (or the ant). Reddened by the menstrual blood which appeared after the incestuous union between the Earth and her son, the Fox (see p. 51 n. 16), they were set out to dry on an ant-hill. When Amma had fallen asleep, the Fox thought him dead and, donning the fibers taken from his mother, he climbed onto his father's terrace

---

31. This is also very far removed from the explanation offered by Riley (1955:19). According to him, each man tried to attract to himself and assure the possession of additional *nyama*, especially that of a recently deceased relative. The mask enables this capture and, in wearing it, the individual had the feeling that he could capture all or part of the vital force and add it to his own power of control over the supernatural. This is why, according to Riley, the use of the mask in funeral rites was a common practice in Africa.

where he danced a dance that traced the world and its future. Thus the first dance was the dance of divination, but also the dance of death, since the Fox invented it to honor and praise his father whom he thought dead. A bird of prey stole the fibers which were then brought into the reach of human beings. A woman obtained them, and with the help of the adornment, ruled and sowed terror. Finally, men took the garment from the woman and in their turn adorned themselves with it. However, because they had hidden their exploits from the oldest man, this finally led to the events described above in reference to the great wood.[32]

When men put on the fibers, says Ogotemmêli, "it is as if they were dressing as women" (Griaule 1966:161). But the connotations do not end there and are multiple: the scarlet fibers refer to the sun; damp, they refer to the fecundity of women, dry, to their sterility; the red color refers to menstrual blood, but also to certain aspects of the resurrected Nommo and to the female sex organ: "the red color of woman is comparable to the red fibers of the mask which are themselves like the leaves of the stalk of ripe millet, that is to say, a symbol of death" (Griaule and Dieterlen 1965:363–64) Given this complexity, of which I have given only a glimpse, it is apparent that the interpretation offered by Calame-Griaule (1965:283, 442, 445), for whom the *nyama* of masks is the *nyama* of the dead and masked men represent and identify with the dead, seems, to say the least, a bit short. Indeed, the multiple connotations of the fibers complement what was described above about masks: the latter indeed recall a series of events, but from the perspective of death, in opposition to the other perspective, that of the gift of the word. In the variation of the myth just summarized, the fibers, the essential element of the costume of the mask, are the clue connecting, on the one hand, the various disorders which bring about the introduction of death into creation and the world of men, but also, on the other hand, the various restorations of order which have made the world what it is today.

To what extent does the learned tradition modify the perspective opened by the narrative of the carving of the first animal mask? I shall limit myself to the example of the *kanaga* mask which represents the *kommolo tebu* bird, maybe a small bustard

---

32. Griaule 1963:52–63; 1966:159, 175–76.

(Griaule 1963:470–71). This mask is crowned by a sort of "cross of Lorraine" on the extremities of which are four short extensions directed toward the sky on the upper branch and turned downward on the lower one (fig. 9). At the popular level, the *kanaga* is explained in two stages (Griaule 1963:475). There is first of all the narrative constructed on the model just described: "a hunter killed a *kommolo tebu* that he had seen glide through the sky with spread wings, and carved and assembled pieces of wood in his image." The figurine, which is often placed above the shaft, is described as a female genie (*gyinu*) who inhabited the felled tree used to carve the mask. The *nyama* of the genie, deprived of its support, provoked the illness in he who had cut the tree, so the figurine was carved to enable the transfer of this *nyama* to the drawing in red ochra on the wall of the cave. By contrast, according to the learned tradition, one of the forms of the *kanaga* represents the work of Amma, supreme god; the statuettes above are the *nommo die* twins in the invisible sky; the central axis is the axis of the world; the two upper arms, the sacrificed *nommo* and his twin in the visible sky; the two lower arms, Ogo and his twin Yasigui on the earth. A variation of the *kanaga* represents the insect *barankamaza* who secured the ark of Nommo to earth; when the *kanaga* dances in a public place, the Dogon sing "*e e e barankamaza*" to imitate the cries made by the ancestors when the insect took control of the ark. In another variation, the *kanaga* represents Ogo in his form as a fox on his back, with his four paws in the air, dying of thirst and imploring Amma.[33]

Given the actual state of our knowledge, it seems particularly vain to attempt to determine for each mask whether the learned tradition conveys in whole or in part an interpretation that was belatedly applied to a mask which did in fact represent what the popular version tells us,[34] or whether the popular version is a simplification of the learned tradition, or perhaps a disguised form, for use by the uninitiated, representing the cosmogonic events which are in fact recalled by the mask. Actually, while for the purposes of this discussion I have distin-

---

33. Griaule and Dieterlen 1965:171–73, 444. See also Krieger and Kutscher 1960:19; Maquet 1968:268; and above, notes 15 and 16 of this chapter.

34. See in particular the thesis vehemently supported by Bernolles 1966:143.

9. *Kanaga* mask. From Griaule 1963:471.

guished various types of masks on the basis of their particular appearance (things, living beings), the Dogon would include them all in one category, as related in the words of Ogotemmêli: "The society of masks is the entire world. And when it moves onto the public square, it dances the way of the world, it dances the system of the world" (Griaule 1966:179).

In summary, it is possible to say that at the first level, masks represent the elements of the Dogon cosmos, that is to say, they are descriptions of what the world is and how it functions; here, the masks are understood principally on the basis of their "appearance" (two-storied house, granary door, bustard, hare, Peul, etc.). But by dancing the system of the world, the dancers intend to recall creation and the events that made the world what it is —an aspect that is particularly emphasized in the explanations given by the "learned" tradition. At this second level, the same masks can then reflect primordial events which explain why and how the world became the way the Dogon experience it today. Neither level contradicts the other, but each corresponds to a different point of view and a different degree of sophistication in the comprehension of the masked ritual.

What conclusions can be drawn from this brief overview? First, a Dogon mask can have significance without necessarily representing a "spirit." Second, even when a mask represents a particular being, the Dogon can aim at recalling through it not only that being but the events with which he is associated. Consequently, to explain the Dogon masks by merely affirming that they represent spirits would amount to biasing the facts from several points of view, most seriously by overlooking that the masks represent the cosmos and the events that made it what it is.[35]

Do the Dogon constitute a particular case or can these conclusions be equally applied to other traditions? Let us first of all look at some zoomorphological masks. Among the Bambara (Mali), the lion (dyara) is the symbol of calm and serene knowledge, the basis of education and socialization; he is divine knowledge proposed as a model to man (Zahan 1960:150). The mask or "head" of Komo, whose morphology borrows elements from the heads of the hyena and the crocodile, also reveals a cosmological symbolism that is extremely complex, since the Bambara affirm that all things in the universe are represented in this mask (Dieterlen and Cissé 1972:51). The principal masks governing societies of young people in Timbuktu and Buguni refer to the cosmic legend: "the lion symbolizes the Smith and the upper tree, the goat, the griot (or his wife) and the middle tree, and the elephant, the prisoner and the lower tree" (Pâques 1964:139). Among the Dan (Ivory Coast and Liberia) the mask of the toucan recalls the events that brought God to create the

---

35. Griaule 1963:790; Griaule 1966:178–81.

earth.[36] Similarly, one could perhaps compare the Dan mask of the chimpanzee with masks found elsewhere which represent the fomenter of disorder in the form of an obscene monkey.[37] These few examples demonstrate the principle, which in my view is fundamental, that a zoomorphological mask can be emblematic or recall various cosmological elements or events, is attested to elsewhere, not only among the Dogon. These masks confirm that "the morphology does not in any way betray the proper function of a particular mask" (Vandenhoute 1948:3).

This conclusion is even more evident in the idea of the cosmos, the system of the world: note first of all that what was said about Dogon masks can be equally applied to their neighbors, the Bozo, Bambara, and Marka, who in front of spectators enact a complete aesthetic presentation of the various episodes of the myth and its characters. The spectator, always sensitive to the beauty or ugliness of the mask, to the active, solemn, or comic deployment of the ceremony, sees the elements and events relating the history of the universe paraded before him in an order that follows the stages of this cosmogony. Each spectator participates in them, each according to his own level of knowledge (Dieterlen 1960:53–54). Thus, among the Bambara, the legend of how the first mask of the *n'domo* was sculpted is, at another level, one of numerous legends treating the creation of man, this mask representing the image of man as he came from the hands of God. "That is to say that this object has a more profound meaning than its form and use by the initiates allows us to suppose at first glance" (Zahan 1960:74, 78). The Bobo (Burkina Faso) possess masks of leaves which they consider to be the oldest and most important masks since they are the exact model of what was revealed to men by Wuro, the supreme God, at the end of the cosmogonic age. These masks work to reestablish broken equilibrium so that the order established in the cosmos may continue to exist. In certain ceremonies, the masks adopt an east-west direction as their axis of progression, conforming to the ap-

---

36. Fischer and Himmelheber 1976:119–23. On the controversy over whether or not the Dan mask represents an ancestor, see Vandenhoute 1948:3 and Himmelheber 1965:83.

37. Fischer and Himmelheber 1976:105–9. See Dieterlen 1960:54. In expressing social disorder, the mask of the chimpanzee teaches social order according to Wells 1977:23; a slightly different explanation appears in E. Fischer 1978:22.

parent path of the sun; they thus follow the movements imprinted in creation as a whole and contribute to maintaining its rhythm.[38] Among the Senoufo (Ivory Coast, Mali, Burkina Faso) the *kponiougo* ("head" or "face" of Poro), recalls the original state of the world as the mythological narratives describe it. For the initiated, it evokes the original situation of the universe before its organization by the divine demiurge Koulo Tiolo.[39]

The Gelede festival of the Yoruba (Nigeria) honors "our mothers." It publicly recognizes the power of women (old women, ancestresses, or deified women), not only their creative power but also their secret and destructive power which expresses itself in witchcraft. The participants aim then at conciliation with "our mothers the witches" (*àjé*) so that they will use their powers for good rather than for the destruction of the community. The motifs which appear in Gelede masks seem limitless, as they touch upon all aspects of Yoruba life and thought. In this case as well, masks recapitulate the daily, historic, and mythic diversity of the community.[40] Among the Ibo (or Igbo, Nigeria), the *ijele* mask is a great structure (four to six meters in height, and three meters in diameter) that supports numerous figures of men, animals, masked persons; the upper part of this mask is a tableau of the daily activities of man, of the world of spirits and the world of animals and of the forest (fig. 10).[41] In the Bantsaya group of the western Teke (Congo-Brazzaville), the mask of the Kidumu dancer is a "true summary of the culture of that group."[42] Finally, among the Kuba (Zaire), the use of the *mosh'ambooymushall* mask aims, among other things, at recalling the conception, the organization of the world and the promises of Woot, the founding ancestor. The danced and mimed gestures executed during the ceremony imitate as faithfully as possible the exploits accomplished by the mythic ancestor in the founding age.[43]

I do not pretend here that all African masks reveal the traits

---

38. Le Moal 1980:114, 170, 330.
39. Holas 1964:13; Holas 1965:354.
40. H. Drewal 1974b:11; Drewal and Drewal 1983:152–220; Fagg and Pemberton 1982:56; Harper 1970:67.
41. Aniakor 1978:42, 44; Boston 1960:62. This cosmic character is found in the *mbari* houses: Cole 1975:105.
42. Dupré 1968:295; Lehuard 1972:18.
43. Bastin 1984a:335–36 and pl. 351; Mulamba 1982:125.

10. *Ijele* mask. From Aniakor 1978:42.

that appeared so clearly in the Dogon masks. However, the few examples noted here suffice to demonstrate that Dogon masks are not the only ones of their kind and that other masks among other peoples testify to the same concern with displaying the events and with explaining a cosmos, a system of the world. The equation masks = spirits does not do justice to this complexity. For this reason it can not constitute an adequate general explanation of the African ritual mask. How does it fare in other regions in which masking is known?

It has been said of Melanesia that it cultivates the mask in such an intense manner that it should be considered the leading region of the world in this respect (Montandon 1934:728). One could deduce from this that it is easy to say what Melanesian masks are and how they integrate themselves into the rites in this part of the world. However, such is not the case: the great number of studies undertaken in the field reveal a veritable swarm of social and religious forms from which it is difficult to draw a coherent synthesis. The following examples appear to confirm that the equation mask = spirit misses an important aspect of these rituals.[44]

According to Guiart, the neo-Caledonian mask is

> the only sculpted work that represents a precise mythological figure, and not the anonymous collectivity of the ancestors [fig.11]. It is god, the very one who, under the name of Pijeva, with clear skin and a body covered with eyes, leads the dance of the dead in their land under the sea. One sees him glide through the troubled waters of estuaries in the form of a shark, while on earth he takes on the appearance of a lizard, or of bubbles sliding toward the surface at the foot of a cascade; unless he appears precisely in the form of a figure in fact wearing the mask, and its coat of armour made of netting and feathers; one then calls him Gomawe, acknowledging that it is the same god."[45]

---

44. See a number of other examples in chapter 4.
45. Guiart 1963:64–66; also Guiart 1960:30; Guiart 1983:58. On Gomawe, see Guiart 1962, 83–84; Guiart 1966, 129–45. Did the mask belong to immigrants which the chieftainships then adopted? Is it merely a plastic symbol of the chieftainship? See Bensa 1983:68; Guiart 1966:149–50; Guiart 1983:59; Leenhardt 1933:15; Leenhardt 147:68; Leenhardt 1971a:210; Riesenfeld 1950:665.

Spirit, Event, and World System

11. Neo-caledonian mask. From Guiart 1966:93.

The mask does not represent either a deceased person, or an ancestor. According to Guiart, he takes on a quasi-cosmic value, his figure being the guarantor of the whole of the reproductive aspects of the world. Leenhardt had already noted that the theme of the mask was connected to the more general subject of mythic representation.[46] It is therefore the notions of cosmos and mythic representation that dominate.

Among the Mali-Baining (New Britain), the principal goal of the *mandas* ceremony is the representation of events that took place during the mythic times of the beginnings. While a chorus of women sings the history of creation, eighty-four masks represent its various phases: the birth of the ocean, the appearance of the earth, the primordial forest, the flora, the winds, the animals and birds, and when the scene is thus prepared, the appearance of the first human couple and their son.[47] All these dances are held by day; by contrast, the appearance of disorder in the world is represented by nocturnal dances (Laufer 1959:914). It is important to note that, again, certain masks do not represent characters, but events. The *ngoaremchi* masks, for example, represent whirlpools and thus depict the birth of the sea which spread whirling in every direction. As for the *ngavoucha* masks, they show how the earth was separated from the waters.[48] In general, one can therefore affirm with Krantz (1983:211) that "the art of the Baining is an expression, in visual form, of the totality of the world of the Baining."

The *dukduk* society is found in New Britain as well as elsewhere in the Bismarck Archipelago. It includes masks of two kinds: the *tubuan* and the *dukduk*. The *tubuan* is female and the mother of the male *dukduk* to whom she gives birth annually toward the end of the northwest monsoon. The *dukduk* dies at the beginning of the following monsoon, but the *tubuan* never dies, remaining to give birth again to the *dukduk* in the following year. The study of this society has been influencend by the vari-

---

46. Guiart 1960:30; Leenhardt 1933:18–19; Leenhardt 1954:9; Leenhardt 1971b:32.
47. Laufer 1959:908–9; Laufer 1970:179–82. Cf. Valentine 1961:42.
48. Laufer 1970:181. In other subgroups of the Baining, one finds, under the name of *ngoaremchi* or *goaremki*, masks which have been interpreted as representing either the return of the mythic ancestor in a boat loaded with food and objects, or a horizontal crescent of the moon, or a snake emerging from the water. The term *ngoaremchi* signifies the whirlpool, the eddy, the foam. Hesse and Aerts 1979:28–29; Krantz 1983:210; Laufer 1970:181.

ous theories which have been in circulation since the end of the nineteenth century. I mention it briefly here since it should serve as a reminder to proceed with caution. Rivers, for example, has little doubt that the members of the *dukduk* society are meant to represent the dead; furthermore, in the relationship between the two masks, Rivers sees the result of the addition of a solar cult brought into an older tradition by a migration.[49] In contrast, for Peekel there is no doubt that these masks represent the moon in two different phases. He informs us, nevertheless, that the natives call these masks *beo*, which means bird; the form and the behavior of the masks show that it is a *casoar*, a bird which plays an important role in myths of this region. For Nevermann, the myth of the death and resurrection of the spirit-bird was behind the origination of the *dukduk* society. This myth was accompanied by a cult which degenerated, yielding the *dukduk* society observed by missionaries and ethnologists. Finally, for Leenhardt the *tubuan* is both an eternal mask—which is neither destroyed nor created, but is "awakened" when fashioned—and a figure of authority whose power is exercised through wealth, considered not in terms of fortune, but as accumulated vitality. According to Leenhardt, there is no doubt that this figure is a mythical ancestor.[50] I do not have the pretension to decide on that here.

Among the various regions of New Guinea, the Sepik River region is one of the best known for its art and also one of the most richly represented in Western museums. I shall only consider here those figures called *mai*. These are costumes consisting of a painted cone placed on the head of a dancer whose body is wrapped in a cylinder attached at the shoulder. Both cone and cylinder are covered with leaves and flowers and adorned with shells and feathers. The wearer is hidden to the calf. An artificial face is fixed to the cone above the head of the wearer (Stanek 1983:160). The masks of this type often appear in groups of four: two male masks and two female masks which are described as being brothers and sisters. This group of four is always linked

---

49. Rivers 1914:2, 511, 525. Rivers bases his interpretation on the fact that *duka* is the word for "ghost" on Santa Cruz. This etymological argument, proposed by Codrington (1891, 70), had already been accepted by Frobenius 1897–98:70. As for the word *tubuan*, it means old woman, female ancestor, according to Peekel 1937–38:64.

50. Peekel 1937–38:66–67, 69. Nevermann 1933:162; Nevermann 1972:124. Leenhardt 1947:44, Leenhardt 1971a:209.

to a particular clan, and the masks bear the distinguishing features of the clan's totemic relationship. The masked figures are called *ngoal*, which means "ancestor on the father's side." Yet, they do more than represent mythical beings or ancestors. In the course of their lives, these beings underwent various transformations, various avatars, which are translated by the elements of the entire masked figure into a visual depiction of the history and metamorphoses of the characters represented. Furthermore, the appearance of these masks is accompanied by the recitation of mythic texts and totemic names, amplified by means of a bamboo megaphone. The combination of these diverse elements suggests that an attempt is being made to represent simultaneously the mythic character and the primordial events in which he was involved. This brief summary does not, of course, pretend to exhaust the extremely complex meaning of these figures.[51]

In conclusion, let us turn briefly to the western Elema (Gulf of Papouasia) also known as Orokolo. They have ceremonies called *kovave* which aim at distracting and propitiating the spirits of the bush. The masks that intervene at this occasion represent spirits of the bush each with his own individuality, name and characteristics.[52] The Orokolo also have a complex ceremonial cycle called *hevehe* which can last as long as twenty years. Two types of masks appear there in particular: the *eharo* and the *hevehe*. The *eharo* take on a great variety of forms; essentially, they represent either creatures playing an important role in myths, or totemic creatures such as birds, fish, insects, reptiles, dogs, trees. These *eharo* are used as much as a means of comic distraction as to represent mythic events.[53] During the ceremonial cycle, a sea creature (*mahevehe*) goes repeatedly to the men's

---

51. See Museum für Völkerkunde Basel 1970:66; Stanek 1983:160–62. Cf. Hauser-Schäublin 1976–77:137–45; Kaufmann 1968:101, 104.

52. F. Williams 1940:150–51 and pl. 16; also Coquet 1983:146; Kiki 1968: 42–45.

53. Mamiya and Sumnik 1982:19; cf. Coquet 1983:153–54. In this case as in many others, it would be more judicious to speak in the past because when F. Williams studied the Orokolo, during the thirties, the *hevehe* tradition was already in full decline; when Herbert A. Brown went to the same region in the beginning of the fifties, the ceremonies had practically ceased to exist (Mamiya and Sumnik 1982:7). On the role tax played in this disappearance, see Kiki 1968:48. On the *hevehe* ceremonies see F. Williams 1940; Mamiya and Sumnik 1982, who also reproduce some of the photos taken by Williams; Coquet 1983; Kiki 1968:46–48; Krantz 1983:140–42.

house where it leaves some of its "daughters," either the *hevehe* masks (F. Williams 1940:224) or the materials used in the fabrication of *hevehe* masks (according to Coquet 1983:150). In fact, these masks not only represent beings from the sea; their names reveal that they represent mythic creatures of the forest, the sea and the air. The *hevehe* ceremonial cycles correspond to the periods during which these beings stay, dance and celebrate in the company of humans (F. Williams 1940:262).

These few examples are not enough on which to base general conclusions on Melanesian masks. However, they do allow one to observe that in Melanesia as well, masks do not necessarily represent the dead, but primordial beings and mythical ancestors, culture heros and gods. As in the African examples, the dramatization of events seems essential, to the extent that certain masks seem to represent important moments of creation, but no particular figure.

"The mask is found throughout the whole world, even in North America," Beeman tells us.[54] Why does he use the word "even"? It is not explained. The fact remains that ritual masks are indeed present in America and that they played more than a negligible role in the elaboration of theories about masks in general. Does one find at least in some American traditions elements similar to those found in a number of African and Melanesian masks? I shall limit myself, here again, to a sampling of those societies which are among those most frequently cited in the discussion of American masks.

After a stay of more than four years in the north of Alaska, between 1877 and 1881, Nelson brought back a number of objects and various notes and observations on the traditions of the Inuit of the Bering Straits. "Unfortunately," he added, "I failed to secure the data by which the entire significance of customs and beliefs connected with masks can be solved satisfactorily. I trust, however, that the present notes, with the explanations and descriptions of the masks, may serve as a foundation for more successful study of these subjects in the future; the field is now open, but in a few years the customs of this people will be so modified that it will be difficult to obtain reliable data."[55] He was

---

54. William Beeman in Gründ and Khaznadar 1982:54.
55. Nelson 1899:394–96. Iconography and details on Nelson and his ethnographic collection in Fitzhugh and Kaplan 1982.

right about the rapid acculturation of the Inuit traditions and this made later studies all the more difficult.[56] It seems evident, nevertheless, that masks of the *inua* type recall the ancient times, when all animated beings had a double existence, taking either a human or animal form at will (fig. 12). These masks

> recall the original double nature. The animal and his human double, the *inua*, are inscribed in the same face, presented either simultaneously, or, with the aid of an apparatus of moving shutters that open and close, alternatively. The primitive state is thus restored, when exterior form was a mask that one set aside at will in order to appear as a man or an animal, changing appearance, but not in essence. The animal on the mask is not divinized nor necessarily representing a totemic ancestor. It recalls a time—whose episodes the dancer brings to life—when the separation was not yet realized (Lot-Falck 1960:9).

Once again, there is no question of interpreting all Inuit masks in light of what has just been said about *inua* masks, but it would be just as erroneous to neglect this important aspect of the dramatization of episodes of a primordial history.

The Kwakiutl (Northwest Pacific coast) are particularly well known for their fantastic masks, especially for their "mechanical" and "transforming" masks, which are articulated by mobile pieces mounted on hinges and manipulated by the wearer by means of strings and straps. There are some whose faces open like a double-door to reveal a second, or even a third face; others have moveable jaws, etc.[57] These masks were interpreted in various manners: for Montandon (1934:730), they reveal the human personality of some animals; for Mauss (1938:269), they are "superimposed totems"; for W. A. Kenyon (1961:45), when the mask springs open, it reveals a second mythical figure.

How does Kwakiutl myth help us interpret these masks? In the beginning there were only animals on earth. After a series of events, including a struggle between the mink and the crow, on the one hand, and the wolf on the other, the world became what

---

56. See for example remarks by Disselhoff 1936:181 and VanStone 1968–69:839.
57. Müller 1962:300; Lévi-Strauss 1960a:23.

12. Mask representing a bear and its *inua*. From Nelson 1899, pl. XCV.

we know it to be today. Some of the animals changed into men; the others remained what they were. This is how the "ancestors" or "first ones" appeared; during their eventful voyages, they received the ownership of clans from the gods (Müller 1962:302–3). It is these events that numerous masks recall, which are not limited however to dramatizing the transformation of animals into "first" men, but also enact other episodes of this history of origins. Boas (1890:7–8) describes a mask whose outer face is that of a deer and whose inner face is human (fig. 13). This mask "refers to the tradition of the origin of the deer, which originally was a man, but was transformed, on account of his intention to kill the son of the deity, into its present shape." In other cases, the faces of the mask can also express two states of mind of the same character; thus a mask which, when closed, represents the incensed ancestor combatting his rivals will, when opened, show the same ancestor, victorious and full of joy, distributing presents (Bédouin 1967:47). In yet other cases, the masked dance does not directly recall the adventures of a mythic figure, but rather recreates the dance given to the ancestor by a mythic being with whom he was in contact (Holm 1972:10). These masks evidently aim at much more than the mere representation of spirits. They aim at the dramatization of events, and are even capable of provoking true dramatic reversals, or sensational developments—coups de théâtre—as Lévi-Strauss rightly observed (1960a:23).

Turning now to the Southwestern United States, I shall examine masked figures which the Zuñi Indians of New Mexico call *kokos* in their own language, but which they also call *kachinas*, as do the Hopi. It is this second term that, following most authors, I shall adopt here. "The distinctive character of the Pueblo masks, is that they are derived from an abstract conception," Cazeneuve tells us (1957a:233). All the same, this abstraction is not only decorative, but profoundly meaningful. On the one hand, through its colors, the design refers to the directions in space and also refers to the seasons and to the various works of men. On the other hand, each of the materials used corresponds to a particular symbolism. In order not to lose this symbolic complexity, an apprenticeship is required during which the Zuñi slowly familiarize themselves with the constituent elements of masks. In this way, "the Zuñi children learn from earliest childhood to recognize the various insignia of the Cocoskachinas from dolls which are scrupulous copies" (Müller 1962:290). All boys must be initiated into the society of *kachinas*, which is done in two stages: the first between ages five and nine, and the second between the ages of ten and fourteen (Tedlock 1979:502).

The origin of the *kachinas* goes back to the mythical period. Summarizing the very complicated narrative of primordial events to a considerable degree, the Zuñis believe certain

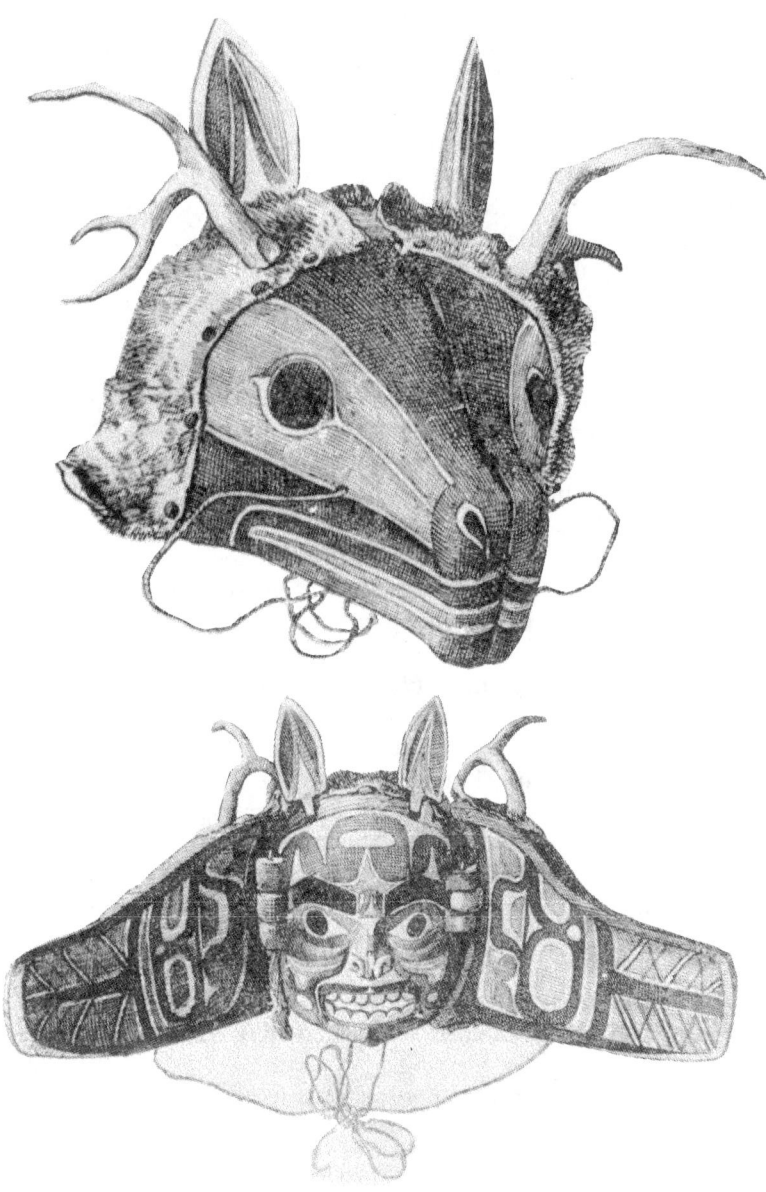

13. Kwakiutl deer-human mask. From Waite 1966:282.

kachinas are the result of an incest between brother and sister and others of the double metamorphosis of a group of children (Cazeneuve 1957a:72–78). In the old days, the *kachinas* regularly left their village at the bottom of the lake to visit humans, distract them with their dances, and bring rain and fertility. Unfortunately, after each of these visits, the women followed them to their village and died.[58] To put an end to this tragic consequence, the *kachinas* decided no longer to come in visible form; they asked humans to make masks resembling those that they themselves wore, and since that time, when the Zuñi wear these masks, the *kachinas* are present, invisible, among them.[59] As for the masked dances, they recall the various episodes of mythology and consist also, particularly in the Shalako ceremony, of a mimetic representation of the *kachinas'* action when they want to send rain to the Zuñi. Here too it is not only a matter of representing the "spirits" but, above all, of dramatizing actions.

For various reasons (acculturation, forced or not, extinction of populations following epidemics or genocide), the available information on masked rites and their symbolism in South America is often extremely sparse. For this reason I shall only briefly mention two traditions.

Among the Tukano (Cubeo) and the Arawak (Kaua, Siusi) of Rio Uaupés and Rio Icana, a death is the occasion of extended masked dances. However, Zerries notes (1962:433) that these dances are not simply intended to appease the spirit of the dead, to drive him away or to keep bad demons from following through with their misdeeds. They are also supposed to bring good fortune and fecundity to the village and to its inhabitants, to farms, and to all nature; their meaning is therefore much more general. This tradition finds its justification in mythical times: when death appeared for the first time in the Cubeo world, it was the culture hero Kuwai who taught men to make bark masks and to paint them in such a way that they could celebrate the

---

58. Tedlock 1979:502. Bunzel (1932:607) simply says that after their departure, someone died. Variations are in Cazeneuve 1957a:77.

59. Cazeneuve (1957a:77–78) speaks of a spiritual presence in the mask. The myth related by Bunzel (1932:607) says simply: "when you dance with them we shall come and stand before you"; this implies an invisible presence, but not necessarily an "incarnation" in the mask. On the other hand, an inhabitant of Isleta declared to Parsons that the *kachinas* incorporate themselves in those who don their masks "just like the *padre* when in the Mass he eats the body of Christ" (Parsons 1929:154).

ceremony of mourning. By way of their masks, the Cubeo aim to represent the totality of living creatures in their world. Their masked dances are mimetic, each illustrating a gesture or distinctive movement of the creature represented (Goldman 1979:221–31). There is therefore a dramatization of a cosmos.

The Karaja (middle course of the Araguaia) have various types of masks; the most remarkable of which are the "cylindrical hats ornamented with a mosaic of feathers whose design makes reference to the animal that is being represented, but in such a way that it is barely intelligible to the uninitiated. The hats for dancing include long fiber capes, which are placed on the shoulders and hips" (Zerries 1962:437–38). The mythic references of several of these masks are known to us. Thus, certain among them evoke "a couple of supernatural parrots, about which a myth relates the descent to the realm of men."[60] Similarly, the "dance of the aruana" bears the name of the fish whose form the Karaja had before becoming men. In fact, one variation of the myth recalls that in the beginning the Karaja lived under the water in the form of fish (aruana). One day, one of these fish swam through a hole and traveled as far as the upper world. Coming onto the beach, he found the upper world very pleasant. When he went back underwater, the other aruana listened to his tale and also wanted to explore the upper world. They slid through the hole, explored the beach, hunted, ate fruit and honey, mixed corn with yams and manioc, thus inventing stew. After a siesta, they wanted to go back underwater, but could not find the hole. They were therefore forced to remain in the upper world and transformed into humans, built houses, made canoes, ate stews, and danced the aruana dance. The choreography of the dance also refers to the story of two mythic heros who marry two green parrots who in turn reveal themselves to be women and whose children will be the first Karaja.[61]

The remarks made above about African and Melanesian masks are therefore equally applicable to America, where masks are found that represent the totality of living creatures populating the world of their wearers, mythic beings and ancestors, culture heroes, and even gods. Consequently, what can be observed in conclusion to this chapter?

---

60. Lévi-Strauss 1960a:21; cf. Dietschy 1960:3–4.
61. Dietschy 1960:3–4; 1970–71:48.

First of all, there are masks that seem to represent neither spirits, nor characters, but events, moments of cosmogony. Therefore, if the affirmation "masks represent spirits" is to hold, these masks must be considered exceptions; however, nothing in their ritual behavior or in the prohibitions attached to them would justify that they be distinguished from the others in this way. In fact, these mask-events attract attention to a fact that is very widely held, but which the affirmation "masks represent spirits" unintentionally eclipses: masked rituals which represent particular figures are rarely limited to this alone; the figures are placed in their context recalling events with which they were associated. Perhaps it would be better to reverse the usual order of the discourse and, instead of saying that a mask represents such and such a figure in its context, rather say that the necessity of this mask stems from the desire to represent such and such an event, no matter which figure the protagonist may be. The emphasis is thus shifted from the person to the events, which are generally the founding events of the world, of humanity, of the clan, or of a particular institution. Thus, in certain societies, the dramatization can refer to acts of the supreme god himself, while in others it is the primary ancestors of the clan or the culture heroes who come into play. Through its intervention, the mask can also link a moment in life or a particular event to its model at the time of the beginnings. It mediates between the current particular case and the mythic model. This function is especially evident at the time of a death (see the following chapter), but it is also brought out at initiation ceremonies and at times when order is to be reestablished. In such cases, the determining principle remains the representation of the system of the world, or the events which founded the institution or the practices under consideration.

Therefore, masked rituals often play a pedagogical role of the first order; they are a remarkable audio-visual means of teaching about what this world is, and what it means to live in this world. They therefore take on the significance of emblems of identity since, in representing the founding events and the system of the world, they reveal what it means to be Bambara, Mali-Baining, or Cubeo.[62] In so doing, they also express the type

---

62. They often reinforce the stereotypical representations of the neighboring populations and do not hesitate to include an imitation of the

of social contract on which the society is based, which explains—at least as much as the anonymity bestowed by the mask—the role played by the masking institutions in maintaining social control. The extent to which they deal with identity is also one of the principal reasons why the masked ritual often endures even after Islamicization or Christianization of the society has caused the figures and events that are staged to lose their religious character.

Paradoxically perhaps, it is precisely because of the polyvalence of the masked ritual and its capacity to survive the disappearance of one of its dimensions that one may be tempted to ask if, and to what extent, the masks and rituals which were discussed above are or were truly religious. Such a question raises a certain number of difficulties regarding the societies studied, the available evidence, and the diversity of approaches adopted by the various scholars. Actually, in societies without writing, what we call "the religious" is such an integral part of the whole way of life that it is generally not experienced or thought about as an element that can be separated from the whole. In the same way, it is sometimes difficult to distinguish "religious" masks from "profane" masks since the degree of sacralization of a mask can depend more on the circumstances than on its type. As noted above, for example, the same *eharo* masks are used as much for comic distraction as for the representation of mythic events. Furthermore, comic or satirical episodes are frequently integral to ceremonies whose religious character cannot be doubted, but it is not always possible to identify where one begins or the other ends. This phenomenon is very widespread in Africa, but this is not the only region in which it is found. Non-Eskimo eyewitnesses to the old Inuit dances only rarely understood what was taking place, so it is now difficult to separate strictly religious dances from those that were both religious and secular, or only secular.[63] The dances are a total event within which it is not always easy to make such distinctions, all the more so given that scholars on whose works we must rely do not necessarily use the same criteria and definitions. In referring to Inuit masks, for example, Hipszer (1967:87)

---

anthropologist who has come to study them (for example, Griaule 1963: 585 n.1).
  63. Ray 1975:25.

declares that it is better to risk "erring on one point or another than to abandon these masks to a certainly inaccurate religious interpretation. Of course, the models represented may be characters of a myth, but no spirit animates them except the happy inspiration of the sculptor who carved them, the poet-musician who composed the songs, the dancers who animated these sculptures." This seems to mean that for a mask to be considered religious a spirit must animate it or "incarnate" itself in it, which seems an excessively restrictive criterion (see chapter 6). Another example is the graded societies in Vanuatu: they are obviously institutions of sociopolitical integration but do they have a religious character or not? Here again, the answers vary, on the one hand, because some speak of these societies as they have observed them, while others reconstruct what they think may have been the role of these institutions in the past and, on the other hand, because these authors also differ on the conditions that a phenomenon must fulfill in order to be called religious.

If religion is defined as an institution consisting of culturally patterned interaction with culturally postulated superhuman beings (Spiro 1966:96), there is no doubt that, in general, the ritual complexes described above are religious. This is not to say that they do not fulfill other important functions (social, psychological, economic) since there is no "pure" religious phenomenon, that is to say a phenomenon that is uniquely and exclusively religious (Eliade 1959b:11).

In the majority of examples that I have cited, the figures enacted are primordial beings, mythic ancestors, culture heroes, and gods,[64] who are not usually included in the category of "spirits," and above all not in that of "spirits of the dead" since many such figures never died. Is it possible at this point to conclude that the dead are absent from masked rituals? Certainly not, and in the following chapter I shall describe certain aspects of rituals in which masks explicitly represent dead humans.

---

64. Zerries (1962:433) speaks of "liturgical representation of gods by masks."

CHAPTER 4

The Mask, the Dead, and Its Model

IF THERE is one type of mask that the literature constantly associates with the representation of the dead, that is to say with actual historical beings who are deceased, it is certainly the skull-mask, in which some specialists were tempted to see the most primitive form of the mask (Nevermann 1972:123). These skulls, whole or partial, worn on the top of the head or in front of the face, decorated, remodeled, or covered with skin, have elicited numerous speculations. Frobenius positioned them within a logical development beginning with the use of the complete skull, moving on to the skull-mask and finally ending with the mask sculpted in wood.[1] Of course, such speculations fed the interpretation of prehistoric documents as well. Indeed, paleontologists considered that certain collections of bones, certain marks or fractures on long bones and skulls could only be the result of the action of man. On the basis of ethnographic parallels, they then proposed explanations based on head-hunting, cannibalism, the cult of skulls, and then, the use of all or part of the skull as a mask.[2] Modern research, however, has revealed natural phenomena which could explain, in part at least, what could seem extraordinary in the first half of this century.[3] Thus, Vallois observes that only in the Hallstatt epoch of central Europe (Iron age) do we find pieces whose function possibly could be attributed to masking, though this is not certain.[4]

The skull-mask exists in the three main regions in which masks are found. In Africa, using a technique which is particular to the Cross River region, it is sometimes covered with skin, a technique which is also used to cover wooden supports. In America, the technique of remodeling and decorating skulls with turquoise was used by the Aztecs, among others. But it is the

---

1. Frobenius 1897–98:162–64; Frobenius 1898:185.
2. For example, Breuil and Lantier 1959:299–306; Maringer 1982.
3. For example, Binford 1981; Binford and Ho 1985:413–16.
4. Vallois 1971, 212–14, citing Vlček and Kukla, 1959; A differing opinion is found in Lumley 1985:175; see also chapter 2 above.

Melanesian examples which provided the material for the most lively speculations.

In Melanesia, the technique consisted of remodeling or molding over all or part of the skull with a sort of wax, painting it, and often adorning it with glued human hair. This technique was not limited to the making of masks but was also used to make funerary mannequins called *rambaramp* in the south of Malekula, and for the preparation of remodeled heads found especially in the Sepik region in New Guinea. These heads were kept in various manners: some were nailed to special pointed stands in cult houses, others exposed in dwelling houses or kept there in a sort of net or bag. This same technique also served for the exposition of human heads on wooden props.[5] Because of the identical nature of the technique used, all the remodeled skulls were sometimes considered to belong to a single and unique category (fig. 14).[6] Some scholars also insisted that they must have represented the recently deceased, who were known to the spectators, and that those who fashioned them sought to create the greatest possible resemblance to the deceased. Some even wanted to see in them the origin of the art of the portrait (Lips 1959:235). This conception is probably valid for the *rambaramp*: in order to make these, care was taken, for example, to reproduce the proportions of the limbs of the deceased on the mannequin by means of measurements taken on the bones of the skeleton (Guiart 1949:75). But as far as the skull-masks were concerned, this insistence on resemblance must be tempered. Bartels (1896:241) already noted that this theory probably only applied to 19 of 36 masks that he had examined, and recent studies have reduced even this proportion (Helfrich 1985: 130–31).

Basing his theory primarily on the wide diffusion of the remodeling technique, Frobenius supposed that at a certain epoch, the skull-mask must have been much more widespread in Melanesia (1897–98:69, 163–64). More recently, however, Damm (1969) made a strong case in favor of a much more decisive distinction between skull-masks and other remodeled heads. He points out that with some few exceptions, all the Oceanian skull-masks that we know of come from the Gazelle

---

5. Bühler 1969:100, 194–98; M. F. Girard 1954:256.
6. For example, Frobenius 1897–98:163; Speiser 1934:170–71.

14. Baining remodeled skull, New Britain.
From Guiart 1963, fig. 280.

Peninsula (New Britain).[7] According to Damm, they can be classed in two types: (1) faces that have been completely remodeled with open eyes and reconstructed nose and (2) faces in which only the lower half is remodeled with occluded eyes and unretouched nose of the skull. Since the observers of the last century paid only little attention to the function and meaning of these masks, and given that their explanations are often contradictory, many of the questions that are raised about them will never be resolved. Therefore, it is impossible to say with any certainty how the masks of the second type were worn and whether they participated in a dance or not. As for type 1, we know that it was used in dances accompanied by the beating of a drum and the songs of women. But we have no idea of the details of these dances or of the texts that accompanied them. Damm (1969:113) speaks of "ecstatic dances," but the available documents are much too poor to warrant any interpretation whatsoever, whether it be this one or another. Other Melanesian masks representing the dead nevertheless provide a general context within which it is justifiable to situate the skull-masks.

Let us examine first of all the *malanggan* of New Ireland. This term refers simultaneously to certain masks and sculptures, to the complex of ceremonies and festivals with which they are associated, and to their particular style, the last usage from a genetico-chronological list formulated by Speiser (1941:34–38). One of the particularly striking characteristics of the *malanggan* is the richness of frequently repeated motifs: human beings, human heads, birds, fish and snakes of varied species, as well as pigs or pigs heads, all reproduced in the most varied combinations.[8]

Various explanations were given for the ritual complex of the *malanggan*. The differences in explanations were especially influenced by the period in which the ritual was observed, the epoch in which the interpretation was formulated, as well as the school of thought to which the author belonged. Recent studies heavily favor the socioeconomic aspect. As a result, the *malang-*

---

7. For a different approach to the problem, a criticism of sources and a discussion on the origin of ceremonial skulls, their diffusion and their link with other elements of culture, see Helfrich 1985.

8. Bühler 1969:180–203; Guiart 1963:53, 55, 292–301; Helfrich 1973; Museum für Völkerkunde Basel 1970:22–27.

gan as is often described as a festival of commemoration offered in honor of one or several deceased, each represented by a sculpted figure. Organizing a *malanggan* would essentially serve to assure or to increase the prestige of the living.[9] To understand how, one must know that the *malanggan*, whose celebration often takes place more than a year after the death, calls for considerable expenditures, which therefore presupposes a collaboration among clan members of the deceased. This is why it can be said that a "principal function of the rituals of Malanggan is to confirm and tighten the social links between individuals and among groups" (M. F. Girard 1954:261). From this point of view, the obligations of the organizing clan can be studied in the framework of ceremonial systems of exchange, which are widely diffused in Melanesia and are often compared to the "potlatch" of the Northwest coast of America.[10] The socioeconomic function of the *malanggan* does not stop there: it also marks the lifting of prohibitions which must be observed by members of the family of the deceased. Moreover, at the time of the ceremony, plots of land are reapportioned after handling concerns that follow the death of an adult (Lomas 1979:56, 60).

There could be therefore no question of minimizing the socioeconomic role played by the *malanggan*, nor by any of the ceremonies in which masks intervene; however, it must be pointed out that these festivals also have a meaning that transcends that of a simple festival of commemoration. This is suggested, for example, by the fact that initiation ceremonies take place on this occasion. Moreover, in the majority of cases, birds reproduced in the *malanggan* represent the founders of the clan in their animal form, and certain fish and snakes are also directly linked to particular clans. The use of proper names to designate the types of *malanggan* also suggests a link with mythic beings. Since only very little is known of myths themselves, it is not possible to determine the exact meaning of all of these figures, but when such facts are known, it becomes evident that the sculptor indeed transcribed a mythology in them (Leenhardt 1947:46). Therefore, the representation or reenactment of the primordial events of creation appear to be the prin-

---

9. Guiart 1963:50–51; M. F. Girard 1954:261.
10. Guiart 1963:34; Serpenti 1976:179; A critical comparative study appears in Gregory 1980.

cipal function of the *malanggan* and of the celebrations that are associated with them (Bühler 1969:187). It would probably be correct to speak in the past tense: in modern times, the loss of traditional beliefs has indeed reached such a degree that any confirmation of a religious meaning in the field has become impossible. For the historian of religions, however, such a meaning nevertheless remains perceptible in the ritual elements which have survived.[11]

Of the different types of masks that participate in the ceremonies (Helfrich 1973:18–39), one of the forms represents the mythical and historic ancestors as a group; it is worked in a much more elaborate manner and supplied with many more attributes than the masks that represent persons who have recently died. The latter are made in a much simpler manner and each of them bears the name of a particular deceased person (Bühler 1969:200). In his interpretation, Guiart maintains that the rite, which represents the image of the deceased along with a number of decorative or mythic themes, "does in no way aim at influencing the status of these dead in the world beyond, nor even at offering any satisfaction to the dead." According to him, there would be in that case a need for prestige, "the already remote death of a beloved person serving as pretext to a ceremonial complex aiming at the exaltation of the group" (Guiart 1963:51). M. F. Girard points out this "confusion between the dead and God" elsewhere in Melanesia and wonders if it is not made easier by the social structure, that is to say by the lack of historic perspective caused by the equivalency between the generation of the grandson and that of the grandfather (M. F. Girard 1954:257, 264).

The interpretation of Guiart, as much as Girard's hypothesis, appears singularly partial if the various aspects of the ritual and its context are taken into account. It is possible to respond to Guiart, for example, that the change of status of the deceased already appears, at least indirectly, in the fact that the *malanggan* signals the end of the mourning period and the redistribution of land. And if the ritual aims neither at influencing the status of the dead nor at offering them satisfaction, it is then difficult to understand why all sorts of ills are liable to befall the members of a deceased's family for whom no *malanggan* has

---

11. M. F. Girard 1954:262; Zelenietz and Grant 1980:116.

been celebrated (Walden 1940:12). As for the recently deceased, it is more plausible to think that the ritual does indeed intend to change their status, especially to help them safely reach their appointed place within the land of the dead. Toward this end the deceased are "organically incorporated," to use Bühler's terms (1969:187), in a festival that reproduces the myth of creation and the myth of origin of their clan. Such a festival almost inevitably includes the representation of events which provoked the irruption of death into the world of men and evokes as well the original solution which was found for this problem. As a consequence, there is good reason to suppose that the ritual helps to solve the problem posed by the dead by recalling how this very problem was resolved in the primordial time. It is, moreover, particularly interesting to note that the *malanggan* is a ritual complex within which both the initiation of the young members of the community and the transition of the dead to their new status proceed. I shall return to this connection in reference to other Melanesian rituals.

The Asmat of southwest New Guinea (Irian Jaya) have a masked ritual, the *jipae*, which imposes a great burden of obligation as much on relatives of the deceased as on the wearers of masks.[12] The preparation of masks takes between four and five months, and during this time, the men who are connected with the making of the masks are supported by the ones who will wear the masks. The latter are provided with food by the relatives of the dead commemorated at the ceremony. Moreover, the masked performers act as substitutes for the dead and adopt the surviving children.

The *jipae* is in general presented as a ritual of expulsion.[13] In this ceremony, the dangerous deceased, and especially the victims of headhunters, the children and great warriors, are represented by masked men. Toward evening, when the time for the ritual arrives, the masked men come out of the woods and begin to dance, imitating the waddling gait of the cassowary (fig. 15). This dance continues through the night with the official performers taking turns with their relatives. The opening and closing moves are danced by the eldest brother of the actor. At sunrise the masked actors go to the men's clubhouse, followed by the women. Suddenly, the men of

---

12. Van Renselaar and Mellema 1956:11–13; Wassing 1977:39 and pl.28–30.
13. Van Renselaar and Mellema 1956:11–13; Guiart 1963:66; Bédouin 1967:61.

15. *Jipae* mask. From Wassing 1977:42.

the village attack the masked performers with sticks, driving them into the men's clubhouse accompanied by much noise. This is the end of the ritual proper.

In the *jipae*, masks thus explicitly represent the dead. But it would be wrong to remain satisfied with this observation, since these masks are not limited to representing the dead but also adopt several solar characteristics: the celebration of the ritual begins at nightfall, at the moment when, according to the Asmat, the sun puts on its mask to descend into the realm of the dead, thought to be in the West. The dancers imitate the waddling of the cassowary, a bird that the Asmat link with the sun. The ritual ends at dawn, that is to say, when the sun leaves the land of the dead and sheds its mask.

This solar symbolism is also present among other peoples of the south of New Guinea. I shall return to this later in considering other rituals, and so it is worth briefly considering it here. In the southeast of the region inhabited by the Asmat, among the Marind-anim, whose territory extends along the coast from the southern mouth of the straits that separate New Guinea from Frederik Hendrik Island to about fifteen miles east of Merauke, a myth of the origin of man tells the following story: the dema (primordial beings) made a great feast underground in the far west of Marind territory. Thereupon they went eastward, traveling underground (in the myth, the fact that both the feast and the journey eastward were underground is an important feature). On the surface of the earth, a dema-dog hears the dema burrowing along on their eastward journey. He follows the sounds and, on the banks of a creek, he starts digging. Water wells up and out come a number of peculiar beings of fish-like appearance. They look like catfish, but they are in fact human beings, who have neither mouths nor ears and whose arms, legs, fingers, and toes are still one with their bodies. The intervention of a stork-dema and the fire-dema gives them their definitive human form. The humans then leave and go westward, traveling day and night till they arrive in their present territory. The first to go, Woryu, will also be the first to die. He has brought his drum, Mingui, which the dead beat ever since, when they celebrate a dance. He follows the entire coast westward till he arrives in the country of the Yab-anim on the lower Digul, where all the dead have since gone. This land of the dead is identified with the place of sunset or a place beyond sunset.[14]

The path of the sun therefore symbolizes the path of human existence (van Baal 1966:219); it is the model, the referent, of the existence of the first man, and consequently, of men in general. This explains the extreme importance given to the East-West axis, an importance that is found among other populations of the region, among the Elema of Orokolo (F. Williams 1940:33) and among the Kiwai, for example. Among the latter, who live in the estuary of the river Fly in the Gulf of Papua, the men's house is oriented according to this axis, and during ceremonies, one enters by the door of the eastern gable; the opposite door at the West indicates the direction of the land of the dead. It is said that the sun carries the spirit of the deceased with it as far as the land of

---

14. Van Baal 1966:199–211; cf. Nevermann 1972:117–18.

the dead. During funerals, the body is carried with the head facing toward the West and it is in this position that it is exposed on a platform where it will decompose (Landtman 1927:257–63). One could find numerous examples, in Melanesia as well as elsewhere in the world (Eliade 1959b:125–28), but it will suffice here to note that, among a certain number of populations in the south of New Guinea, from the Asmat to the Elema, the path of the sun, the journey traversed by culture heroes, and the human life cycle, are united in a very rich symbolic relationship that does not neglect the "obscure zone" of solar symbolism, especially the connection with the world of the dead and initiation.

Returning now to the *jipae* of the Asmat, it is unfortunate the sources make it impossible to determine with certainty if this dance only evokes the cassowary sun, if it stages what supposedly happens at the same moment in the world beyond, or if it explicitly recalls primordial events in which this bird would have played a role. These three perspectives are not, for that matter, mutually exclusive. One thing nevertheless seems evident: through the go-between of the mask, the deceased is identified with the cassowary sun and this identification facilitates his passage to the world beyond.

According to van Renselaar, the masked dancers were symbolically killed at sunrise, in order to prevent the dead from coming back should they wish to follow the example of the sun. Following that, the masks are stripped of their ornaments and stored in the men's house. They are no longer of any value and will not be worn again except for a possible war expedition, as a means of frightening the enemy. To complete the interpretation of this episode, it would be necessary to compare it with various other "murders" witnessed in New Guinea or in other populations of Melanesia.[15] Unfortunately these "murders" have until now received no satisfying explanation. Layard thought he had found the answer in a ritual from Malekula, the ne-leng, which I shall discuss later; in this ritual the "victim" is the Guardian of the world beyond who keeps the dead from gaining access to this world and threatens to devour him. The murder, in this case, enables the deceased to attain the land of the dead, while in the interpretation reported by van Renselaar, it keeps the dead from returning. It is difficult to neglect such a difference. It should

---

15. A. Lewis 1922:9; J. Poole 1943:224; F. Williams 1940:373–76.

nevertheless be pointed out that this theme of murder is not limited to Melanesia (see for example the Brazilian case in Hartmann 1977:106), nor to masked figures.[16] The problem is made all the more complex in that it is sometimes difficult to distinguish the theme of "murder" from variations of another theme which is just as widespread, in which the first dead person felt no urgency to leave the land of the living. Bothered by the odor, the living decided to chase him away and force him to go to the land of the dead.[17] The staged enactment of this theme also frequently includes a simulated combat. Is it possible to compare the "murder" with cases in which masked dancers must make gifts to the relatives of the deceased whom they have personified in order to relieve and compensate for the violent emotions of unhappiness and mourning that they have provoked (Pouwer 1956:384)? Or to compare it with cases in which dancers (who do not wear masks, in this case) must still pay compensation to those whom they have caused to cry, even though they have already undergone serious burns to the shoulders inflicted upon them by the overwrought relatives of the deceased (Schieffelin 1976:24, 204–10)? From a psychological point of view, could the "murder" perhaps constitute a similar compensation? This question is far from simple and it is better to confine the discussion, for the time being, to the interpretation furnished by van Renselaar.

The masks lose all their ritual value at the end of the *jipae*. This rather widespread phenomenon often surprised observers of masking societies. Thus, Williams wondered why the *hevehe* of the Elema should be killed and destroyed at the end of a ritual cycle, only to be recreated in the next cycle, when they might pass from one into the other as if living throughout (fig. 16). He was astonished to see the products of years of industry and art thus perish in an few fiery moments.[18] The same reasoning could have held with regard to the *malanggan*, which, before the arrival of whites, were also destroyed by fire at the end of the ceremonies (Bühler 1969:187). Western astonishment in the face of these abandonments and destructions reveals a double prejudice: interest in the object as a work of art places a higher value on the "final

---

16. Deacon 1934b:461–68; Layard 1942:384–85.
17. Nevermann 1972:118. See also van Baal 1966:200, in which the first man to die takes advantage of an eclipse of the sun to leave his tomb, forcing his widow to chase him away.
18. F. Williams 1940:375–76; cf. Kiki 1968:48.

16. *Hevehe* mask. From F. Williams 1940, pl. 38.

product" and minimizes the ritual value of its fabrication; at the same time, there is a tendency to regard the ceremonies as spectacles, as representations, and consider that all that preceded them finds meaning in these representations. This is a very distorted vision of these ritual cycles. In fact, the fabrication of the *malanggan*, for example, punctuated with dances, sacrifices and offerings, with its fixed periods each having a name and covering a determined space of time, is itself a ritual in which the phases of creation of the archetype object are reproduced (M. F. Girard 1954:264). Therefore, it is essential that in the next cycle this repetition be taken up again from the beginning, that is to say, starting with the process of fabrication of the different objects. This is also the case for a number of masks and most probably explains how they can be destroyed or allowed to rot without regret at the end of a cycle.[19] But that unfortunately would not suffice to explain the theme of "murder."

The Kiwai, for whom as mentioned above the solar symbolism assumes a particular importance, have a ritual called *horiomu* whose description, given by Landtman, can be summarized as follows: the whole of the male population takes part in the ceremony, representing a large cast of different supernatural characters, each character or group bearing a marked individuality. Some of the dancers are supposed to represent individual spirits, particularly those of people recently dead, and they resort to various means to keep up the illusion before the women. At the burial of a dead man his height is measured with the aid of a stick, and during the *horiomu*, that spirit is impersonated by a man of the same height. In the case in which the spirit of a dead child appears, the women are told that he has grown after death. Each spirit wears the ornaments of the dead person he represents. To make the deception complete, the ornaments are afterward sent out to be inspected by the women, and they are never worn by dancers other than the supposed owners.[20] According to Landtman, the dead require to be celebrated in the *horiomu* ritual, and, therefore, the people are anxious that each one of their recently departed relatives be represented. They ask each other to

---

19. Cf. for example Bastin 1984b:41; Borgatti 1982:36; Cole 1975:105; Goldman 1979:222; Offiong 1982:197–207; and above, chapter 3, on the Dogon great wood.
20. Landtman 1927:327, 335. On "illusion" and "deception," see below, chapter 7.

undertake this office, giving the dancers presents of food by way of reward (Landtman 1927:335). This interpretation was taken up textually by Lévy-Bruhl (1963a:131), while Nevermann saw in the *horiomu* the mark of a "religion that insists most especially on the cult of the dead and resorts to masked actors to play the role of the deceased" (1972:120).

It is difficult to be satisfied with these explanations. In fact, if the *horiomu* had as its goal the celebration of the dead in general, or was the manifestation of a cult of the dead, there should be evidence of a concern that all the dead, recent or not, be honored. This is not the case. Why then this insistence on the recent dead and why is such importance attached to their being represented in ritual? There is reason to believe that in this case too, this particular preoccupation with the recently dead refers to the ritual necessity of facilitating the passage of the deceased to the land of the dead. Only this interpretation explains why it is so important that all the recently deceased be personified, and why "anyone who acts as a spirit at the *horiomu* will afterwards be assisted by the real ghost when spearing dugongs" (Landtman 1927:335). Is it not natural that the deceased assist someone who in turn helped him attain the land of the dead? If there is hardly any doubt the masked dancers help the dead gain their final destination and attain their new status, the sources unfortunately do not allow one to determine if this aim is accomplished by recalling primordial events, that is, in having the deceased play the role of the first dead person, a god, a culture hero or a particular ancestor.

Let us turn now to a type of dance performed throughout the territory of the island of Malekula (Vanuatu), called *ne-leng* in the district of Seniang (Southwest of Malekula), or *na-ling* in the North and *na-leng* on Atchin (a small island very near the eastern coast of Malekula). These *ne-leng* are spectacular dances of great formal precision performed during the daytime before an audience composed of neighboring populations, among others, who also can participate on this occasion. The dances vary greatly according to the place where they are observed: in some cases, it involves masked dancers, whereas in others the dancers have their faces covered with veils, above which are the carved or modeled images of the characters they represent. Still elsewhere, the dancers are painted to indicate the figures they represent. Sometimes a number of different performances are extended over a rather long period, while elsewhere there is only one.

I shall limit myself to one example, observed by Deacon (1934b:469–74), in the district of Seniang. In this *ne-leng*, all the protagonists represented in the distinct dances observed by Layard on Atchin, as well as a certain number of figures not witnessed on Atchin, are regrouped in a single dramatic performance which, according to Layard, supplies the key to the whole ritual complex.[21] A group of fifteen men take position at the center of the dancing ground. They are arranged in five columns of three men each and form a labyrinthine structure which recalls the geometric drawings also observed in Malekula.[22] In addition to this "chorus" and to the principal dancer, the participants include another ten men and two women who each have a particular title, and individually or in pairs, play a distinct role in the representation.

Deacon acknowledged his ignorance of the meaning of the performance (1934b:474). For his part, Layard based his interpretation on the knowledge that he had of other similar rituals: most notably, he had the opportunity to dance in a *ne-leng* on Atchin. Layard saw in the dance a dramatization of the journey of the dead (1936:153). Thus, according to him, the principal dancer corresponded to the ghost of the dead on this journey (1936:164). Various aspects of the dance confirm this interpretation. For example, one character is named "the man who shoots the *ne-leng*." He sings a song that says "he shoots at the *sap*," which is to say at Temes Savsap, the guardian of the world beyond. When the dead arrive in front of this guardian, she rubs out half of the labyrinthine drawing called "the path" and devours any of the dead who are unable to reconstitute it. This part of the *ne-leng* closely resembles the adventures of the deceased warrior who, when unable to complete the "path," ran back to the land of the living to take his bow and arrow, killed the guardian of the abode of the dead and ultimately succeeded in attaining the land of the dead.[23]

Even while affirming that the *na-leng* dances are based on a mortuary ritual, Layard does not interpret the *ne-leng* as being preoccupied with the deceased, but rather as a ritual of initiation in which the principal dancer, although seen to correspond to the

---

21. My description of this dance is considerably summarized and reduced to only a few elements; the reader might want to refer either to the account given by Deacon, or to the presentation and interpretation of it provided by Layard (1936:147–70; 1942:336–44).

22. Deacon 1934a; Layard 1936; Layard 1942:649–83.

23. Deacon 1934a:130–31; Layard 1934:125; Layard 1936:167.

ghost of the dead man, clearly is a living neophyte hoping for his admission. In his interpretation, Layard grounds himself to a great extent on his conviction that, in Malekulan dances, all characters meant to represent ghosts wear masks. However, as the principal dancer described by Deacon does not wear a mask (in the strict sense of the word) but a headdress, it follows that he does not represent a dead person but rather a living candidate participating in some living rite (Layard 1936:151–52). This problem of the distinction between mask and headpiece was constantly present in the ethnography of Melanesia. In the last century, Codrington already concerned himself with this in regard to the *tamate* of the Banks Islands (1891:77–80). Ever since, the question has been taken up continuously; it recently came up again, for example, regarding the rites of the Kilenge (northwest of New Britain): Dark (1973) speaks of masks while Zelenietz and Grant (1980) maintain that they are hats. In fact, this question recalls the much larger problem of the definition of the mask, which was covered at the beginning of this book. Without pretending to resolve this question in any definitive way here, it is important to recognize that although it is tempting to mark a break in the continuity between some masks and some headdresses as objects, it is often difficult to justify this in the field as this break is not necessarily found in the role played by these adornments in the rituals where they are observed. It would not in any case be possible to draw from this distinction any conclusions as to what a dancer represents.

Considering what is known of Melanesia in general and of Malekula in particular, Layard's interpretation can be—and was—questioned. Thus Nevermann (1972:110–11) considered that the principal dancer of the *ne-leng* "incarnates" the deceased; for him, this dance would be executed in such a way as to guarantee the deceased a successful journey to the world beyond. This interpretation does not necessarily contradict that of Layard. In fact, an essential part of the initiation consists in learning the geometric drawings and in preparing oneself thus to encounter the guardian of the beyond, an encounter comparable to a post-mortem initiatory trial.[24] Consequently, the deceased, when he passes this test, is represented by a neophyte. And since the dance refers to the paradigm of this scenario, the *ne-leng* would, at least in certain cases, stage events happening at three levels simultaneously, but conflated,

---

24. Eliade 1959a:128; cf. van Baal 1966:203–4.

each identified with the other: the living rite for the neophyte, the post-mortem trial for the deceased, and the primordial events for the mythic figure. The dancer would then be at the same time the neophyte, the deceased, and the paradigmatic figure. Through the identification of the deceased with his model, he would help the deceased to attain the land of the dead without difficulty. The *neleng* would therefore be preoccupied, among other things, with the initiation of the living and with the accession of the dead to their new status, both functions being sometimes combined in a single ritual while they remained distinct in other cases.

In chapter 3, I briefly mentioned the masked ceremonies (*mandas*), of a sub-group of the Baining, the Mali (southeast of the Gazelle Peninsula, New Britain) and described how the masks represented various phases of the history of creation there. It is interesting to note briefly here that the first day of these *mandas* is dedicated to the memory of those who died during the preceding year. On this occasion, two *sölevep* masks appear which represent vertebrae. Unfortunately, while Laufer describes the various steps of the dance as well as the manifestations of grief that were observed, he tells us nothing of the exact meaning of these two masks and their behavior (Laufer 1970:178–79). On the second day of the ceremony the representation of the primordial events begins, and with it, the active participation of young initiates.[25] Although the interpretation of the first day of the ceremony cannot be pushed very far, it is none the less interesting to point out that here again are three elements that were noted above: the preoccupation with the recently deceased expressed in the framework of a ceremony which recalls the primordial time and serves as a background to initiation.

To conclude, let us move to the ceremony called *mbii-kawane* (literally "spirit-platform") which Pouwer observed at Mimika (Irian Jaya). The *mbii-kawane* is part of a ritual closely connected with the death of one or several members of the community. With this ritual, Pouwer tells us (1956:375), enthusiastic tribute is paid to recently deceased individuals of some standing, in order to ensure that their spirits withdraw satisfied and content to the land of the dead, believed to be located far away in the mountains. The dead are represented by masked men. In the case observed by Pouwer, two deceased persons were represented on the stage and it was

---

25. Laufer 1959:930; Laufer 1970:179.

obvious that personal, familial, and group considerations had played a role in the choice of persons whom it was appropriate to honor.

The masked ceremony is preceded in the afternoon by dances executed on a platform by women. The first couple of masked performers emerges from the forest in the early evening. They wildly toss their fringes into the air, wave their arms, and stumble like drunkards. When they prepare to mount the platform, the deceased's three closest relatives spin around them in a paroxysm of emotion, singing a lament. The masked figures then clamber on to the platform where they sit, legs dangling. Immediately, the men and women standing in front of the platform seize them by the legs, thighs, feet, and backs, and rub them, tug and pull at them, as they are wont to do with the mortal remains of a dead relative at the height of their grief. They weep passionately and ceaselessly, calling the deceased by name (Pouwer 1956:382). Then a pantomime is played which demonstrates the proficiency of the deceased during their lifetime. The masked dancers challenge the onlookers, wondering whether the living will be able to get along without the dead. The living reply that they know all the tricks (of the pig hunt, of fishing, etc.) and that, as a consequence, the dead are not indispensable; there is no need for them to remain with the living since the latter can manage without them. This pantomime is repeated several times (five in the example reported by Pouwer 1956:383), and each time the masks are worn by new dancers. Theoretically, all husbands of sisters and daughters of the deceased are supposed to act as impersonators, but time is too short to allow for it. After a time, the spirits get up and leave the village at a jog, on their own initiative. They are not driven away.[26]

There is no doubt that in this ritual the masks represent deceased members of the community. Also in this case, they personify individuals who have recently died and, once again, there is an element that causes us to think that this ritual is not limited to representing deceased human beings: when the first couple of masked performers emerge from the forest, the village headman loudly calls out the names of two culture heroes who are supposed to have caused a migration by their violent behavior and to whom the ori-

---

26. Pouwer 1956:384. Cf. the tukuna mask (Brazil) that passes from head to head during the initiation of young girls: Hartmann 1967, commentary on photograph number 112.

gins of this masquerade are ascribed (Pouwer 1956:381). Therefore, is it not reasonable to suppose that the name of the culture heroes is pronounced because the masks, even while personifying the dead, also represent these heroes? In this case, the recently deceased would therefore also be identified with paradigmatic figures.

To grasp the meaning of the rituals just summarized, it is necessary to recall that for a number of peoples in Melanesia, as elsewhere in the world, funerals only bring a provisory solution to the disorder introduced by death. They are followed by an extremely delicate period during which the transformations that follow death are not achieved. Several risks accompany this period. First, the uncontrolled presence of the spiritual elements of the dead among the living presents a potential danger (of contagion, of seduction). It is therefore appropriate to ensure that these spiritual elements no longer wander in the world of the living but arrive at the place and achieve the status that must be theirs. Therefore, a ritual that favors and enables the accession of the dead to his new state is executed, for, as Layard pointed out very well, it is not death, but ritual which opens up the way to future life.[27] Since the ritual is necessary for the dead to reach their definitive status, it follows that the deceased for whom the ritual is not celebrated remains in a state of instability and profound dissatisfaction. He is consequently liable to act against the living, not necessarily in a spirit of wrathful revenge, but in such a way as to prompt them to celebrate the appropriate ritual. This danger is added to that of the presence of the spiritual elements of the dead among the living. Among other things, the reestablishment of order effected by the ritual enables both these risks to be allayed. As a result, there is a relief for both the living and the dead following the performance of the ceremony. The fears expressed regarding the dead and the relief felt after the fulfillment of the ritual have often been interpreted as resulting from a general fear of the dead. This is most probably wrong since it is not all the dead who are feared but only those whose status has not been settled.[28]

As described above, the prescribed ritual is often very costly. It can impoverish a family and, in certain cases, even cause them to convert to Christianity or to Islam.[29] It is within this type of ritual

---

27. Layard 1934:118; cf. Hertz 1907:58.
28. For more on the problem of the fear of the dead, see chapter 5.
29. Abdel Rasoul 1956:172; Hudson 1966:342–43. Cf. Adams 1986:47; Hertz 1907:52–53.

that the masks representing the dead generally intervene. Even if the sources are rather lacking in precise and detailed information, it is possible to draw some conclusions. For example, there is no question of just any individual deciding, simply because he wants to, to organize a ritual in which he would represent any dead. The wearer must be related to the deceased (to a proscribed degree), or he must be part of a clan or a village entitled to represent this person as a result of sometimes complex relations based on reciprocity and exchange. The wearing of this mask is therefore a service, one which can be the source of honor and prestige, certainly, but which can also bring with it rather heavy obligations, such as the adoption of the children of the deceased among the Asmat.

Studies of the mask have dealt again and again with the relation of the wearer of the mask with the figure represented by the mask, a relation which was most often presented as implying the dissolution of the wearer's ego, the incarnation of the spirit in the wearer.[30] Completely taken by this relationship between wearer and mask, the authors seem not to have perceived that the main purpose of the mask might be to associate, not (or not only) the wearer with the spirit of the dead, but above all the dead with his model (first dead, culture hero, etc.). This seems, however, the most important element in the rituals just summarized. This identification of the dead with his model takes various forms, which are situated between two extreme poles. In certain cases, the appearance of the masked figure is entirely fixed by tradition; it is a paradigmatic figure and nothing is done to draw it closer to that of the deceased. In this case, it is in the attitude of the familiars that the identification becomes manifest: the living behave toward the masked figure as they would toward the deceased that they mourn. This does not mean the wearer of the mask has become the deceased, but rather the deceased and his model are assimilated with each other. In other cases, a considerable effort is made to have the masked figure resemble the deceased as much as possible, in which case the assimilation with the paradigmatic figure is marked by the text that is recited or sung, or in the steps of the dance that is performed. Although it is sometimes possible to wonder if what was represented in the ritual corresponded to the primordial events or to what was happening to the deceased in the beyond at the time of the ceremony, in the end this is a false problem. As a matter of fact,

---

30. This interpretation is discussed in detail in chapter 6.

what the deceased experiences in the world beyond corresponds to what happened at the time of the beginnings in such a way that the deceased can only follow the itinerary traced at the origin by his model and go through the stages and trials that the paradigmatic figure knew. As one of the very goals of initiation is precisely to transmit the knowledge of this itinerary and of these trials so that the initiate will be able to succeed in his own passage, it is not surprising that participating in this ritual marks a stage of initiation and that the preparation of the dead and worries about the dead can be combined in it. Within this ritual, women play an important role, one of whose aspects consists in confirming and validating this identification by behaving toward the mask as they would toward the deceased himself.[31] To take this ritual role as a pretext for claiming that the women are the object of a deception and that they do not know that they are dealing with masked men amounts to misunderstanding an essential element of this type of ceremony.[32]

These remarks are able to be applied also to a certain number of funerary masks, too. Since the last century, various types of masks which were found on mortuary remains, on mummies, on urns containing the ashes of the dead, among the funerary furniture gathered in tombs, etc. have been grouped under this label. Some of these masks are realistic: they seem to attempt a portrait or in some instances were directly molded on the face of the dead; others, sometimes called "idealist," reveal traits which, by all indications, are not those of the deceased (with intermediary positions between these two extremes, such as idealized or stylized portraits, for example); others finally have no true face at all. In some cases, the mask may have been worn by a living person during a funerary ritual, while in other cases nothing would indicate such a use. Some authors do not despair of finding the unique origin and retracing the communal history of a variety of traditions which are extremely removed from one another both in time and space, yet are brought together under the notion of the funerary mask. Ancient Egypt, Mycenae, Etruria, ancient Rome, ancient China, Siberia, Tibet, pre-Columbian America, and America of the eighteenth and nineteenth centuries, provide fertile ground for such attempts.

The category of "funerary mask" does not cover a well-defined

---

31. Compare with the ritual described by Groves in New Ireland (1936:226) or, in Brazil, with what Schultz reports (1963–65:116).
32. See chapter 7.

class of masks. As a result, it is not surprising that it has given rise to various interpretations. All the same, taking into account the considerable variations that can be found from one tradition to another, it seems that funerary masks are created with two fundamental ideas in mind: on the one hand, to prevent the spiritual element(s) of the dead from wandering among the living (by offering them a new support, instigating or obliging the dead to leave the land of the living, enabling him to see the land of spirits); and on the other hand, to ensure that the deceased easily reaches his rightful place in the world beyond. In this second aspect, the identification with a paradigm plays a role which is not negligible: it can be seen in the traits of the mask, or even in the very fact of wearing a mask, or through other elements of the funerary ritual. Among the Egyptians, for example, Osiris was regularly represented as a mummified king, such that the mummification of the deceased and the use of a casket in the form of a mummy reinforced the identification of the dead with Osiris.

In this chapter, I have approached only some Melanesian rituals. It goes without saying that, to be complete, this survey would have to be followed by the examination of a number of similar ceremonies observed elsewhere in Melanesia and in the world. This is not necessary, however, given my specific goals in this chapter: the examples cited above suffice to show that even masks which explicitly represent the dead can be interpreted as having more than this single function. Indeed, the Melanesian rituals prove that by enabling the dead to play the role of his mythic model and at the same time recalling the primordial events and the stages of the journeys of the dead, the mask realizes a process whose significance, complexity, and meaning greatly transcends what the simple equation "mask = spirit of the dead" would have us think.

CHAPTER 5

Mask, Psychoanalysis, and Ambivalence Toward the Dead

THE THEME of the fear of the dead is very widespread and dates far back into the literature of history of religions and ethnology. As early as 1871, Tylor affirmed that it was quite usual for savage tribes to live in terror of the souls of the dead and to consider them to be harmful spirits. As a counterbalance to the malevolence of the dead, Tylor found the benevolence of the ancestors. Happily for man's anticipation of death, he stated, and for the treatment of the sick and the aged, thoughts of horror and hatred do not preponderate in the ideas of deified ancestors, who are regarded on the whole as kindly patron spirits, at least to their own kinsfolk and worshippers. Frazer also noted that the general attitude of "primitive man" toward the spirits of the dead was very different from ours in that, on the whole, it was dominated by fear rather than by affection. For Frazer, the cases in which primitives did not manifest this fear were only exceptions to the rule. Therefore, according to him, it was understandable that the primitive sought to guard himself by all the means at his command and made a concerted effort to send the spirits away and finally, to keep them at a distance. Westermarck thought that death was commonly regarded as the gravest of misfortunes; hence the dead were believed to be exceedingly dissatisfied with their fate. According to him, the "primitives" made no distinction between a violent and a natural death and thought that a person only died if he was killed, by magic if not by force, and that such a death naturally tended to make the soul vengeful and ill-tempered.[1]

These conceptions were in the air at the turn of the century when Sigmund Freud seized upon them and gave them a psychoanalytic explanation that can be summarized as follows: the death of a loved one elicits the satisfaction of an unconscious wish which might actually have brought about this death if it had had the power.

---

1. Tylor 1958:197–99. Frazer 1933–36, 1:10, 13, 167. Westermarck 1906–08, 2:534–35.

In almost every case where there is an intense emotional attachment to a particular person we find that behind the tender love there is a concealed hostility in the unconscious. This is the classical example, the prototype, of the ambivalence of human emotions. . . . Both of the two sets of feelings (the affectionate and the hostile), which, as we have good reason to believe, exist toward the dead person, seek to take effect at the time of the bereavement, as mourning and as satisfaction. There is bound to be a conflict between these two contrary feelings. . . . The process is dealt with . . . by the special psychical mechanism known in psycho-analysis . . . by the name of "projection." The hostility, of which the survivors know nothing and moreover wish to know nothing, is ejected from internal perception into the external world, and thus detached from them and pushed on to someone else. It is no longer true that they are rejoicing to be rid of the dead man; on the contrary, they are mourning for him; but, strange to say, *he* has turned into a wicked demon ready to gloat over their misfortunes and eager to kill them. It then becomes necessary for them, the survivors, to defend themselves against this evil enemy; they are relieved of pressure from within, but have only exchanged it for oppression from without. . . . It is quite possible that the whole concept of demons was derived from the important relation of the living to the dead. The ambivalence inherent in that relation was expressed in the subsequent course of human development by the fact that, from the same root, it gave rise to two completely opposed psychical structures: on the one hand fear of demons and ghosts and on the other hand veneration of ancestors (Freud 1950:60–65).

Drawing from both the thesis of the fear of the dead and the psychoanalytic interpretation, Meuli derived an explanation of the behavior of the masks which can be presented in four points: (1) masks represent the spirits of the dead; (2) it is a widespread belief that the deceased, even the closest and dearest, manifests his power first of all through anger and evil; (3) the psychoanalytical hypothesis of the ambivalence of feelings explains the survivors' bad conscience and the need to expiate the resulting guilt; (4) as a result, this hypothesis explains the comportment of masks as well.² Meuli's opinion was and still is very widely cited, not only in history of religions but also in fields associated with though not derived from it. Folklorists, who are now generally very critical of the theses of Meuli on European masks, tend to be much less so in regard to his interpretation of masks for peoples without writing or his psychoanalytic explanation of their behavior, an explanation that was even presented as being "the most interesting aspect of Meuli's theory."³ In 1987, a folklorist could still write that Meuli's theory of the cult of the dead "could offer a basis for a tentative interpretation of masquerades of mid-winter carnival customs" (Röllin 1987:66). The discussion of Meuli's theses is therefore not anachronistic. A thorough discussion would ideally require investigating all the facts alleged by Meuli—or even by Freud—and reexamining his interpretation. Obviously it is hardly possible to do so here, and, consequently, I shall limit myself to a rapid examination of the four points of Meuli's thesis.

Meuli bases his theory on the principle that the masks of peoples without writing represent the spirits of the dead.⁴ As described above, this affirmation unfortunately is not verifiable, since even a brief survey of the principal regions in which masking is known (Africa, Melanesia, America) shows that most of the characters represented are primordial beings, mythic ancestors, culture heroes, and gods, of which a great number never died. Moreover, the masks that explicitly represent the dead are not necessarily limited to so doing, but aim at identifying the deceased with his mythic model. It is possible, therefore, to contest the validity of any theory interpreting the masks of the peoples without writing as representing for the most part spirits of the dead.

According to Meuli, masks are malevolent: they seek to avenge the dead and, toward this end, they plunder, rob, hit, even kill whomever they encounter. For this reason, during the time of masking, paths are left clear and people shut themselves up in their houses. At the same time, people also wish for this domination by the masks; they expose themselves to the spirits, allowing themselves to be beaten and stripped, punished and humiliated, offering them presents, drink, and food. Such penance relieves

---

2. Meuli 1932–33:1749–50, 1754; cf. Meuli 1943:45.
3. Chappaz-Wirthner 1974:79. See above, note 15, chap. 1.
4. Meuli 1932–33, col. 1746; 1943:47; 1967:69.

their conscience; it is an act of expiation that brings peace and well being. As spirits of the dead, the masks are therefore both wicked and good: wicked for avenging the dead and good when they have been appeased through veneration and respect and by the presents that are offered them. At the same time, the periods of license and anarchy that correspond to the time of masking are a safety-valve for those aggressive tendencies which the structures of society must repress with the greatest rigor.[5]

Here again, the proposed description hardly corresponds to what anthropology has shown us. Violent, anarchic, or "liberating" behaviors are certainly not the dominant trait of the masks of peoples without writing. On the contrary, mask wearers often take a great deal of trouble to learn and rehearse, sometimes for months, steps, synchronized combined movements, or learning texts, in order to perform, often in perfect synchrony. Therefore, far from being allowed to give free rein to his darker instincts (Meuli 1967:82–83), the dancer must exercise total concentration and be perfectly conscious of what he does, in order to follow the steps and rhythms prescribed by tradition.[6] Moreover, in at least some of the examples where the masked figure apparently manifests an "anarchic" behavior, it seems that it often represents the mythic fomenter of disorder rather than the wickedness of the dead.[7] Finally, in cases where the masks seem to have as their avowed goal terrorizing the non-masked, further investigation reveals the existence of complex ritual traditions whose aims greatly surpass that of eventually quenching a darker instinct.[8] Consequently, beginning with the description and the analysis of the implications of the facts, Meuli's interpretation of the behavior of ritual masks seems to be faulty. Was it perhaps unduly influenced by the theories formed on the basis of masks from Europe and Asia? In that case, Meuli does not bear the whole responsibility for this distortion, as it was at times already present in anthropologists' initial descriptions of the facts. In fact, when the ethnographic study of the mask began, it was very natural that the first scholars often turned to Greco-Roman Antiquity for the typology that enabled them to understand the phenomena and to

---

5. Meuli 1932–33:1749–50; 1967:71–4.
6. I return to this aspect in chapter 6.
7. See note 37, chap. 3.
8. See chapter 7.

classify the masks, or for comparisons that enabled them to explain the ethnographic documents. This is how Gorgo became a type of mask in Melanesia, and how African double-faced masks came to be called "Janus," while it was much more difficult to find a name for masks with three or four faces![9] Therefore, can it be astonishing that, in certain cases, this chosen model colored the element belonging to the exotic civilization under investigation? The course of this confusion of civilizations did not run in only one direction. The fascination that ethnographic evidence held for specialists of Antiquity also gave rise to theories that presented Antiquity through these various foreign models, as is the case, for example, with certain studies on the origin of the Greek theater (Jeanmaire 1951:322).

If the masks cannot be considered as representing the spirits of the dead for the most part, and if their behavior cannot be defined as being essentially liberating, what of the validity of ethnological views serving as the basis of the Freudian explanation taken up by Meuli, that is to say, essentially, the notions of fear of the dead and ambivalence of feelings toward the dead? This problem can be approached by examining the traditions of a particular people.

It is only in exceptional cases that the Dogon (Mali) would bury a woman who had died while pregnant: the woman was struck while she was in a state that, for the Dogon, represented her essential quality, fecundity, and the same misadventure could happen to the earth that would receive her (Ortoli 1941:67). This fear of contamination is equally important regarding death itself. Actually, the idea that death spreads by contagion is well documented among peoples without writing; it is of the greatest importance for understanding many of their conceptions and mortuary rituals. To neglect this notion often leads to a misinterpretation of the many precautions taken as reflecting a fear of the dead, while they are explained just as well, and often much better, by the fear of the contagious character of death. Thus, when Opler states that, among the Apaches, "the time during which the living and the

---

9. Speiser 1937:355; cf. Leach 1954; Nicklin 1974:14–15; Underwood 1948:13. The case of the Gorgo is interesting: it is merely by analogy with Antiquity that Speiser called a type of Melanesian mask "Gorgo." However, some art historians believe the presence of these "Gorgos" in Oceania could very probably be explained by diffusion. See Fraser 1966:51 and above, note 23, chap. 1.

dead are in contact is reduced to a minimum, a logical procedure in view of the dread sickness it is believed can be contracted from the dead, from the sight of the corpse, or from the possessions of the deceased." Is it truly a case of fear of the dead, as he believes, or is it not rather the contagion of death that is in question?[10]

Returning, for example, to the Dogon and their myth which relates various problems that appeared after the death of Dyongou Sérou in his intermediary state as a snake, and that of Lebe in human form (Griaule 1963:70–73): after these events, the myth adds, death spread by contagion and many people began to die. The unrestrained presence of the spiritual elements of the dead among the living presented three dangers to society: (1) the risk of contagion, (2) overcrowding provoked by their increased number, and (3) their attempted seduction of the living in order to find companions. It was therefore necessary to ensure that these spiritual elements no longer wandered in the world of the living but reached their appointed place and status. This is why *dama*, the ritual that ends the period of mourning, is executed. The most important part of this ritual consists of a masked dance with a simulated fight on the terrace of the dead man's house. Various interpretations are proposed: at a certain level, the masks serve to cause the souls of the dead to flee; at another level, Griaule's informant, Ogotemmêli, reveals that on the narrow rectangle of earth, which symbolizes the celestial regions, the group of the masks integrate the soul of the deceased in their activity and carry it out of the earthly realm.[11] At any level these interpretations agree as to the goal pursued, which is to restore order following the dangerous situation of instability created by death and the temporary solution effected by the funerals. In this context, the danger that the dead represent could not be attributed to their "wickedness": countless myths and narratives relate that this danger is caused by the disorder that death introduced into the natural order, death itself often being conceived as the result of a series of disorders. Therefore, the function of the rituals is to extenuate these disorders and to restore order.

As mentioned in chapter 4, these rituals are often very costly. Among the Dogon, all the participants are the invited guests of the

---

10. Opler 1936:84, 93; cf. Hertz 1907:62.
11. Griaule 1963:72; Griaule 1966:170; cf. Griaule and Dieterlen 1965:379–80. See above, chapter 3.

family of the deceased and, among other duties, they must offer them beer in quantities in direct proportion to the number of *dama*s that the deceased himself had taken part in. To these demands other factors are added, among which the familial prestige is not the least concern (Griaule 1963:780–82). This is why the family usually waits to attend to several deceased members at one time, and then celebrates a collective *dama*. This allows the family to distribute the expenditures, but it obviously causes the number of dead whose status is not settled to accumulate. This results in running two principal risks: on the one hand, there is the danger described above which comes from the mere presence of the spiritual elements of the dead among the living; on the other hand, there is the risk that the dead will try to prompt the living to celebrate their *dama*. An example will clarify this second danger: Ambara (one of the Dogon informants for the French ethnologists) was hit in the eye by a grain of rice leaving him blind in that eye. He thought that it was the consequence of his negligence in carrying out his obligation to celebrate the *dama* for his father (Calame-Griaule 1965:406 n.3). At first glance, this anecdote might seem to corroborate the theses of Freud and Meuli as to the wickedness of the deceased parent. Yet, the anger of the deceased, if there were in fact any anger, had nothing to do with death itself. From the Dogon point of view, if Ambara had celebrated the *dama*, his father would not have caused his blindness. Consequently, the deceased acted under the influence of the anxiety and unhappiness caused by his unstable and unsettled situation, not under the impulse of a sentiment linked to his death per se or coming from a particularly wicked character. The goal of this act was to prompt Ambara to do his duty and celebrate the *dama*. Ogotemmêli clearly denied the thesis of vengeance by the dead upheld by Freud and Meuli since he affirms that "this disorder is only a warning addressed to the living, the goal of anxious souls being not vengeance but an alert given to humans, a call by the deceased to put things in order" (Griaule 1966:172).

The story of Ambara's father happened during that extremely delicate period when the various transformations that follow death are not yet completed, a period when, as I have stated, the status of the deceased is not yet settled. As seen in chapter 4, death in itself is not a sufficient condition for reaching the realm of the dead or the rank of ancestor. The performance of the ritual defined by tradition is the condition *sine qua non*. The circumstances in which death occurs also play a role (age, type of illness, violent death, etc.) as well as, in a number of cases, the physical and psychic integrity of the deceased. As a general rule, it can be said that the dead who are feared as being ill-tempered and malignant toward the living are those deceased whose status, for one reason or another, has not been settled. Tylor himself provides a significant amount of evidence in this regard since, in support of his thesis of the fear of the dead, he cites the spirits of the unburied dead, souls of wizards and shamans, lepers and beggars, people killed by the plague or violence, bachelors or women who died in childbirth (Tylor 1958:197–98). This enumeration is confirmed by more recent works. Thus in Africa, "the deceased witches, men deprived of funerals, those who perished through drowning, or struck by lightning . . . are, most often, condemned to wander in the bush . . . Always wicked and avid for vengeance, they terrorize the living who force themselves, however, to appease their wrath" (Thomas and Luneau 1969:62). "In a number of American religions, a special realm of the dead is reserved for women who died in childbirth, to all those who were struck by lightning, who committed suicide, as well as to those who drowned and to a few other individuals struck by a sudden and violent death. . . . The unburied dead and those who did not benefit from funerary rites are also separated from the mass of the dead. While the first group, with the exception of suicide cases, usually fare better than those who have a common death, those who remain without a tomb in general lead the lugubrious existence of a ghost on earth" (Hultkrantz 1976:783–84). Finally, throughout Oceania, there is nothing more dangerous than the ghost of a man who has been the victim of a murder and for whom the funerary rites were not performed (Guiart 1963:127). Some rituals specifically address this category of dangerous dead, for example, the *jipae* of Asmat in New Guinea, which concerns itself particularly with children, great warriors and victims of head-hunters (see chapter 4). Women who have died in childbirth also present a particular danger in Melanesia (Codrington 1891:275) where, in general, the happy dead are considered to be good, whereas unhappy spirits are wicked (Nevermann 1972:105–10).

It is apparent then that, contrary to what Westermarck believed, peoples without writing sometimes introduce very fine distinctions between the various circumstances of death and the relations between the living and the dead. Contesting Tylor's theory, Jensen affirmed that the dead who were loved and those who were feared actually constituted two completely different categories. He added that the dead who were feared were those who were never admitted to the realm of the dead.[12] It is preferable to speak here of the dead whose status has not yet been settled, even while recalling that it is also necessary to take into account cases where the character of the deceased is merely the persistence of his mortal character (Spiro 1952:497) and of those where the dead are divided between several realms.[13]

Patterns that exist for the dead are equally valid, *mutatis mutandis*, for the ancestors. In this connection, it is necessary to return to the confusion that often exists in the sources between the dead and the various types of ancestors, a confusion which was rightly deplored by Stöhr (1968:219). These two notions are often used synonymously, as if to say that any ancestor was necessarily dead and that any of the dead were necessarily ancestors. However, such is not the case since there are ancestors who never died in the traditional sense, and a number of deceased who are not eligible to become ancestors. I make no pretension of treating here this extremely vast problem to which societies have brought diverse solutions. I shall only raise the point that to become an ancestor it is often a condition that the person have died after a certain age, having had children and accumulated experience and material goods. In this sense, children, young people, generally do not become ancestors. Moreover, the deceased must not have been "abnormal" either, whether physically or psychically, just as death must not have been the result of a degrading illness such as leprosy.

J. Clyde Mitchell asserted that "ancestors seem to be normally ambivalent, inflicting punishment to demonstrate their legitimate authority and exercising benevolence when appealed to" (in Fortes and Dieterlen 1965:18). Again it is necessary to agree on the meaning of the term "ambivalence" in order to avoid any confusion. In

---

12. Jensen 1963:308; cf. the notions of "unincorporated or "incorporated" death in Bradbury 1968:131.
13. These facts must have been well known. It is therefore less than surprising that in 1975 one could still seriously ask whether the fear of the spirit of a member of the family was a specific instance of the general fear of the dead or if, conversely, this general fear were the extension of the first phenomenon of the local and somewhat prior fear of the familiar ghost: Tuzin 1975:557.

psychology, ambivalence signifies the simultaneous presence of attitudes and feelings of opposed tendencies, such as love and hate, toward a single object. One should use the term *ambivalence* only "in the analysis of specific conflicts in which the positive and negative components of the affective attitude are simultaneously present, indissoluble, and constitute a non-dialectical opposition, beyond which the subject who says yes and no at the same time cannot go" (Laplanche and Pontalis 1971:19–21). However, in Mitchell's remark, the simultaneity of the feelings disappears. Indeed, what Mitchell means to say, is that the ancestors can be alternately good or bad, according to the case. It is obvious that this description does not fit the definition of ambivalence such as Freud conceived it.[14] Yet, it must be said in its defense that it corresponds with the ethnographic facts. In fact, the role of the ancestors can be largely summarized by saying that they are "not uniformly benevolent or malevolent. They are just and their justice is directed at enforcing the moral and religious norms and values on which the social order rests. When misfortune occurs and is interpreted as a punitive, or to be more exact, corrective intervention by the ancestors, they are believed to have acted rightfully, not wantonly" (Fortes 1965:136).

Both in summary and conclusion, it is important to repeat that it is impossible to describe the masks of the peoples without writing as representing spirits of the dead for the most part. It is equally abusive to attribute the wickedness of some spirits to the fact of their death: this wickedness is the result of a particular fate which preceded death (which can be the result of an individual's failing to accomplish his destiny in life such as it is conceived by his/her society), or of a particular kind of death (ignominious sickness, violent death, etc.), or of difficulties sustained after death (absence of funerary ritual, for example). In no case is it a general question of a phenomenon that would affect all the dead. The dead as much as the ancestors can be alternately benevolent and malevolent; the character that they demonstrate or the attitude that they adopt depend either on the circumstances peculiar to the deceased person, or on the conduct of the living. Consequently, it is not possible to juxtapose fear of the dead with the veneration of ancestors, generally speaking, as Tylor, followed by Freud, suggests. Furthermore, it seems false to consider that there is ambivalence with regard either

---

14. For example Freud 1950:29; Freud 1952:53–54.

to the dead, or to the ancestors, since there is no simultaneity of contradictory feelings. Rather, distinction is made according to the case and the circumstances. Therefore, the very bases of Meuli's psychoanalytical interpretation of the behavior of ritual masks fall through, calling for a revision that must hold much more closely to what ethnology and the history of religions has taught us about these masks and the rites in which they participate.

Part Three

The Mask, Its Wearer, and Women

CHAPTER 6

The Ritual Mask and Its Wearer

"THE WEARER of the mask not only represents the spirit in question, he becomes, he is, this spirit." Already present in the works of the end of last century (for example, Nelson 1899:395), this affirmation has been continually repeated and elaborated, up through the present day, in a considerable number of publications devoted to masks. Despite this apparent consensus, it seems to be a worthy idea to test it here with some anthropological data, not to verify whether or not there are cases that correspond to this interpretation, but to determine whether if it is possible to justify transforming it, as has been done so often before, into a general rule, valid for all ritual masks.

To situate the debate in its context, let us go back to the works of Lévy-Bruhl. According to him, when one says that the masked figures represent ancestors, "'represent' must be understood here in the literal etymological sense in which the primitives would take this word, if they used it: *to cause to be present again, to make something which has disappeared reappear*. As long as the actors and dancers wear these masks, and from the single fact that the masks are worn on them, they are not only the representatives of the dead and of the ancestors which these masks depict: they actually become them and for a time, they really are these dead and these ancestors. . . . To put on a mask is not, as for us, a simple disguise under which the individual remains what he is. It is to submit to a real transformation" (Lévy-Bruhl 1963a:124–25). After this declaration of a perfectly clear principle, Lévy-Bruhl nevertheless questions himself: "When these actors, costumed and masked, 'represent' the spirits and the dead, do they believe in their actual presence within themselves? Are they conscious of a transformation of their personality, or do they still know that they are playing a role?" (1963a:130). The examination of some examples results in an answer which is much less clear than his declaration of principle, since he is forced to conclude that "without a doubt, the actors often take recourse in 'tricks,' to delude the uninformed spectators that the mysterious beings that they see dancing before them are the spirits themselves, and not their neighbors in the flesh. But it should not be immediately concluded that there is fraud and duplicity in this. The actors can, up to a certain point, be sincere and share in the illusion that they create. It is the immediate effect of the participation that is accomplished through them" (Lévy-Bruhl 1963a:131).

Lévy-Bruhl's interpretation thus oscillates between two poles. On the one hand, there is the theory, which is clear: there is an "actual transformation" of the wearer. On the other hand, there are facts and the evidence that must be explained and integrated, something which is not easily done. Actually, since the wearer is conscious of creating an illusion (it is only "up to a certain point" that he can share in it, says Lévy-Bruhl), the "actual transformation" is not complete, or is valid only for the uninitiated public. However, as I shall describe in chapter 7, the uninitiated participants, in great majority, are not "deceived," which would seem to negate this aspect of the interpretation offered by Lévy-Bruhl. But the ambiguity of Lévy-Bruhl's position and the difficulties that it brings with it prefigure the core of the inevitable problems encountered when approaching ritual masks on the basis of a general hypothesis of an "actual transformation" of the wearer, problems that I shall try to sketch out briefly.

The corollary of Lévy-Bruhl's hypothesis would have it that, if those whom he calls "primitives" can perceive an "actual transformation" where a contemporary Westerner would rather tend to see, for example, actors playing a role, or a symbolic presence, it is because their fundamental conceptions are different from ours, indeed because their mode of thought is different from ours.[1] Lévy-Bruhl is not alone in this opinion; numerous authors take up this hypothesis, whether explicitly or implicitly. Indeed, an exami-

---

1. Lévy-Bruhl's opinion on this point evolved with time. His first works oppose the "primitive mentality" (prelogical) with "modern mentality" in a much more radical way than do his later works, which especially abandon the notion of "prelogical mentality" and seem to admit that every human mind carries in it both a tendency to what Lévy-Bruhl calls the "mystic mentality" and a possibility to reason logically, the first being simply more generally put to use in "primitive" societies (Lévy-Bruhl 1949:60–64; Cazeneuve 1967:96). The question of the existence and the nature of a "primitive mentality" has not ceased to haunt ethnology and history of religions. See one of its most recent reappearances (unfortunately rather confused) in Wiebe 1987; on certain epistemological issues at stake in this problem, see Penner 1986. It should be noted that these two authors only take into account the literature available in English as do many North American historians of religions.

nation of the literature shows that the "actual transformation" of the wearer of the mask is hardly conceivable other than in terms of the existence of a "mentality" different from ours.[2]

For Eliade, for example, this "actual transformation" is only a particular case of a general rule: "This series of facts falls under a 'law' well known to the history of religions: *one becomes what one displays*. The wearers of masks *are* really the mythical ancestors portrayed by their masks" (Eliade 1968:153). This author is, therefore, consistent when he conceives of an "archaic consciousness" different, in particular, from that of a person in the Judeo-Christian civilizations; in fact, the first chapter of his *Myth of the Eternal Return (Cosmos and History)* opens with an exposé on the "primitive mentality."[3] All the same, Eliade reintroduces a certain ambiguity, similar to what exists in Lévy-Bruhl's work, when he declares that behind a mask, a man ceases to be himself, that he becomes, *at least in appearance*, another (Eliade 1958–67:878; emphasis mine). By the very fact of admitting that the wearer might become another only in appearance, has the "law" defined above not been cast into doubt?

More recently, in a study devoted to the African mask, Cole notes that "for us of the Western world who are not prone to accept incarnation, it is perhaps incomprehensible that Africans *do* believe in the spirits they have created, but it is nonetheless true. The masker, the wearer, who is now 'ridden' or imbued by the spirit, also believes in his own new and altered state. His personal character and behavior are modified, fused with those of the spirit he creates and becomes. Human individuality is lifted from him. He is not himself. There are occasions in some cultures when the mask wearer becomes truly possessed by spirits and, thus disassociated from his normal personality and being."[4] Besides the impor-

---

2. It is said, notes Valentine, "that non-literate peoples believe that their masked figures actually are spirits or other non-human beings, and that the primitive masker is convinced that he literally becomes whatever his disguise signifies. This interpretation of masking has been particularly emphasized and developed by scholars interested in demonstrating that the mental functioning of non-literate peoples sets them sharply apart from modern society" (Valentine 1961:4).
3. Eliade 1949:17. This is also the case work of Gruyter (1941:5–8).
4. Cole 1985:20. This text is sufficient to show that the problem discussed here is not a dated one—far from it. Let us again recall, however, that in the context of the Forty-Third International Congress of Americanists, a symposium devoted to masks was held and that it too raised once again the question of the ontological status of the wearer of the mask. See Halpin 1983; cf. Halpin 1979:46ff.

tant methodological problems which Cole raises—Do Africans really think that they have created the spirits in which they believe?—this text, which is as recent as 1985, reiterates the ambiguities already present in the interpretations of Lévy-Bruhl and Eliade.

To a great extent, the arguments presented are circular: on the one hand, the hypothesis of a "primitive mentality" explains why and how certain peoples can perceive an actual transformation of the wearer of the mask, while, on the other hand, the hypothesis of an "actual transformation" is considered to demonstrate the existence of a "primitive mentality." In the face of this methodological ambiguity, the only solution rests in returning to the documents with a mind as free from prejudice as possible, to verify whether these documents elicit or truly confirm the theory that suggests that the "actual transformation" of the wearer is the "law" enabling one to understand the relation between the wearer and his mask and between the other participants and the masked figure. The theory examined here was applied to societies once identified as "primitive" and which are now called "without writing." To avoid any misunderstanding, let me state that while I do not consider the dichotomy "primitive/civilized" or "without/with writing" to be valid (see note 4, Introduction), in the discussion that follows I refer to documents concerning these peoples in order to test the theory described above.

Verification is far from easy since it is not only a matter of controlling facts, but also their interpretation. To illustrate the difficulties encountered, let us take Leroi-Gourhan's favorite analogy (1964:1–2), that of the intelligent being coming from another stellar system and participating, for example, in a celebration of the Eucharist in a Catholic church and in a Reformed temple. Having seen the ritual, he learns the "founding myth" in its different versions.[5] If he learns only this, he will be very much at a loss to say with any certainty in what manner the participants considered the Christ to be present in this sacrament in each of the churches visited. To advance along this line, he would need, on the one hand, to interview the participants and, on the other, to know a whole theological tradition, either through a study of the texts, or by familiarizing himself with it through knowledgeable informants. Now, as for masking societies, only rarely do scholars possess the

---

5. Mt 26:26–29; Mk 14:22–25; Lk 22:15–20; 1 Cor 11:23–26.

elements that would enable them to make judgements in all certainty. They know the ritual, although often in a makeshift way; sometimes they know the founding myth as well; but only in exceptional cases can they go further. It is especially rare that they have access to a detailed analysis of the semantic content of the terms employed; now, expressions like "real," "really," "in reality," readily used to express how the man wearing the mask "becomes" or "is" the being represented, are preeminently "trap-terms" (Lalande 1960:900–902).

Are African, Melanesian or Amerindian societies capable of living their relationship to the masked figure other than from the perspective of an "actual transformation"? Are they capable of making the distinction between the sign and the thing signified? Certainly they are, and two examples will suffice to confirm this. Among the Lakalai of New Britain, Valentine (1961:6, 42) found no evidence of any belief that a man donning a mask becomes something other than a man or that masked figures are non-human beings of any sort. According to him, the vast majority of Lakalai masks do not represent or resemble supernatural beings and are not intended to give anyone the impression that they are spirits of any sort. Those that are made in the likeness of supernatural beings are purely dramatic representations and there is no suggestion that even the uninitiated believe that they are actual spirits.

Among the Dogon, the wearer of the mask is not considered as "becoming" or "being" the spirit represented by the mask (much less so given that certain masks represent a series of events that took place in the primordial time rather than beings) but instead as the "anonymous mover" of the mask (Griaule 1963:795), a very relative anonymity, moreover, since the peculiar qualities of each dancer are known and recognized, at least by the initiated public.[6] Moreover, Griaule very clearly denied the widely accepted theory cited above. In fact he made it clear that "the Dogon do not conform to the idea that we generally maintain of the attitude of a

---

6. See for example Leiris and Delange 1967:141. Among the Wè, the singers identify the wearer by allusion, "giving his nicknames or the names of his intimate friends, wife, or family, so it is not difficult for local people to decipher his identity" (Adams 1986:48). Cf. Adelman 1975:40 and further below, chapter 7. Also recall that in certain funerary rituals, the tradition specifies precisely who must wear the mask; the wearer is thus inevitably known (see chapter 4).

Black regarding the images that he creates. Far from being fooled by the appearances or the material effects of the rite, he is conscious of the difference existing between the thing represented and its image. He has a word, *bibile* or *bilay*, to translate the terms of reproduction, image, resemblance, double. . . . A photograph is the *bibile* of the person who is represented. The shadow of a living being is called *bibile* because it reproduces the outline, attitudes, movements of that being. By extension, this word is applied to all that which has an appearance of life yet is not animated. . . . The masked dancer is called *imina bibile*, appearance, reproduction of the mask."[7]

It is interesting to recall that the above text was published in 1938 in a work which, since that time, has been certainly the most generally cited book by authors concerned with the mask. However, this did not prevent the majority of these authors from maintaining that, because of his particular mentality (or of his archaic level of consciousness, etc.), the man from societies without writing believes that the wearer "becomes" the spirit represented by the mask, precisely what Griaule had already refuted in 1938. This persistence of the theory despite the documented evidence that contradicts it warranted serious examination, which might take place in the context of the study of cultural modes undertaken by Eliade (1978:11–29). In any event, it would appear difficult from this point on to consider the theory of the "actual transformation" as universally valid.

To take literally the idea that the wearer of the mask becomes—*is*—the spirit represented by the mask seems to lead to a second corollary: that the wearer is possessed by the spirit in question. Indeed, this conclusion was reached by Meuli, who writes of "sacred possession"; by Nevermann, who tells us that the wearer of the mask is subject to a possession when he uses masks of ancestors or demons; and by Beier, for whom every Yoruba, though fully aware that there is a human being under the mask, believes that the spirit of the deceased may be brought to enter into the masquerader during the dance. According to Beier, every true Egungun will enter into a state of possession when he will actually speak with a new voice; the Egungun's altered voice therefore is not a "ventriloquist's trick" but an indication of trance.[8]

---

7. Griaule 1963:792 n.4, 795 n.1.
8. Meuli 1967:82; Nevermann 1972:123; Beier 1956:383–85; 1958:34; but

The hypothesis of an "actual transformation" indeed presents the following alternative: either to admit the transformation is real as much for the wearer as for the uninitiated spectator, or to admit that the transformation is only real for a naive audience, that it is only in the eyes of the uninitiated that the wearer becomes a spirit. In the first case, possession is the logical consequence, and it becomes necessary to reject the numerous testimonies in which initiates affirm that only the uninitiated believe that they are really dealing with spirits. In the second case, it becomes necessary to accept the image of a society and an institution divided in two, having on one side the initiates playing a role and using various "tricks" (Lévy-Bruhl's term) to create an illusion, and on the other side, the uninitiated who mistakenly believe themselves to be truly in the presence of the spirit. All of this despite the numerous testimonies showing that these uninitiated, in fact, are not "deceived" either.[9]

Unable to escape this dilemma without renouncing their fundamental thesis, some authors attempt to reconcile the content of each of these positions. This is, for example, what Caillois does when, refusing to oppose the notion of the actor playing a role with that of a wearer becoming the spirit of the mask, he tries to establish a chronological link between them. From this viewpoint,

> the wearer is not taken in at the beginning, but he rapidly succumbs to the frenzy that transports him. . . . He then incarnates, temporarily, the frightening powers, he mimes them, he identifies with them, and soon alienated, falling victim to the delirium, he believes himself truly to be the god whose form he at first attempted to emulate with the help of a masterly or childish disguise. . . . This is the victory of pretense: the simulation results in a possession that is not simulated. Following the delirium and the frenzy that the simulation provoked, the actor comes back to consciousness

---

cf. Hipszer 1966:60. See various explanations of the "voice of the mask" in Dieterlen and Cissé 1972:50; Himmelheber 1938:6; Little 1967:242–43.

9. Some of the testimonies mentioned here will be presented in chapter 7. For Tischner, the alternative is limited to two causes that produce the same effect, without the other aspects being envisioned: "In wearing a mask, the wearer loses his own Self, either because he believes himself to have really become the spirit of the ancestor, or because the uninitiated, beginning with women and children, believe it" (Tischner and Hewicker 1954:viii).

in a daze and a state of exhaustion which leaves him with only a confused, bewildered memory of what happened inside him, without him.[10]

This text is again very close to Lévy-Bruhl since there is hardly any difference between the actors who, according to Lévy-Bruhl, share in the illusion that they create, and the masker who, according to Caillois, ends up truly believing himself to be the god whose form he has taken. Caillois' conclusion is indeed the logical consequence of the principle stated at the outset, but does it correspond to a general reality? Unfortunately not, as it is a widely attested fact that the masked dance is not necessarily associated with the phenomenon of possession. For this reason, other authors take pains to avoid the trap by affirming, for example, that "even when there is no crisis of possession in the strict sense of the word . . . the individual is no longer himself, it is the god who acts through him."[11] But from a certain point of view, an actor playing a role is no longer himself either, showing once again the extent to which it is difficult to distinguish between the two interpretations.

In my opinion, we must first and above all know whether the wearer is acting in full consciousness or if everything is taking place "without him," as Caillois puts it, since we find here an old misunderstanding which has associated the mask with delirium and frenzy, and which it would be well to dispel. Under the influence of theories on European masks and after examination of some "primitive" examples which at first sight seemed to correspond with these interpretations, some scholars were indeed led to explanations of the mask as catharsis and to the association between mask, delirium, and frenzy. The distinctive feature of these theories is that they are centered on the wearer of the mask and explain the phenomenon of the mask by a desire, a need, even an instinct, on the part of the wearer. There are various ways

---

10. Caillois 1967:186, 171–72; cf. Caillois 1960:140–41; Caillois 1962.
11. Maquet 1968:266. Also see the periphrases used by Cole 1985:20 or the "unconscious phenomenon of autosuggestion" of Villeminot and Villeminot 1966:265. Gill (1982:72) reports a Hopi example that "expresses the paradox of how one is at once enacting an impersonation but is also transformed into what he is impersonating. It is described in terms of perspective. One best 'sees' the reality that oneself is manifesting by wearing the mask; while looking through its eyeholes, one gains a view from the vantage of the audience and is able to know the reality it presents."

in which they are expressed, from among which I shall select three examples: masks, Leiris states, are "instruments through which men are able to repudiate their usual personality to become, as long as they are dressed in them, beings from a zone verging on the supernatural." According to Buraud, the strange instinct that drives men to mask themselves responds to man's aspiration to "escape from himself, to enrich himself in new types of existences, to incarnate himself in multiple personalities, and in order to feel its fullness and powers multiply, to identify himself with the demoniac or celestial forces of the universe." Finally, Bédouin confirms, masks "can play this role because [they are] essentially an instrument of metamorphosis."[12]

These psychological explanations revert to the theory that human individuality is perceived to be centered in the face, specifically in the expression of the eyes: when we wish to depersonalize a photograph, to give it an anonymous character, do we not omit the eyes?[13] Thus, focusing his thought on the Western mentality, Bachelard deduces that "the mask is the will to have a new future, a will not only to command one's own face, but to reform one's face, to have *from then on* a new face."[14] If these conclusions are applied to the whole field of ritual masks, two equally unacceptable errors are committed. First, the feeling of self-liberation experienced by the masked Westerner is thus projected on to African, Melanesian, or Amerindian societies. Second, is becomes easy to indulge in what Evans-Pritchard (1965:43) termed the "if I were a horse" type of guesswork: we project ourselves upon the other, we abandon ourselves to the illusion that we can, without difficulty, put ourselves in the other's place, and we attribute to him the reasons and feelings that would drive us to act as he does.

Yet, a close examination of ethnographic data would prompt us, by way of a first approximation, to apply *cum grano salis* to the masked dancer what Hubert and Mauss (1904:95) said of the magician: "The magician cannot be conceived as an individual acting out of personal interest, for himself and through his own means, but as a sort of civil servant, invested by the society with an authority in which he is himself committed to believing." The notion

---

12. Leiris and Delange 1967:130; Buraud 1948:93; Bédouin 1967:9.
13. H. Faure 1965:32. Some interesting therapeutic applications were drawn from this phenomenon: see Pollaczek and Homefield 1954.
14. Bachelard in Kuhn 1957:11. An echo of this theory is found in the explanations of the mask given by Honigmann 1977:278, for example.

of a civil servant is, of course, very far from that of the liberated, metamorphosed man, escaping from himself; it is nevertheless closer to reality. The idea of service was particularly apparent in the rites examined in chapter 4. It is also apparent among the Dogon, for example, where wearing the mask is an obligatory service. This service demands, on the one hand, considerable material efforts and, on the other hand, "an intellectual and moral education that provides each, as he advances in age, with an increasingly complete idea about the system of the world, the functioning of the supernatural, the organization of human society; memory is constantly kept alive by a slow but regular apprenticeship in the secret language which also presupposes a certain ability of elocution. From the moral point of view, it teaches with strict discipline and a lively feeling of responsibility."[15] These demands are very widely confirmed: Abua boys (Nigeria) are trained for up to six moons in the secrets of the society and in dancing with the masks (Eyo 1974:55). Among the Ibo (Nigeria), the plays are rehearsed intensively at night, sometimes over a period of months, before they are shown (Boston 1960:60). Among the Mali-Baining (New Britain), the novices study the steps of the dance with their godfathers and learn to correctly maintain their masks in balance with the aid of two strings held in each hand (Laufer 1970:178). The impersonation of some of the Zuñi kachinas (New Mexico) involves year-long duties; the men elected to this office must say daily prayers and attend nightly or weekly meetings and rehearsals.[16] Many other examples of this kind exist.[17]

Therefore, far from giving himself over to his delirium and frenzy, the dancer must be fully concentrated and aware of what he is doing in order to follow the steps and the rhythms, to use the peculiar voice associated with the mask, and where the case demands it, to recite the correct text. There is no trace of delirium or frenzy in this description of the dance of the *dyaraw* (lions) masks among the Bambara, for example: "The slow rhythm of the 'lions'' movements, their ordered, measured gestures, their gazes and

---

15. Griaule 1963:786–87. Those who abstain from dancing when there is an outing of the masks are subject to a fine of 800 cauris (Paulme 1940:250) or 30,000 cauris (Griaule 1963:262). Cf. Adams 1987:46; Offiong 1982:197.
16. Tedlock 1979:502; Wilson 1956:28–29.
17. To move outside the three regions of the world I am considering, see for example the rules to which the dancers of the Tibetan *'chams* are subject: Nebesky-Wojkowitz 1976:75.

The Ritual Mask and Its Wearer 127

their imperturbable appearance are moreover signs of the presence and the majesty of the divine. Their dance, synchronized down to the least posture, strives for a representation of the infallibility of God and the transcendent character of his science" (Zahan 1960:151–52). No frenzy is found either in the Dogon funerary rite or during the masked dance on the terrace of the deceased's house; on the contrary, "the performances of the actors are serious and full of meaning."[18] Nor do the African, Melanesian and American rituals, to which I briefly alluded in part 2, give the impression of involving an escape from the self, a delirium, or a frenzy.

The care given to the preparation of the participants is better understood if one accepts that the wearer of the mask remains conscious and responsible. The Bobo provide a very telling illustration:

> The wearer risks death. This risk comes from the fact that the tasks that certain masks, such as the *dada* . . . and, above all, the *gwala* of initiation, must accomplish are so serious that the least liturgical error committed by the wearer during the ritual is thought to provoke the vengeance of Dwo. Added to that is the fact that the mask in itself is charged . . . with dangerous forces. But there is yet another reason why wearing the mask is dreaded. One of the rituals to be carried out is a beating which, in order to be faithful to the custom, the mask must execute mercilessly. However, it is not rare that young people, cruelly wounded, or members of their family, take revenge at a later time, by poisoning the wearer of the mask (who is known since . . . his identity is revealed during the rituals).[19]

Thus, not only is the wearer considered responsible by the god (Dwo), but also by the "beneficiaries" of the beating. This is evidence that can not be reconciled with the hypothesis of an "actual transformation" but which can help to explain why those who are called to wear masks feel very vulnerable and often take every sort of precaution to protect themselves from witches who could pro-

---

18. Griaule 1963:789; compare with the exalted description given by Buraud, 1948:91.
19. Le Moal 1980:258 n.4.

voke a potentially disastrous error or accident. For, to fall, to loose one's mask, to forget to transform one's voice, etc., is to commit a liturgical error. In a representation of the events that founded the order of the world, for example, every error represents a disorder and, as such, must be expiated or ransomed. In certain cases, it is also feared that the character represented would consider an error to be a mark of disrespect and that this would cause him to seek vengeance.[20]

Is this to say that the masked figures are only actors playing a role, without any power or extra-human entity present during the ritual? They can be, but this is not necessarily the case. Numerous documents have shown that the mask is often charged with a force, a power that may come from the material of which it is made, from the treatment which it has undergone or from sacrifices offered to it, as well as from the figure represented who moreover can be not only a character but an event or one of those immaterial, incorporeal, invisible, impersonal substances, endowed with supernatural forces and powers, that is found in a number of traditional religions. Indeed, the choice of elements that make up the costume and the mask is rarely attributed only to the availability of the materials and to the ease with which they can be worked. These elements are also chosen for their symbolic character, or even for the power that inhabits them. This is why it is important, in West Africa as it is in New Britain, for example, that the leaves forming the costume be as fresh as possible.[21] This is also why the Iroquois would carve their False Faces from a living tree, without cutting it down, only cleaving them away at the end of their work; the mask thus participated in the life of the tree, which survived the ablation (Fenton 1941:423).

The care that is taken with masks that are to be used several times often aims at restoring their powers to them; at the same time, the treatment or the feeding of the mask may have the value of a sacrifice, with the mask becoming the functional equivalent of an altar. Among the Bobo, "at Muna, Dwo has no other altar than the *muturu* mask that presides over the ceremonies and on whose

---

20. See Adams 1986:48, 50; Griaule 1963:348, 355, 383, 795; Holas 1952:100; Lafargue 1971:131–33; Lafargue 1973:88; McNaughton 1979:38–39; Speck 1949:78; Wilson 1956:29. The error of the wearer can either turn against him or have repercussions on all or part of the community. I shall return to this in Chapter 7.

21. Le Moal 1980:170; Weil 1971:282; Bateson 1932:336.

head the blood sacrifices are made. Furthermore, the head of an active mask may receive sacrifices even when a fixed altar exists. . . . The *sibe molo* mask thus can be considered a mobile substitute for the Dwo altar that it represents (Dwosa) which is too dangerous to approach" (Le Moal 1980:328). Among the Dan, the spirit represented by a mask is always more closely linked to its manifestation, that is to say to the mask itself, than to the owner or to the wearer of this mask (Fischer and Himmelheber 1976:8), a fact which Harley confirms in reporting that after having executed his ritual dance, a dancer made a sacrifice to his mask, thus demonstrating that it was the mask, not the wearer, that mattered (Harley 1950:5). For the women's society, *sande*, of the Mende (Sierra Leone), the spirit inhabits the mask (Richards 1973:71). Among the Seneca (Iroquois), it is the mask itself that is important, confirmed by the existence of miniature maskettes, shaped like full-size False-Faces, which are treated like masks and have the same powers but which, of course, are not worn.[22] Recall, as well, the Zuñi myth: at the beginning, the *kachinas* would come to the village in visible form. To avoid the troubles that accompanied their departure, they taught the masked ritual to men and, ever since, when the Zuñi wear the masks the *kachinas* are present, invisible, among them.[23] The myth therefore insists on the difference between two situations: on the one hand, there is the time of the origin, the visible coming, *in concreto*, of the *kachinas*, and on the other hand, their current invisible presence. Would an interpretation of the latter on the basis of an "actual transformation," not be a blurring of the very distinction that the myth underlined?

The force present in a mask can be more or less powerful, dangerous or virulent, depending on the masks and the circumstances of their intervention. Among the Iroquois, this force seems to persist and cause anyone who suddenly finds him or herself face to face with a mask to risk being struck by the illness caused by the False-Faces; this is why masks must be set aside and wrapped, or hung with their face against the wall.[24] In the explanations given at the first level of Dogon learning, explanations that essentially portray masks as having served to capture the vital

---

22. Sturtevant 1983:45; cf. Speck 1955:70–71.
23. Bunzel 1932:607; see above, p. 76 n. 59.
24. Fenton 1941:423; Hendry 1964:387; Keppler 1941:39; Sturtevant 1983:46.

force (*nyama*) of deceased beings, it is obvious that this vital force is temporarily present in the mask itself and not in the wearer. Indeed, from this viewpoint, the mask was fashioned precisely in the likeness of the deceased in the aim of fooling his vital force into entering the new container and abandoning the wandering state harmful to humans; the mask therefore was used as a therapeutic transfer and it is only when, in its turn, it had been emptied of any dangerous spiritual element that it was worn for the dance.[25] For the Bobo, "the power of a mask is most intense in the place in the bush where it has just been made. . . . The virulence of some masks during their action in the bush is such that a mere Bobo, even an initiated elder, could not stand it. It is then the smith who must wear the mask, although it is owned by the Bobo farmers, in order to bring it from the point where it was made to the outskirts of the village, where the rites will take place. At this moment, the Bobo again take possession of their mask, but it is still overflowing with injurious forces. . . . The power of the mask decreases after the strictly religious ceremonies. It is still appreciable during the closing dances, but becomes more tolerable when the mask finally enters the village. At that point it can be, as the situation allows, worn by initiates of an lower standing" (Le Moal 1980:257–58). It seems obvious that the power of the mask is not incarnate in the wearer, transforming him; the wearer does, however, enter into contact with it when he puts the mask on, hence the qualities that are demanded of him (initiation) and the preparation that he must undergo (purification, abstention from sexual intercourse, etc.).

The power can also reside in other elements of adornment or of the costume. Among the Igbirra (Nigeria), it is present in the accessories and not in the mask itself (Unrug 1983:56). As for the costume, its importance has been both overestimated and underestimated. Indeed, starting from the hypothesis of an "actual transformation," some authors have theorized, through rationalization, that in order for the illusion to be perfect and the wearer to appear as truly "being" the spirit, it was important that he be completely hidden by his costume. From this came affirmations like "the African mask is always associated with a costume that envelopes the wearer from head to foot" (Himmelheber 1960:6) or "in all of Melanesia, the masked individual completely disappears be-

---

25. Griaule 1963:76–77, 422 –23, cited above, in chapter 3, pp. 56–57.

neath his mask" (Mauss 1967:101). However, a glance at the photographs taken during masked dances, or at the sketches made by ethnographers, is enough to ascertain that neither the African nor the Melanesian mask is always associated with a costume that covers the wearer from head to foot. Even so, it can always be maintained that *originally* all masks must have been accompanied by a costume that entirely hid the wearer.[26] But given the current state of knowledge, this remains impossible to prove.

Nevertheless, it would be absurd to deny the existence of any idea of concealment in the costume of many masks. Several factors, which are not mutually exclusive, may be behind this concealment. It may be that one wants to hide the human nature of the wearer from unmasked participants; however, many witnesses attest that, in a great majority of cases, the uninitiated know perfectly well what to expect (see chapter 7). Therefore, this concealment comes under the category of prohibitions: one knows perfectly well that one is dealing with a masked man, but one is not supposed to know it or to speak of it and severe punishment is incurred if this knowledge is made apparent. To a certain extent, therefore, this "secret" is close to that desire, to make the actor disappear behind his role, to efface the personality of the wearer as completely as possible behind the character or event being represented. Concealment, in this sense, does not in any way stem from a desire to deceive the audience, but from a desire to avoid having the wearer be too present as an individual in a scene or a narrative where he has no place.[27] Finally, concealment may aim at protecting the wearer from the powers with which he is to come in contact. The protective function of many liturgical costumes is well known and it seems likely that, in certain cases, the costume worn by the dancer also has this function. Among the Yoruba, a myth relates that "Ifa instructed Orunmila to put on a mask, headtie, and anklets for protection as he was going to the grove of the destructive mothers" (H. Drewal 1974a:29).

However, two risks are involved in raising the concealing function of the costume to the level of a general rule: first of all,

---

26. Speiser 1923:77–78. The interpretation given by Speiser also has other origins to which I shall return in chapter 7. It influenced even the study of European masks; for example Rütimeyer 1924:362.

27. See the semiotic analysis proposed by Calame 1986: cf. Ogibenin 1975. When the masks bring a judgement, anonymity, even if only in principle, affirms the transfamilial or transclanic character of this justice.

one risks wrongly considering those outfits where the costume does not entirely hide the wearer to be "degradations." For example, Speiser affirms that the *dukduk* mask (New Britain) underwent a degeneration, visible in the fact that the costume no longer covers the feet and does not extend further than the knees of the wearer, allowing him possibly to be recognized (Speiser 1945:14). Second, and more serious still, is the risk of neglecting a detailed interpretation of the costume, considering it to be primarily for the purpose of concealment and not meaningful in itself. This second attitude is evident among those authors who speak of the costume as a complement to the mask, while it would be more fitting to look upon both as elements of a single whole (again including the accessories of the masked figure, its text if there should be one, its behavior, etc.). The facial part of the mask is not necessarily the most meaningful element of the whole: "In the figure that is created by the combination of the man-animator, the costume, the ornamentation, the accompanying music, song and dance, the mask is only an accessory, and often an interchangeable one. That which defines this 'apparition' is a way of being that is so characteristic that the initiates, at certain moments of the funerary ceremony, recognize without any difficulty, the men who usually animate the characters of *kouto, taanian, korrigo*, etc., even though they are, for this occasion, naked and without insignias, and are just as effective naked as masked" (Bochet 1965:644). If the costume is not considered in any way other than as hiding the wearer, there is no chance of understanding a mask such as the *onidan* of the Yoruba; in this case, in fact, the wearer wears one costume on top of the other and effects transformations in the course of his dance (Drewal and Drewal 1978:31–33).

Finally, as I have already emphasized, not only can the materials used and their color have their own significance, but so can the details of the costume, the manner and the occasion for which it is worn.[28] Let us return, for example, to the *dyaraw* (lions) masks

---

28. The importance of fibers and their red coloring among the Dogon is known (see above, chapter 3, pp. 58–59); also among the Bobo-Ule and the Nuna (Zwernemann 1978:49; but cf. Le Moal 1980:220 n.3). The color of the costume may underscore the mask's belonging to the superhuman world (Holas 1965:356), or the sex of the mask (Bochet 1959:82). In New Caledonia, black recalls humidity; the dark cloak is a piece of clothing associated with water, humidity, life (Leenhardt 1933:10). In America, colors especially refer to sexual symbolism and to directions in space (Speck 1950:8; 33, 42; Lévi-Strauss 1960a:26).

of the Bambara, which have two mutually exclusive costumes: one the lions wear during the first part of the initiation and one they reserve for the second part of this ritual. The first consists of a series of bracelets, belts, and ankle bracelets of different widths, coarsely woven on one side, with loose fringes on the other. Briefly, it can be said that the fibers represent the teachings and education, since they come from the tree of development and learning. The ornaments are attached at the six essential joints of the body, which correspond to the six great fields of human activity: physical vigor (shoulders), social contact (elbows), work (wrists), reproductive functions (lumbar region), quest for strength (knees), and progress (heels). As for the hood covering the head, it symbolizes the development of the spirit. To educate one's joints and one's mind, is to better human activity, that is to say, man in his exteriority. Thus adorned, the initiate is conscious of conforming to the example of the divinity: this costume of the *dyaraw* is perfectly suited to the first part of the initiation, which is devoted to the death and resurrection of the neophytes, and covers the period of gestation of their spiritual being. But man needs to complete his training toward the total completion of his person which the second phase of initiation will confer upon him. This then is the meaning of the cloak of unwoven fibers that covers the *dyaraw* from head to foot. Entirely enveloping the dancers and transmitting to every parcel of their being the spiritual assets they are lacking, the *n'dege* fibers represent the total man, ready to participate in the divine principle (Zahan 1960:149–51). Beyond the significance of the costume for the comprehension of the meaning of the masked figure, this Bambara example shows that there is not necessarily any degeneration in the costume from a piece of clothing entirely hiding the wearer to a costume that does not totally cover him, since the *dyaraw* actually has both costumes, which are distinguished by differences of meaning, not by any loss of the original function.[29]

In summary, even a brief examination of various anthropological documents is sufficient to disavow entirely the theories that attempt to explain the institution of the ritual mask as the satisfaction of an individual desire or need of the wearer, in particular those interpretations that see in the ritual mask a means of enabling the wearer to let himself go, to liberate his instincts, to es-

---

29. Cf. Eliade 1968:128; Mark 1983;8; Thompson 1974:182.

cape from himself in delirium and frenzy. In a number of cases, the mask appears rather as a service, which is particularly evident when considering its role in funerary rituals or in ceremonies marking the end of the period of mourning (chapter 4). As for the relation between the wearer, his mask, the power, the event or the spirit represented, it is found—according to the available documents—on a continuum ranging from the simple dramatization of a character or a mythic narrative to a possible "actual transformation" of the wearer, including a number of cases where the "supernatural" power or element is present, completely or in part, in the mask, its accessories or the costume. It is therefore impossible to affirm as a general rule that the wearer of the mask becomes, or is, what he displays, in the sense of an "actual transformation."

Why is it, then, that despite the anthropological documents, so many authors have adopted and continue to adhere to the theory of an "actual transformation" as the principle of general explanation. No doubt, this theory corresponds to a romantic image of the "primitive" who reminds us of the old "mythical image of a 'natural man,' beyond history and civilization" (Eliade 1957:39). Perhaps the Westerner's unconscious has not yet "renounced the old dream of encountering contemporaries lingering in an earthly Paradise."[30] This would explain Western nostalgia for a state that makes possible the qualities that the theory attributes to the peoples from societies called primitive, traditional, or without writing. This would also explain the imperious Western need to consider these peoples to be different, as if they were responsible for preserving something that has escaped the West. Finally, it also implicates the division of the field of study of anthropology and history of religions between primitives and civilized, societies with and without writing.[31] I shall not be able to deal with this problem here and shall limit myself to remarking that the Western attitude put up strong resistance to the recognition of the facts, a resistance made obvious by the intellectual contortions which some authors practiced in an attempt to make the facts fit the theory. But it is precisely because these contortions and explanations are too confused and further and further removed from the ethnographic evidence that one is led to reject "actual transformation" as a general

---

30. Eliade 1957:41; cf. Eliade 1967:498.
31. See the detailed methodological examination of this problem in Long 1980; cf. Penner 1986.

interpretation. This theory appears to be an example of "verbose phenomenology, falsely naive mixture, in which the seeming obscurities of the indigenous thought would only be brought out to cover the otherwise all too evident confusions of the ethnographer's thought" (Lévi-Strauss 1960:xlvi).

Chapter 7

The Mask and Women

According to the Viennese school of the "culture circles" or "areas of civilization" (*Kulturkreise*), in a former era women played a leading role in society, and, in order to resist their economic, social, and religious supremacy, men created secret societies. This theory postulates a quasi-organic link between secret societies and masks, the latter of which were considered to be the means used by men to seize power from women and secure their own domination. This link is even noted by authors who do not necessarily accept the theory of matriarchy. Here, summarized in five points, is how Speiser expressed it: (1) the aim of the secret society is to terrorize the uninitiated in general, and women in particular; (2) it achieves this aim with the use of masks, deemed to represent spirits; (3) in order for masks to actually terrorize the uninitiated, it is essential that the latter remain ignorant of the true nature of the masked beings; (4) thus every effort must be made to keep the uninitiated from discovering the truth and to cause them to believe that they are dealing, not with disguised men, but with the spirits themselves; (5) therefore, it is possible to deduce that, at their origin, all masks were accompanied by a costume entirely hiding the wearer.[1]

Some masking societies are also the guardians of traditional order; they can play this role effectively since they are called to represent the cosmic order, the system of the world, and they establish a union among participants that extends beyond the links of family or clan. On this basis, they had an important role in the resistance to colonization and evangelization. This had two complementary consequences: in order to resist, they had to reinforce the secrecy that surrounded them, and this attitude of secrecy and the measures that they adopted to maintain it contributed to the distorted image given of them in the European literature. This image was especially influenced by the prevailing relation between

---

1. Speiser 1923:377–78. Cf. Cole 1985:15–16; Kirby 1985:41, 45; Schmidt 1919–20:554; Webster 1968:75–76.

the sexes in Europe,[2] by the theories on the Germanic *Männerbünde*, as well as by the ideas that circulated on the hidden role of the Roman Catholic Church or the Freemasons.[3] The colonial context and its projections which obscured their reality certainly contributed to mistakenly grouping under the heading of "secret societies" extremely diverse religious and social institutions (including societies of men, societies of age classes, graded societies, cultic societies, etc.) whose differences were underestimated in order to emphasize their common characteristics which, often, did not withstand examination. Speaking of the particular innovations of the secret masking societies, Eliade affirms, for example, that "the most important are: the capital role of the secret, the cruelty of initiatory trials, the predominance of the cult of the Ancestors (personified by the masks) and the absence of the Supreme Being in the ceremonies."[4] It is immediately apparent that, defined in this way, many of the masking societies briefly mentioned in the preceding chapters would not enter into this general category. The *ava* of the Dogon, for example, does not include cruel trials.[5] It so happens that the Supreme Being is present in the ceremonies in which this society participates, since, as described in chapter 3, some masks specifically dramatize his acts of creation. Furthermore, the *ava* is not truly a secret society: it is a men's association in which all circumcised males from certain Dogon villages take part. Also, it is proven, as much in Africa as in Melanesia, that masks can very well exist independently from any secret society and that certain secret societies only belatedly adopted the mask, which existed outside of them.[6] This beautiful edifice appears then to be built on sand.

---

2. Missionaries and colonial officials "encouraged" the redefinition of the roles of each sex in the societies in which they were active. See Sanday 1981:157.

3. Azevedo 1980:13–14; Leleur 1979–80:170; Ottenberg and Knudsen 1985:40, 94. Anthropological theories often tell more about the anthropologists than about their subject matter, notes Leach 1967:46.

4. Eliade 1959a:149. Elsewhere, Eliade uses the same text to define the secret societies in general: Eliade 1971:227.

5. Griaule 1963:786–87; cf. ibid., pp. 183–90.

6. E. Fischer 1980:81; Laufer 1959:909; Leenhardt 1971a:209; Leenhardt 1971b:31; Siegmann 1980:94. At the beginning of the nineteenth century, the Iroquois (Seneca) prophet, Handsome Lake, sought to destroy the societies and orders that conserved the older religious rites. To resist, these societies became secret and terrorized those who would betray them. At this point a new mask appears, made of wood, over which was stretched a rabbit-skin stained with

For the Viennese school, these secret societies were supposedly created to struggle against the power of women, against matriarchy, a notion that postulates a politico-juridical system in which power is held by women and where the genealogical links follow the maternal line (matrilineal descent).[7] This school unfortunately was never able to prove satisfactorily the existence of this matriarchal stage or cycle. First of all, "no actual society, as 'primitive' as it might be, has a matriarchal regime defined as such."[8] Moreover, from a methodological point of view, scholars reproached this school for the significant imbalance between the weight of its theoretical presuppositions and that of the available data; it was accused of having leapt at synthesis before it had pursued an exhaustive analysis, and of having thus reached conclusions that were a mere fabric of the imagination.[9] Finally, anthropological and ethnographic research has greatly evolved since its time, in particular concerning the study of the forms of power, of kinship relations, and of the localization of marriages. As a result, it is no longer possible today to accept a schema postulating and explaining, as did the *Kulturkreislehre*, a complex associating matriarchy, secret societies, and ritual masks.

This theoretical schema must be abandoned. But some of the facts used by this school to bolster its theory remain, and still require an explanation. Thus, it is true that many peoples think that it is women who discovered masks and who possessed them in the old days: "Legends are told such as the one of the masked being who revealed himself to women near a well; but in their stupidity, they did not know how to treat him properly and turned him over to men. Another is about those women who, thanks to their ownership of the masks, had at one time tyrannized men until the day when, by trickery, men robbed the women of the masks, thus reversing the relations between the sexes" (Himmelheber 1960:20).

---

blood. This mask was supposed to represent the face of a traitor as he would look when drowned for his infamy (Parker 1909:162–63, 181; Krusche 1975:173–74). This is a clear example of a masking society belatedly taking certain characteristics of a secret society under the influence of historic factors having nothing to do with the struggle between the sexes.

7. Historic in Eliade 1963:102–4; Heine-Geldern 1964:412; Lowie 1966:156–60, 177–95.

8. Panoff and Perrin 1973:174.

9. Kroeber and Holt 1920:457, 460; attempts at refutation in Schmidt 1919–20:553–63. Summary of the main criticisms addressed to the historicocultural school in Lowie 1966:185; Vansina 1961:148–50; Zimoń 1986:251–56.

The Mask and Women

What is striking about the theme of the discovery by the women is its very wide dissemination. Examples are to be found in all three of the masking regions considered in the preceding chapters. Nevertheless, it is important to refrain from drawing hasty conclusions about this kind of tradition that, first of all, raises a methodological problem.

For example, in the case of the Dogon, whose "popular" myth recounting the discovery of the fibers by a woman makes explicit reference to a matriarchy, "the men, seeing that the material of the Andoumboulou was a means of domination, decided to steal it from the women. For up until then, it was women who ruled over men, even going so far as to bully them, every day taking a greater share of power. If this state of affairs had lasted, men would have become women's slaves" (Griaule 1963:61). At first sight, this narrative seems to support those who hold to the thesis of matriarchy. But consider another fragment of the same Dogon myth: "In those days, the women took stars to give to children. . . . When the children were tired of these toys, the mothers put them back in their place" (Griaule 1963:48). It would not occur to anyone to consider that the sentence "in those days, the women took stars to give to children" relates a memory of an actual historic period. By contrast, some do not hesitate to consider another sentence appearing a bit further on in the myth as a historic reminiscence: "in those days, women ruled over men." It is obvious that the difference of treatment between the two sentences comes from that the fact that the interpreter is ready to accept a given theoretical schema, that of the power of women in the past.

Narratives such as the Dogon myth, which relate that thanks to the masks women tyrannized men until the day when these masks were stolen from them, suffer the same inconsistency: if women knew the nature of the masks since they had worn them, how then would the men have been able to terrorize the women with these same masks? Moreover, would this not imply that women should, through tradition, still know today the exact nature of the masks?[10] What then would be the significance of the demand on them for secrecy? In fact, when comparing this first

---

10. "Because women once made masks they know that the disguised figures are ordinary men garbed in sacred costumes," confirms Valentine 1961:41. But also see below, note 30, chap. 7.

type of narrative with the second explanation, which says that women discovered masks, but did not know what to do with them—some informers add, "out of their own stupidity"—and gave them to men, it is necessary to ask whether or not the main function of all these myths is to explain and justify the present situation of women vis-à-vis masks. This would be accomplished either by making allusion to their stupidity or to some other fault or incapacity of women, or by projecting onto the men of the past the current situation of women, exaggerating it at times (it is the tyranny of women that forced men to react), and thus enabling men to justify their current power and to ease their conscience since, in both cases, it would be in some way women's own fault that they lost the masks. Although this psychological interpretation may explain how men justify the loss of masks by women, it does not explain why this tradition is so widespread.[11]

The myth of the discovery of masks by women is inscribed in a wider tradition. Actually, according to the myths of a great many societies, women are considered as the first owners of a number of important sacred and ritual objects (totemic emblems, bull-roarers, masks, ceremonial songs and dances, etc.); they are also the source of many institutions and aspects of culture, and play a determinant role as well in the events that made the world and the human condition what they are now. When we are told that a woman is responsible for the advent of the ocean, the withdrawal of God or the distancing of the celestial vault, that she introduced death to earth, that she possessed fire, these affirmations can hardly be taken literally as "historical memories." Without pretending that these narratives contain no echo of social, cultural or economic revolutions, it would be judicious to look for their meaning at a more symbolic level. As in the Dogon example cited above, these myths of discovery or of the first ownership by women are often linked with the idea that in those days, it was the women who exercised power. If these narratives cannot be considered references to an anterior historical period, in what context can they be placed? Since I do not have the leisure to indulge here in the long developments that this issue deserves, I shall only propose a few elements of response, which will necessarily be open to criticism given their inevitably sketchy nature.

---

11. See the hypothesis by Sanday (1981:181) according to which this type of myth is found in societies in which women have considerable informal power.

The division of the cosmos into male and female subsystems is certainly one of the oldest basic principles of human cognition, one of the most fundamental means humans have used to order reality. The male/female dichotomy, combined with the prohibition of incest, is the basis of classificatory activity through which humans establish a sociocultural order (Leleur 1979–80:163–64). Male/female entities nevertheless are not constituted by the simple recognition of anatomical differences: the most distinctive element is the female power of reproduction. This fertility appears contradictory since it is accompanied by a negative effect, impurity, whose ambiguous sign is menstrual blood. This is also the mark of woman as a cyclical subject: "cyclical because of the menses, woman is potentially also regular in giving birth. Periodicity is at the outset the condition of fertility; but fertility condemns the very regularity that enabled it. Periodicity means therefore much more . . . : it is the woman who engenders it; it is she who regularly expels impure blood. For that reason, fertility is necessarily female, whether the contribution of the male in conception is explicitly acknowledged or not" (Guidieri 1975:113 n.9).

Due to its physiological structure, the female model enjoys considerable weight, against which the male model is essentially constituted by negation.[12] The male individual, born of a woman and nourished by her, is from his birth impregnated with feminine elements; in order for the young male to be able to become a man, he must rid himself of these feminine elements and separate himself from their source, his mother. Forced to construct his identity by proclaiming himself different from the woman, the man must develop and attribute to himself a sociocultural role likely to confer upon him an importance that is at least equal to that of the woman. He therefore reserves, more or less exclusively for himself, certain domains (relations with the sacred, relationship with the dead and the ancestors) and certain activities or techniques. He also establishes a more or less marked hierarchy between the sexes. The problem with which he is presented is twofold: how can a man become a man and remain one, given that any rupture of the separation between the male and the female, or anything drawing them together, risks a fusion and a consequent loss of identity, or worse: since the male/female sub-systems are funda-

---

12. Imitation also arises, for example in the creation of procedures for the ridding of impurity which are inspired by menstruation.

mental constitutive elements of the total conceptual system, any violation to their integrity, any confusion between them, in turn risks provoking a catastrophic collapse of this system. This is why the boundary between the two subsystems is marked and guarded by so many prohibitions. The subsystems are a function of the total system which, in its turn, is modified by any change within the subsystems. It can thus be expected that the contents of the male/female entities and the tension prevailing between them varies from one society to another as much as in time; however, societies with comparable socioeconomic structures and historic traditions could nevertheless present similarities in the manner in which they live this dichotomy (Whyte 1977–78:12–13).

It is in the perspective of this relation/opposition between male/female that the myths of the discovery or of the first ownership of masks by women followed by a transfer to men must be placed. Depending on the case, these myths demarcate the boundaries of the realms particular to each sex, justify the hierarchy of the sexes, and legitimate the exclusion of women by exposing the reasons for the transfer to men. They usually do so by recalling that the women themselves are responsible for it: because of their stupidity or ignorance, they did not know what to do with their discovery and had to turn to men; they tyrannized men who were forced to rebel; an enemy attacked and the women, incapable of conducting war, had to concede power to men; the spirit of the ritual object refused contact with the women when it saw that they menstruate; or, quite simply, the women of former times, of their own accord, gave the object of the ritual to men.

This approach offers us an alternative solution to the historicocultural interpretation but it does not solve all the problems associated with masks. Indeed, the myth of discovery by women is known by societies with masks as well as by those without them. In the current state of analysis, it therefore does not clarify the reasons why certain societies use masks and others do not. Furthermore, the myth of discovery by women is not the only explanation given for the origin of masks: there are a number of other themes (masks given by the supreme god or by the culture hero or heroes, masks seen in dreams by men, discovery by diviners, by children, by a brother and his sister, etc.) and, in the absence of systematic studies on this question already denounced in chapter 1, it is not possible to say to what other possible differences these variations refer. Finally, if the preceding general remarks enable us to see from another angle the background against which some masking traditions take shape, it is nevertheless true that many works, most of which are no longer based on the hypothesis of matriarchy,[13] continue to describe the relation of masks to women as one of a general incompatibility, women being moreover presented as credulous and ignorant about masks. As in the preceding chapters, I shall test this hypothesis of incompatibility, credulity, and ignorance by confronting it with African, Melanesian, and American data.

At the outset it must be pointed out that the mask/woman relationship is more complex and differentiated than it at first seems. Indeed, the prohibitions to which the women are subject sometimes only cover a particular part of the mask, or a particular circumstance. Thus, among the Kono (Guinea), while "the owner of the mask will take every useful precaution to shelter the facial part of the mask from profane glances, the ceremonial costume, by contrast, can be exposed to the eyes of all" (Holas 1952:35). The Karaja women (Brazil) have no right to look at either the masks without the dancers who wear them, or, during the dance, the dancers without their masks.[14] In other cases, masks can be seen by the uninitiated, but only when they cannot be closely watched.[15] Perhaps these prohibitions could be explained by the desire to keep the uninitiated from realizing the composite character of the mask, i.e., that there is both a mask and a wearer. Nevertheless, the Kono example above is not really clarified by this hypothesis, and it does not explain many other cases either, such as that of the following Dogon example.

During the period of preparation or celebration of the ritual called *dama* which ends the period of mourning, when two women fight and when the loincloth of one of them falls, one of the men who witnesses it seizes a drum and, beating the rhythm of a masked dance, shouts the ritual cry three times. All the young men of the village, thus alerted, come out with the masks that they keep at home or run to get them from the shelter in the bush. They hurry toward the place of the dispute, holding the wooden or the fiber masks either in their hands or hung from their belts. When

---

13. Yet, even in 1985, some scholars had not renounced this explanation: Cole (1985:15–16), for example.
14. Krause 1910:115; cf. Adams 1986:46; Gow-Smith 1925:97.
15. Rivers 1914, 1:90; Haddon 1893:154.

all the men are gathered, the ritual cry is again shouted three times and all the women shut themselves in their houses. The initiates and the old men who have already celebrated two *sigui* sit under the *sene* tree. During this time, the youth, carrying their material and shouting, spread out in the village and finally come together as a group before the old men to ask them for justice (Griaule 1963:384).

I shall not dwell here on the reasons that make a fight and the falling of a loincloth an event of such gravity. What is particularly interesting here, is that the women flee and shut themselves away in their houses, even though the young men are recognizable, since they do not necessarily have their masks on their faces but carry them in their hands or on their belts. There is no question of saying here that the women are "terrorized" because they think they are dealing with spirits. The complexity of the situation is even more apparent when one recalls that the women attend the masked dances, when the young men appear dressed in the whole costume. They do not manifest any "terror" at that time; it is only when an accident happens to a masker that the women withdraw or cover their faces, on pain of a fine, since, as Griaule relates, the wearer would find himself in danger of death if he were to be recognized (Griaule 1963:383). Therefore, a situation exists where, on the one hand, men holding their masks (consequently recognizable but apparently not at risk) cause the women to flee; and, on the other hand, masked men (risking death if they are recognized) are looked upon without danger by the women and uninitiated. In the case of the Dogon, it is therefore obviously impossible to explain the behavior of women by pretending that they do not know the nature of masks and are consequently terrified. The case of the Dogon is not unique. To provide an additional example, consider what happens in Owo (Nigeria) during a ceremony in which masked figures walk in the street in a solemn procession. As they approach Uka ward, the women of that part of town run screaming into their houses, closing doors and windows behind them, while women from other quarters follow the troupe of masks without any apparent qualms.[16] As a first conclusion, which

---

16. Poynor 1978:71 and n.30. Among the Iroquois, there were circumstances where the dancers came out without their masks and ceremonies in which all the masks were supposed to be present, where those that were not worn in front of the face were held in the hand or hung from a belt. Certain men thus carried two or three masks (Tooker 1970:61, 65, 77; cf. Speck 1949:95).

will have to be further elaborated upon later, if the women are "terrorized," it is by the consequences of failing to respect the behavior that tradition expects of them; it is certainly not because they do not know with whom they are dealing.

When examining the relations that exist between masks and women, it is impossible to ignore the particular position that certain women occupy within the masking society, a position that Frobenius considered as probably constituting a survival from the matriarchal stage (1898:260). Of course, each case should be individually analyzed in detail, but I must limit myself to citing, as examples, the cases of women who are admitted to the secrets of the masks of men, such as the *yasigine* of the Dogon, the *dzogo-néa lyopou* of the Kono, the *mabole* of the Mende.[17] In certain cases, women contribute to the preparation of masks or dancers, or are entrusted with the care and preservation of the masks and other ritual objects otherwise prohibited to women. Among the Yoruba, for example, before the ceremony, the women wash and repaint the masks. Among the Elema of Orokolo, the women prepare the costume of *sago* leaves for the *hevehe* masks; in certain Baining communities, the women help the men to make the masks. Among the Navajo, it is an old woman who is the caretaker of the masks used in the Yehbechai ceremony; this is also the case among the Wè (Ivory Coast).[18] In addition, the wives of chiefs and the wives of the heads of initiation societies are sometimes initiated into the secrets of masks.[19] The wives of the chiefs of the Bambara Komo, for example, are instructed in the secrets of the society so that they are able to observe the prohibitions associated with them (Dieterlen and Cissé 1972:35). In the *gbon* initiation society of the Toura of Ivory Coast, the first wife of the principal specialist in charms, as well as her eldest daughter, are both initiated to a high degree; they "carry a great influence over the affairs of men, the opinion of the first being especially decisive in everything concerning the associations of masks" (Holas 1962:158). Among the Sulka (New Britain), the *kheng* (superior woman) was assimilated

---

17. On the *yasigine*, see especially Dieterlen 1956:128–29; Griaule 1963:266–78, 336–40, 386–89, 765; Griaule and Dieterlen 1965:35, 378–79; Paulme 1940:251. On the *dzogo-néa lyopou*, see Holas 1952:139–40. On the *mabole*, see Little 1967:245–46; Reinhardt 1979:234.
18. Heyden 1977:18; F. Williams 1940:238; Jeudy-Ballini 1984:23–24; Newcomb 1956:41; Adams 1986:48.
19. Vormann 1911:419, 427; Bastin 1969:3–4.

to a male initiate; she therefore knew both the female secrets and the male secrets: "it is a remarkable fact that in a society where the traditional principle of order is that of the separation of the sexes, the only individual to officially hold the entirety of knowledge was a woman" (Jeudy-Ballini 1984:31). Finally, from a more general point of view, numerous elderly women are exceptions to the rule that all women be excluded from masking rites.[20] The simple enumeration of these numerous specific cases provides a measure the importance of the exceptions to the rule of the incompatibility between women and masks, as well as to the rule of women's ignorance about the masks.

As for children, another class of uninitiated, they also participate in certain masked rituals.[21] They often have their own masks but also sometimes use masks imitating those of the adults. These imitations have, among other things, a pedagogical function aimed at familiarizing the child with the characteristics of various masks. From this point of view, these imitation-masks are comparable to the *kachina* dolls of the Zuñi, to the figurines of the Karaja, and to the *samba* of the Tikar (Cameroon).[22]

Many scholars compare the ritual use of masks to a theatrical representation and the uninitiated to an audience. It is apparent that, in all of these examples, the masks do not chase the women away. On the contrary, the women participate to varying degrees in the representation: in some cases, they sing with the masks; on other occasions, they joke and they dance with some of them, while they must not see others.[23] Sometimes, their contribution

---

20. Guiart 1966:6; Himmelheber 1966:107; Landtman 1927:173; Nevermann 1972:127; Ptak 1977:198; Rivers 1914, 2:511. The Hua (New Guinea) present a particularly interesting case: the postmenopausal woman with three or more children was formally initiated; took up residence in the men's house, where she was shown the secrets of male society. The postmenopausal woman with one or two children, on the other hand, retained her status of uninitiated outsider (Meigs 1984:65, 67).

21. Ankermann 1899:45; Baer 1974:14–15; Baer 1976–77:104–05; Boston 1960:56–57; Drewal and Drewal 1975:36; Foss 1973:25 and fig. 4; Harper 1970:71–72; Heyden 1977:14, 18–19; Krause 1910:101, 110, 112; Speck 1949:98; Vrydagh 1968:228; Zahan 1960:37–128. Also verified outside the three regions considered here: for example, Rütimeyer 1917:361–62; Hummel 1961, which includes interesting remarks on the distribution of children's masquerades in Eurasia.

22. Müller 1962:290; Hartmann 1973:9–10; Krause 1910:98–102; Joseph 1974:50.

23. Fischer and Himmelheber 1976:16, 41, 93, 120. Holas 1947:63; V. Turner 1967:240.

reverses the generally recognized mask/women relation. As among the Lengua of Gran Chaco, who represent the dangers threatening the young girl at the onset of puberty with a masked dance: masked boys, representing evil spirits, attempt to draw near the young girl, but the women make them flee (Zerries 1962:439–40).

In most cases, masks are worn by men. There are of course exceptions where masks worn by women appear, especially in ceremonies during which young girls are initiated. Unfortunately, very little information exists about these ceremonies or about the symbolism and the exact meanings of the masks that perform on these occasions. Among them, the helmet mask of the *bondo* or *sande* women's societies of Sierra Leone and Liberia is probably the most often cited example (fig. 17),[24] but masks worn by women are present elsewhere in Africa, as well as in the two other regions taken into consideration here (Melanesia and America).[25]

Consider, for example, the *manlou-kplon* or *kohoun*, a Kono mask (Guinea), which is kept by a woman, the *dzogo-néa*, in a basket woven of vegetable fibers and covered with a red cloth. This *dzogo-néa* is always an old woman, no longer having sexual relations and living alone in a hut situated at the edge of the village, at the spot where the footpath leads to the grove reserved for women's meetings. She is the president of *sande* and the mistress of excision-initiations. In some regions of Kono country, the mask warns men, with a special song, of its impending outing, so that they can hide in their houses; it is then simply held in the hand by the *dzogo-néa* herself. Elsewhere, the mask, which is then always "dressed," goes out in public on the occasion of the *sande* initiations and, in these circumstances, it is worn by a young female specialist, all dressed in red (Holas 1952:137–38). Regarding this mask, a situation comparable to that observed among the Dogon is found, but with reversed roles for the two sexes. And the same question is raised: is it reasonable to think that the men are "ter-

---

24. See for example Hinckley 1980; Lamp 1985: Phillips 1978; Phillips 1980; Reinhardt 1979; Richards 1973; Richards 1974.

25. Avdeev 1964:432; Bastin 1984b:95 n.5; Boas 1890:10; Hartmann 1967:14 and commentary on photographs numbers 146, 150–152, 156; Hartmann 1968:123–27; Laufer 1959:909–10; Nicklin 1974:15. Perhaps it is appropriate to mention as well in this context finger masks which, according to the majority of authors, were worn by the women among the Inuit of the Bering Sea: Dall 1884:123; Disselhoff 1936:181; Laguna 1936:585.

17. Mask of the Mende female society, *sande*. From Hinckley 1980:30.

rorized" by the mask when the *dzogo-néa* holds it in her hand, while they are not when they are in the presence of the complete mask? And what must one make of what happens among the Gola (Liberia) at the time of the passage of power between the *poro* (men's society) and the *sande* (women's society)? At this time the women and all the uninitiated retreat into their houses, closing doors and shutters, while the great spirit of the *poro* is led outside of the region by the men. Then, the men flee into the houses while the *zogbea* (male water spirits of high lineage), represented by masks worn by women of high rank in *sande*, spread out in the village.[26] In other cases, men and women flee together; thus, among the Chokwe (Angola), at the arrival of the Cikungu mask, men and women shut themselves in their huts since this mask can only be seen without danger by the great chiefs or important people (Bastin 1984b:43).

As mentioned in the Dogon example above, it is hardly possible to explain the behaviors as the result of terror and ignorance on the part of those concerned regarding the true nature of the masks. And these cases could be further augmented since many of the best-documented ethnographic reports insist that women, in particular, know the true nature of the masks and that a large gap often separates that which they are supposed to know from that which they actually know.[27] Indeed, in many societies with masks the uninitiated *must* not speak of these things, or he *must* only speak of them in a certain manner, or he is *supposed* to ignore certain things. Among the Dogon a woman must never speak of the masks nor let it be understood that she doubts certain explanations given by the men of their practices. Conversely, it is forbidden for any man to converse with a woman about matters concerning the society of masks.[28] With considerable schematization, it is possible to construct a general framework of three levels of discourse: (1) the (secret) discourse the initiates hold among themselves; (2) the discourse the initiates hold with uninitiated or that both groups can exchange; (3) the discourse the uninitiated

---

26. Azevedo 1973:132; cf. Bastin 1984b:95 n.5.
27. Boggiani 1900, 2:72; Boston 1960:55–56; Crowley 1972:28; H. Drewal 1974a:29; Himmelheber 1960:6, 12; Jensen 1933:150; Kaufmann 1968:96; Merriam 1978:93, 94; Pouwer 1956:384–85; Ritzenthaler 1953:24; Valentine 1961:48. Also see Forge 1966:26; Guiart 1962:134–35; Harley 1950:5; Laufer 1959:910; Zerries 1962:440. Cf. Moore 1738 cited in Mark 1983:12.
28. Griaule 1963:383; cf. Paulme 1940:251.

hold among themselves, which may contain counter-secrets or include all or part of discourse 1 and, on those grounds, must also remain secret (the initiates must not know that the uninitiated know and communicate this knowledge among themselves). From a psychological and social point of view, these secrets reinforce and protect the identity of the various groups and subgroups (since all the initiates and all the uninitiated do not share the same degree of knowledge or ignorance), and even the identity of the persons.[29] It is obvious that these secrets and the discourses that explain them authorize manipulations enabling certain subgroups to secure the power for themselves.[30] Hence the temptation for some scholars to describe the societies of masks only from the point of view of social and political control, an interpretation that I shall examine more closely.

Various dangers threaten women (but not only women, as will be seen below) that are, in one way or another, involved in breaking prohibitions surrounding masks. These are generally divided into three groups. I shall initially consider the first two, namely, testimonies that affirm that the guilty would be put to death (by the men, by the shaman, etc.); and those that let it be understood that sickness or death is the direct consequence of breaking the prohibition, without men having to intervene. The two groups are not always clearly defined, as Deacon notes: in many cases the informants affirm that a woman must not touch or see the masks "on pain of death," without always making clear whether this would be the automatic result of her transgression or if the woman would be put to death by the men. In certain cases, both versions exist for the same people. Thus, Gow-Smith states that the karaja woman may be punished by death, whereas Dietschy merely notes that contact with a mask is fatal for a woman.[31]

---

29. See the semiotic analysis of these discourses in Schwimmer 1981.

30. On this subject, it would be erroneous to juxtapose men against women as if each could be considered a homogeneous group. Jeudy-Ballini (1984:32–33) notes that, among the Sulka of New Britain, the old women sell to naive young girls the fiction that the masks are mythic beings sprung from the rocks of the bush. "Thus, women are not satisfied with enduring the supposedly mystified status conferred upon them by men, since in becoming mystifiers in their turn, they propagate among the uninitiated of both sexes a fiction which they do not themselves believe; in so doing, they give advance warning of the use that the uninitiated male will make of the same mystifying discourse in support of the dominant ideology, once they are officially introduced to the esoteric knowledge."

31. Deacon 1934b:432, n.2; Gow-Smith 1925:98; Dietschy 1960:3.

Cases belonging to the first group (death as punishment inflicted by the men) abound in Africa as well as in Melanesia and in America. Since their formulation is almost identical everywhere, I shall not expand on it here, except to point out that in numerous cases, the informants affirm that death was the punishment inflicted "in the old days" without always making clear whether those "old days" refer to a historic past, for example the precolonial era, or if they reflect back to a mythic period.[32] By contrast, it is interesting to cite some of the consequences of transgressions of prohibitions included in the second group: a rite of purification must be performed without delay in order to avoid unfortunate consequences, even death (Holas 1964:15 for the Senoufo); the woman is either possessed or goes mad (Redinha 1956:18 for the Lunda-Batshioko group in Angola); the woman contracts leprosy (V. Turner 1967:240–41 for the Ndembu of Zambia); the woman has a miscarriage (Zemp 1965:457–58 for the Dan of Ivory Coast); the woman would be possessed by evil forces or would deliver a stillborn child (Unrug 1983:55 for the Igbirra of Nigeria); if they discover the truth, they die that night (Haddon 1893:154 for the Torres Straits); the woman would become sterile; if she chanced to conceive, her offspring would either be an idiot or die (J. Poole 1943:224 for the Baining of New Britain); the woman is taken ill and may even die (Pouwer 1956:385 for Mimika, New Guinea).[33]

Among these dangers, some of which correspond to social death, several speak of harm to the woman's fertility. Is it solely a matter of a discourse in which the men do not believe but which they hold in order to terrorize the women and to keep them under their control, or is it justifiable to see in this something more profoundly experienced? Here again, it is dangerous to generalize and the examples should suggest some prudence:

There is first of all the case of the *dama* (the end of the period of mourning) of the Hogon, formerly the political chief, judge and religious head of the Dogon, and currently their religious leader. When this rite is celebrated, the women of the Sanga region, both

---

32. See for example Bastin 1969:4; Boas 1897:435; Bolens 1967:62; Boston 1960:55; Lafargue 1971:121; Vormann 1911:418.

33. The risks mentioned do not necessarily concern women only; other non-initiates are just as much in danger: see for example Peek 1983:36; Thiam 1966:27. In Malekula, a man who is unmarried is afraid to make *nalawan* masks lest in the future some harm should befall his children (Deacon 1934b:426).

young and old, perform a curious parody of masked dances to which the men are this time amused spectators. Unable to touch the actual masks, the women merely imitate them by means of makeshift accessories (Calame-Griaule 1956:298–300). A second example is the "secret" rite performed during the funeral of a woman, which also demonstrates that the old women know more about masks than people pretend, as Calame-Griaule (1965:300) states. After the dances held on the square, they gather any fibers which may have fallen from the dancer's costumes and carefully place them in the box in which their jewelry is hidden. These symbolic fragments are kept by an old woman of the family who has nothing to fear regarding fertility. When there is a funeral for a woman, they shut themselves in with the corpse, and upon completing its toilette, take out the fibers and very lightly beat the rhythms of the masks on a grinding stone with an iron utensil used for shelling grain. Thus the deceased, who as a woman is not entitled to be honored with masked dances, receives from the other women a small symbolic act of consolation, which also constitutes a secret vengeance toward the men. But the most stinging point is that the latter, at least the best informed among them, know it and tolerate it as a legitimate compensation for the type of frustration endured by the women who are kept away from the masks.

I shall not expand upon the psychological explanation Calame-Griaule gives of this ritual here, but shall limit myself to highlighting three essential aspects of the Dogon data: first, the women are well informed of the true nature of the masks; second, it is their fertility that would be impaired if they enter into contact with the mask; third, and perhaps most important, the women accept this view. Indeed, when the dance is performed with the imitations of masks, the young women participate in the rite; by contrast, only those who have nothing left to lose in the way of fertility risk infringing the prohibitions concerning the actual masks, and in this case the fibers, the importance of which was described in chapter 3. Why would the women respect the prohibition in a secret rite, performed outside the men's control, if they had not interiorized the views to which it refers? In a parallel to these Dogon facts, note that among the Mende, the *sowie* mask of the women's society, *sande*, is accompanied by assistants, one of whose tasks it is to pick up even the smallest pieces of raffia that may fall from the costume. For if a man stepped on such a strand of the sacred costume he would contract genital elephantiasis. Several authors maintain this is also a punishment brought down on a man who spies on *sande* matters (Reinhardt 1979:244-45).

Therefore, the fear of infertility can be experienced by both sexes, in fact by society as a whole. A double relation binds the mask with sterility and death, on the one hand, and with fertility and life, on the other. Indeed, while the mask threatens to bring sterility and death, it can also bring or restore fertility, and this is true in Africa as well as in Melanesia and in America.[34] In order for it to have this therapeutic function, the relation of the mask to fertility and sterility must be experienced in a way that transcends the level of a mere male discourse imposed on women, aiming only to assure their submission. It is furthermore this concern for fertility that probably explains why it is generally old women—or women who are sterile or have undergone several miscarriages—who are permitted to fill ritual roles otherwise forbidden to women.[35]

The third group of dangers that a transgression of the prohibition might involve widens the perspective still further: among the Mandinka of Gambia, for example, it is dangerous for the whole community if an uncircumcised male or any female sees the masker dressing or sees the masker's face. The fertility of all the young women of the community is threatened if any female sees the masker's face or, as usually put, sees the inside of a mask or costume fallen from the masker. The threat to the fertility of the community can only be removed through the punishment of the masker's association (Weil 1971:283). In this case, breaking the prohibition also puts the fertility of women in danger, but the danger is clearly perceived here as threatening the entire community. Therefore, the punishment—whether it is inflicted upon the wearer of the mask, on the woman or uninitiated, or on the masking society—no longer aims at guaranteeing a secret, which is after all illusory, but rather at protecting the fertility of the community, its future, its very life. Similar conceptions, expressed

---

34. For example Dietschy 1960:3; Holas 1947:62; Holas 1954:77, 103, 149; Nevermann 1933:160; Tedlock 1979:502. Cf. Fenton 1937:238; Zemp 1965:464. On the relation of the mask with the menses, see for example Beier, 1968: 6-7; Griaule 1963:353-55; Griaule and Dieterlen 1965:363-64; Paulme 1940:268-70.

35. This explanation seems more plausible than that which is based only on the fact that menopause would put an end to the danger (pollution) that woman represents for man.

under various forms, are found in Melanesia as well as in America. For example, the wooden faces carved by the Kwoma and the Nukuma of northern New Guinea must remain secret from the uninitiated. The primary aim of this secrecy is not to keep the women and children in ignorance and submission; rather, as Kaufmann relates: the Kwoma and the Nukuma are simply persuaded that any contact with these personifications of a small part of supernatural power would have catastrophic consequences for the uninitiated and, indirectly, for the whole of society. A serious illness, death, the dissolution of social order, or even of the world order—such would be the horrible consequences of this contact.[36] This fear of the Kwoma and the Nukuma illustrates in an extremely striking way the risks any rupture of the boundaries separating the male and female subsystems poses for the total conceptual system.

In conclusion, given that the existence of a matriarchal stage or a cycle has not been demonstrated, it is impossible to consider that the masking societies were created as a reaction to the domination by women. Furthermore, these societies are diverse and cannot be grouped under the heading of "secret societies." Finally, the documents reveal an image of the relationship between masks and women to be much more nuanced than the theory founded on the incompatibility, ignorance, and credulity posits. What remains to be understood, now, is why this theory has enjoyed such success, to the point of misleading scholars into ignoring the aspects of their data that did not lead in this direction.

As described above, in a number of masking societies women are either supposed to believe certain explanations given by men or, at the very least, not to express doubts about them. It is easy to imagine that when the anthropologists (men for the most part) presented themselves in these societies, their informants (men in the great majority of cases) gave them information corresponding, on the one hand, to what ought to be said, to what was supposed to be, and, therefore, to what the women were supposed to believe; and on the other hand, to an enhanced vision of what the men themselves knew. The information thus obtained was sometimes held to demonstrate that the masked rituals were deceptions and that they were conceived by a group of incredulous people to

---

36. Kaufmann 1968:101; Kaufmann 1979:331; Krause 1910:98; Métraux 1964:115.

The Mask and Women

dominate a group of credulous ones. The interpretation of these ceremonies sometimes stopped at this point, as if it could be accepted that they had been designed for the sole purpose of dominating women.[37] This also led to the idea that men and women did not believe the same thing: the women were deceived, ignorant of the fact that the masks were worn by men; they were led to believe that the masked figures were truly spirits, while the men believed in an invisible presence of spirits during the masked performance (Landtman 1927:335, for example).

There is nothing extraordinary in anthropologists pausing at this first level of interpretation. What may be surprising, however, is that so few scholars of the nineteenth century and of the beginning of this century attempted to transcend this first stage, to deepen the question. Admittedly, one of the principal causes of this lack of interest is the androcentrism that dominated anthropology. Modern scholars can only be struck by the type of "male complicity" that is apparent in a number of old texts in which the anthropologist (male) does not doubt for a second the information with which his informants (also male) supplied him (according to which the men know what the masks are while women are deceived). Obviously proud to be let in on the secrets of his informants,[38] the anthropologist completely loses his critical faculties. Therefore, it was easy for feminist anthropologists to show "how the degree of male superiority in primitive societies is exaggerated by anthropologists who have been all too eager to find corroboration for their own bias as products of sexist cultures" (Denich 1976:450). However, "if the status and roles of women are misinterpreted and distorted, so inevitably must be those of men. Since the relationship of women and men interlock, the distortion of the roles of men and women leads to a distortion of the total social system."[39]

The ritual mask offers a perfect illustration of this phenomenon: the distortion of the role of women (as deceived) implies that of the role of men (as deceivers) and the erroneous interpretation of the masked ritual as a whole (as deception). Yet, as described above, the best documented accounts relate that the women know

---

37. See Jensen 1933:152. Also Meuli 1943:48. Analysis based on the notion of imposture in Guiart 1962:134–35.

38. The informants perhaps go beyond the expectations of the investigator; Augé 1987:15–16; Vansina 1961:82.

39. Rohrlich-Leavitt 1975:578, cited by Jacobs 1977:232.

perfectly well what the masks are, and there is good reason to think that in general this is true. As a consequence, the women's behavior must be seen from a different perspective, and its interpretation refers not to a "primitive female credulity" that would make of women the dupes of men, but to a system of references touching on the whole of the traditions of the societies considered.

In *Tristes Tropiques* (1962:211), Lévi-Strauss took a step in this direction when, referring to Bororo women, he pointed out that "their real or supposed credulity also had a psychological function: to give, for the benefit of both sexes, an affective and intellectual content to those puppets whose strings the men would perhaps, otherwise, draw with less care." By its tone, this interpretation is nevertheless difficult to uphold since it merely sees the ritual as a "rather sinister farce" and presents us with men who do not really believe in what they do but who continue to do it, aided by women who do not believe either, but who pretend to. Apparent in this view is the echo of former theories according to which the "primitive" seemed to spend most of his ritual activity fooling others and fooling himself. Less pessimistic, Boston thinks that "on the whole it is best to regard the assertion that they are deceived as a dogmatic way of expressing the truth that women support the custom of masking, and that without their support masking could not be continued" (Boston 1960:56).

If, as I believe, nothing justifies the assumption that women act as spectators who pretend to believe in the performance in order to uphold the ritual for psychological or social reasons, how is it possible to explain the emotions they show in the presence of the masks? There is a strong probability that, in most cases, the behavior of the women is akin to an obligatory expression of emotion. I do not deny that women may be afraid of the consequences of their disobedience to the masks, but it is impossible to interpret their behavior in all cases on this basis. Thus, when women manifest terror in the face of the masks, when they recognize in them deceased members of their family and implore them with sobs and tears, it is necessary to ask oneself if this expression of emotion is not an essential and obligatory part of the rite itself (whose function as a form of validation was described in chapter 4), instead of a merely personal reaction to a performance. This convention in no way rules out sincerity, but a sincerity that is addressed to what is represented in the ritual, and a sincerity that cannot be understood unless one first accepts that all the participants may experience the ritual at the level of what is being represented, while remaining perfectly aware of the means used to create the performance.[40]

Now, if the woman is not fooled, if she acts in accordance with what the mask represents and conforms to the norm admitted in her society, she can no longer be considered a spectator: she takes an active part *in* the ritual, a part that can no longer be interpreted as a reaction *to* the ritual. Indeed, when speaking of the masked ritual, it is not enough merely to evoke an image of the men of the community, whose acts alone are meaningful, performing before an audience whose reactions result from its credulity and its ignorance or from some psychological or social generosity. Instead, it is necessary to return to the lesson Mauss gave during the period between the two World Wars when he said: "the spectators get up, sit down, hold their breath. Everything has a meaning, silence itself is a sign."[41]

I am not pretending here, against all evidence, that women are not "excluded from masks" as a general rule. However, what appears to be demonstrated is that the reasons given for this exclusion are hardly tenable and that it is, consequently, necessary to relocate the relation between ritual masks and women. This new investigation will have to start from the point of view that the deeper meaning of masked rituals can only be perceived if one acknowledges that the behavior of everyone concerned is meaningful, the women's as well as the men's, both contributions being at once necessary to the ritual and constitutive of it. Only on this basis is it possible to understand the particular roles that the various traditions attribute to men and to women in their ceremonies.

---

40. See Evans-Pritchard 1965:45; Jensen 1963:27; Mauss 1971.
41. Mauss 1967:238. Cf. La Fontaine 1977:429; Ottenberg 1973:35; Ottenberg 1975:202; Tonkin 1979:246.

Conclusion

AT THE sight of a masked figure, Huizinga tells us, even the contemporary civilized adult is carried beyond ordinary life into a world where the light of day does not reign, into the world of the savage, the child and the poet, which is the world of play. That is why nothing helps modern man in his understanding of savage society as much as his feeling for masks and disguise (1955:26). And, it is tempting to add, nothing has the potential to lead him into greater error, if this "contemporary civilized adult" feels that he attains an intuitive and intimate comprehension of the mask and its meaning. For, instead of turning toward the documents to verify whether or not their analysis can lead to an explanation, he will rather be tempted to look within himself and to interpret his own emotions and rationalizations. This is the origin of what Evans-Pritchard (1965:43–44) qualified as conjectures of the "if I were a horse" type, examples of which were encountered above. The more this "contemporary civilized adult" is persuaded that he knows the facts intuitively, the less he will be inclined to look for the means to test his hypotheses, and the stronger will be his reaction if it is suggested to him that his theory could be mistaken or insufficient. This elementary psychological phenomenon explains, in part at least, how some general theories were elaborated and, above all, how they were able to persist up until the present time in the secondary literature on masks.

In examining some of these theories, it is apparent that from the very beginning difficulties were raised by even the word "mask" which covers, in fact, an extremely wide range of meanings in which various disciplines, and even various authors, have carved out fields which do not necessarily correspond to one another. Depending on whether one insists, for example, on religion, social function, aesthetics, concealment, representation, or incarnation, different elements are included or privileged by the definition. In truth, it is impossible to define *the* mask in a way that satisfies every discipline, every author, and encompasses all the objects, all the adornments and all the institutions that are called "masks".[1]

Beginning with the classic definition that an object is a mask when it covers all or part of the face in order to disguise the wearer or conceal his identity, I have noted that, contrary to what is often written, the mask is not universal and that, although a certain number of works propose hypotheses based on regional studies, there is no general model explaining why some societies have masks and others do not. The same uncertainty applies to the question of the age of the ritual mask since, in the analysis of prehistoric evidence, it appears that the theory or simply the scholar's expectation, his intimate conviction, often weighed more heavily than did the data itself, especially when it was a matter of deciding between a mask and a stylized face or between a masked man and a composite mythical being. Consequently, the existence of ritual masks in Paleolithic times remains doubtful, while the probability of its existence during the Neolithic period grows appreciably. Yet, just as the ritual mask is not present in all contemporary societies, similarly nothing suggests that it was universal at any given moment whatever in prehistory or in history. It is therefore impossible to speak of the universality of the mask.

It nevertheless remains that universality is one of the themes that most frequently recurs in the literature, where it is often presented as an obvious fact. This persistence in the face of doubts and contrary facts confers upon this affirmation a character that transcends that of a simple hypothesis or theory. In this regard, the myths that explain the origin of an institution generally project it into a distant past, the "time of the origins," as a matter of fact. Is this not exactly what a number of texts are doing when they affirm that the origin of the mask goes back to the "dawn of time"? Does this not indicate that the universality of the mask in space and in time partakes of the myth, that is to say, of a myth of the white man?[2]

---

1. This is perhaps the place to recall Guidieri's reflection (1981:1) "I do not know what a mask is. I do know however that this ignorance is shared by others. Like others too, I know masks by the hundreds."

2. It would be interesting to take up the whole of the Western discourse on the mask again, not to verify its adequacy with data, but to analyze what it teaches us as a myth. Such an analysis transcends the framework of this book since it would also necessarily include the examination of the discourse on the popular European traditions such as the carnival, for example.

Conclusion

Aware of the extent of Western projections on the ritual masks, I strived to show the problems raised by the theories I was testing. But in so doing, a few guidelines emerged which in my opinion provided a better orientation to the mass of documents under consideration. Thus, with the help of some examples selected from those regions most often used to elaborate theories on masks (Africa, Melanesia, America), I examined the question of whether by affirming as a general rule that masks represent spirits, or even more specifically, by postulating that they represent the spirits of the dead, we did not risk missing something important. Several conclusions arose from this analysis. First of all, certain masks do not represent a character, strictly speaking, but an event, and they are not any less meaningful because of this; second, most ritual masks represent primordial beings, mythic ancestors, culture heroes and gods, who are not usually included in the category of "spirits" and above all not in that of "spirits of the dead" since many of these figures never died. This being the case, in many of the instances where masks do represent particular beings, they do not do so in a static manner, but put these beings in a context, recalling the events with which they were involved. Furthermore, groups of masks (but also sometimes isolated ones) represent all the creatures belonging to the world of their wearers, or recapitulate the daily historic and mythic diversity of the community. I have concluded that rather than affirming that masks represent spirits, it perhaps would be judicious to shift the accent and emphasize instead, without making it a general rule, that masks often aim, on the one hand, at expressing a cosmos, a system of the world, and on the other hand, at recalling or dramatizing events, which are in general the founding events of the world, of humanity, of the clan, or of a particular institution.

By its intervention, the mask can also associate a particular moment in life or a particular fact to its model. This function is especially obvious in the rituals for the reestablishment of order that follow a death and where the mask associates or identifies the deceased with a model (culture hero, first dead) in order to help the deceased reach his new status. Some were tempted to interpret these ceremonies as being directed only at the living; these scholars consequently privilege explanations based on the need for prestige on the part of the participants or organizers, the exaltation of the group, the reinforcement of social cohesion, the reaffirmation of group values, etc. These are certainly important aspects that must not be neglected. However, "to limit ritual to its communicative aspect would exclude and falsify its significance for those who perform it. Ritual is not done solely to be interpreted: it is also done (and from the point of view of the performers this may be more important) to resolve, alter or demonstrate a situation"; in this case, to help the deceased to reach his new status.[3]

In approaching the relationships between the mask, its wearer, and the rest of the community, and in examining in particular the theory that the wearer becomes the spirit represented by the mask, it seems that we have delved into the heart of the white man's mythic discourse about the "primitive" and his masks. In its purest form, this discourse claims that to don a mask is to undergo an "actual transformation." From this affirmation, two corollaries can be extended: first, if the peoples in question experience the wearing of a mask as engendering an actual transformation, it is because their mode of thought is different from ours (primitive mentality, archaic level of consciousness, confusion between the sign and the signified); and second, this actual transformation implies that, in one way or another, the wearer is possessed by the spirit represented, that he is not himself.

In actuality, the facts show that the wearer generally remains aware and responsible; he must often submit himself to a long apprenticeship, demonstrate great concentration and take precautions to avoid any liturgical error, whether accidental or provoked by a witch. Therefore, the theories that explain the institution of the ritual mask as the satisfaction of a desire or an individual need on the part of the wearer—especially those that see the ritual mask as a means for the wearer to free himself, to liberate his instincts, or to escape outside of himself—correspond to a phantasm or a projection on the part of the Westerner more than to the ethnographic data. According to the sources, the ritual mask stems more from the notion of service rather than from liberation. As for the relationship between the wearer, his mask, his community, the power, and the event or spirit represented, it is placed in a continuum that extends from the simple dramatization of a character or a narrative to the possible actual transformation of the wearer, passing through numerous intermediary cases where a power or a "supernatural" element is present, in whole or in part, in the mask, in its accessories or in the costume. It is therefore impossible

---

3. G. Lewis 1980:35; also see Penner 1986:647-49.

Conclusion

to affirm as a general rule that, in the sense of undergoing an actual transformation, the wearer of the mask becomes, or is, that which he shows.

The other domain where the projections and phantasms of the Westerner weighed and continue to weigh very heavily, is that of the relationship between the mask and women. It is not necessary to return again to the question of matriarchy, a mythic phenomenon if ever there is one, since its existence as a stage or a cycle has never been proven, but simply to recall that it is improper to group extremely diverse religious and social institutions under the expression "secret societies." On closer examination, these institutions show no common characteristics or have only belatedly developed them under the influence of colonization or evangelization, for example. It is now recognized that many of these "secret societies" did not have masks and that others only recently borrowed the use of the mask, which existed outside of them and sometimes were anterior to them. But let me reaffirm that the theories that present women as credulous, ignorant, and terrorized by the masks reflect the androcentrism of anthropology and of the sexist environment in which they emerged. As a matter of fact, the anthropological reports emphasize that the women know the true nature of masks and that an abyss separates what they are supposed to know from what they actually know. If therefore they are "terrorized," it may be caused by the consequences that any disrespect of traditional behavior would have, but it is certainly not because they do not know with whom they are dealing. Moreover, when other attitudes that they display before masks are taken into account, such as manifestations of grief, it appears much more likely that what is exhibited is an obligatory expression of emotion, an expression that is an integral part of the ritual. The profound meaning of the masked rituals can therefore only be perceived by acknowledging that everyone's behavior in them is meaningful, the women's as well as the men's.

In conclusion, and in order to avoid any misunderstanding, it would be well to recall the limits that I placed on this study: it was never my intention to propose a new global interpretation of the ritual mask; the object was simply to verify if a number of propositions, frequently taken up in the literature on masks, in fact had the character of a general rule that had been attributed to them. Doing so obviously restricted the aspects of the mask on which I focused.

I did not, for example, approach the question of aesthetics, which is of considerable importance. A mask may be as it is because it aims at representing a number of things, but a mask is often as it is because it is beautiful, or because it lends itself to the different uses one has for it.[4] Various traditions relate that it is because they found masks beautiful that the people adopted them, sometimes resulting in dramatic consequences. Thus, among the Dogon, it is because the masks and their adornment had seduced the people of Pêguê that they paid to learn their technique, thus introducing misfortune among them. It is because the choreography of the funerals delighted the people of Ogol that they bought a corpse and the right to execute the rites, thus causing a fatal contagion. A number of other regions are equally said to have been contaminated in this way. It is therefore not rash to posit that, in the idea of the Dogon, aesthetic emotion and the spread of death are intimately linked (Griaule 1963:794).

Furthermore, although I did point out the concern and the rigor of the choreographies and dramatizations, I did not engage in a detailed analysis, in part because the generalizations discussed did not touch upon this aspect and, also, it must be said, because data on this dimension of ritual are extremely rare. Now, as Lupu notes (1983:18), "to analyze the precise elaboration of these dramatizations, from the make-up of the masks to the public performance, reveals more of the reality than the constant search for the meaning that too often, for lack of evaluation, results in truisms or in misconstructions. It is probably not by chance that this domain is dealt with very little by anthropologists, as if, among the others, everything must culminate in a meaning, never in an effect. Does not the effect in its dramatization create meaning? All these scenic elements should be brought into relief and transcribed into analytical visual data, in order to exclude words and descriptions as much as possible."

In other respects, I have only noted, without going into it deeply, that the mask could be an identity, emblem, an object of prestige, an affirmation of social status or hierarchy, that it could express and validate political, economic and social realities. Now,

---

4. For example, the Senoufo have minor masked figures whose presence aims at giving luster to the ceremonies by contributing to their animation with dance. They often evoke the appearance of a woman "because it is the most agreeable thing to watch dance" (Bochet 1965:668).

Conclusion

these aspects take on a considerable importance and often suffice to explain why the masked ritual subsists even while the society changes, converts to Islam or to Christianity. Similarly, I have discussed only slightly or not at all the various functions masks fulfill: head of a ceremony, messenger, police officer, judge, etc. Last, but not least of the limitations, I have tested the theories on the basis of the data on which they were elaborated, which means that I have hardly touched upon European masks (or those of European origin) or Asian ones.

Acknowledging these limitations, the study nevertheless brought to light a number of problems the constant reaffirmation of "classic" theses had a tendency to eclipse. Now, to know the problems that ritual masks raise, is already, to a considerable degree, to know ritual masks.[5] The study has also enabled me to draw a few hypotheses, to suggest some paths that, while not leading to a new global interpretation of masks or to a phenomenology of the mask, should still, I hope, enable the reader to mark some bearings and to find an orientation in this vast world of the ritual mask.

---

5. Interviewed on July 18, 1986 by Bernard Pivot of French Television (A2), Georges Dumézil declared in essence: "Those who are looking for something positive to leave behind are working for the museum; what we must leave behind us are problems." I could not put it better.

Bibliography

Abdel-Rasoul, Kawthar. 1956. Funeral Rites in Nigeria. *Wiener volkerkundliche Mitteilungen* 4:167–79.
Adams, Marie Jeanne (Monni). 1986. Women and masks among the western Wè of Ivory Coast. *African Arts* 19, no. 2:46–55, 90.
———. 1987. Problèmes d'identité: Fêtes masquées chez les Wè (Guéré) de l'Ouest ivoirien. *Arts d'Afrique noire* 62:37–48.
Adande, Alexandre. 1955. Fonctions et significations sociales des masques en Afrique noire. *Présence africaine*, n.s., 1:24–38.
Adelman, Kenneth Lee. 1975. The art of the Yaka. *African Arts* 9, no. 1:40–43.
Alon, David. 1985. Letter of July 20, 1985 to the author.
Amiet, Pierre. 1972. *Glyptique susienne des origines à l'époque des Perses achéménides: cachets, sceaux-cylindres et empreintes antiques découverts à Suse de 1913 à 1967*. 2 vols. Paris: Librairie orientaliste Paul Geuthner.
———. 1979. L'iconographie archaïque de l'Iran: quelques documents nouveaux. *Syria* 56:333–52.
Anati, Emmanuel, ed. 1975. *Les religions de la préhistoire: Actes du Valcamonica Symposium '72*. Capo di Ponte: Edizioni del Centro Camuno di Studi Preistorici.
Andree, Richard. 1886. Die Masken in der Völkerkunde. *Archiv für Anthropologie* 16:477–506.
Aniakor, Chike C. 1978. The Igbo Ijele mask. *African Arts* 11, no. 4:42–47, 95.
Ankermann, B. 1899. Eine Tanzmaske der Baining. *Ethnologisches Notizblatt* 2, no. 1:44–48.
Augé, Marc. 1987. Qui est l'autre? Un itinéraire anthropologique. *L'Homme* 103, vol. 27, no. 3:7–26.
Avdeev, Arsenij Dmitrievic. 1964. Aleutische Masken in den Sammlungen des Museums für Anthropologie und Ethnographie der Akademie der Wissenschaften der UdSSR. *Jahrbuch des Museums für Völkerkunde zu Leipzig* (Berlin) 20:413–33.
D'Azevedo, Warren L. 1973. Mask makers and myth in Western Liberia. In *Primitive art and society*, ed. A. Forge, pp. 126–50. London: Oxford University Press.
———. 1980. Gola Poro and Sande: Primal tasks in social custodianship. *Ethnologische Zeitschrift Zürich* no. 1:13–23.

Baer, Gerhard. 1974. The pahotko-masks of the Piro (Eastern Peru). *Bulletin de la Société suisse des américanistes* 38:7–16.

———. 1976–77. Masken der Piro, Shipibo und Matsigenka (Ost-Perú). *Verhandlungen der Naturforschenden Gesellschaft in Basel* 87/88:101–15.

Barguet, P. 1960. Note sur le masque animal dans l'Egypte pharaonique. In *Le masque*. Catalogue of the exhibition held at the Musée Guimet à Paris, pp. 64–66. Paris Musées nationaux.

Barnett, R. D. 1966. Homme masqué ou dieu-ibex? *Syria* 43:259–76.

Bartels, Max. 1896. Über Schädel-Masken aus Neu-Britannien, besonders eine mit einer Kopfverletzung. In *Festschrift für Adolf Bastian zu seinem 70. Geburtstage: 26. Juni 1896*. Berlin: Verlag von Dietrich Reimer (Ernst Vohsen).

Bar-Yosef, Ofer. 1985. *A cave in the desert: Nahal Hemar. 9000-year-old-finds*. Jerusalem: The Israel Museum.

Bastian, Adolf. 1883. Masken und Maskereien. *Zeitschrift für Völkerpsychologie* 14:335–58.

Bastin, Marie-Louise. 1969. Masques et sculptures ngangela. *Baessler-Archiv*, n.s., 17:1–23.

———. 1984a. *Introduction aux arts d'Afrique noire*. Arnouville: Arts d'Afrique.

———. 1984b. Ritual masks of the Chokwe. *African Arts* 17, no. 4:40–45, 92–93, 95–96.

Bateson, Gregory. 1932. Further notes on a snake dance of the Baining. *Oceania* 2 (1931–32):334–41. See also Read, W. J., and Poole, J.

Beaudoin, Gérard. 1984. *Les Dogons du Mali*. Paris: Armand Colin.

Bedaux, R. M. A. 1977. *Tellem: een bijdrage tot de geschiedenis van de Republiek Mali*. Berg en Dal: Afrika Museum.

Bédouin, Jean-Louis. 1967. *Les masques*. Paris: Presses Universitaires de France ("Que sais-je?" no. 905).

Bégouën, Henri, and Henri Breuil. 1958. *Les cavernes du Volp, Trois Frères—Tuc d'Audoubert, à Montesquieu-Avantès (Ariège)*. Paris: Arts et métiers graphiques.

Beier, Ulli. 1956. The Egugun cult. *Nigeria Magazine* 51:380–92.

———. 1958. The Egugun cult among the Yorubas. *Présence africaine* 18–19:33–36.

———. 1968. Gelede masks. *Odù* 6:4–23.

Bensa, Alban. 1983. Le masque dans la région de Touho (aire linguistique cèmuhî), Nouvelle-Calédonie. In *Océanie, le masque au long cours*, ed. F. Lupu, pp. 67–68. Rennes: Ouest-France.

Bernolles, Jacques. 1966. *Permanence de la parure et du masque africains*. Paris: G.-P. Maisonneuve et Larose.

Binford, Lewis R. 1981. *Bones: Ancient men and modern myths*. New York: Academic Press.

Binford, Lewis R., and Chauan Kun Ho. 1985. Taphonomy at a distance:

Zhoukoudian, "The cave home of Beijing Man?" *Current anthropology* 26:413-42.

Birket-Smith, Kaj. 1929. *The caribou eskimos: Their cultural position.* Copenhagen: Gyldendalske Boghandel, Nordisk Forlag.

Bleakley, Robert. 1978. *Masques africains.* Trans. Edith Ochs. Paris: Editions du Chêne (my pagination).

Boas, Franz. 1890. The use of masks and head-ornaments on the North-West Coast of America. *Internationales Archiv für Ethnographie* 3:7-15.

———. 1897. "The social organization and the secret societies of the Kwakiutl Indians," in *Annual Report of the Board of Regents of the Smithsonian Institution for the year ending June 30, 1895: Report of the U.S. National Museum.* Washington: Government Printing Office.

Bochet, Gilbert. 1959. Le poro des Diéli. *Bulletin de l'Institut français d'Afrique noire* 21, B:61-101.

———. 1965. Les masques sénoufo, de la forme à la signification. *Bulletin de l'Institut français d'Afrique noire* 27, B:636-77.

Boggiani, Guido. 1900. Compendio de etnografia paraguaya moderna. *Revista del Instituto Paraguayo*, Año III, 1:40-48, 129-206; 2:49-85.

Bolens, Jacqueline. 1967. Mythe de Jurupari: introduction à une analyse. *L'homme* 7, no. 1:50-66.

Borgatti, Jean M. 1979a. Dead Mothers of Okpella. *African Arts* 12, no. 4:48-57, 91-92.

———. 1979b. *From the hands of Lawrence Ajanaku.* Los Angeles: University of California, Museum of Cultural History.

———. 1982. Age grades, masquerades, and leadership among the Northern Edo. *African Arts* 16, no. 1:36-51, 96.

Borgeaud, Philippe. 1986. Le problème du comparatisme en histoire des religions. *Revue européen des sciences sociales* 24, no. 72:59-75.

Boston, John Shipway. 1960. Some northern Ibo masquerades. *Journal of the Royal Anthropological Institute of Great Britain and Ireland* 90:54-65.

Bradbury, R. E. 1968. Fathers, elders, and ghosts in Edo religion. In *Anthropological approaches to the study of religion*, ed. M. Banton, pp. 127-53. London: Tavistock Publications, Social Science Paperback.

Bravmann, René A. 1974. *Islam and tribal art in West Africa.* London: Cambridge University Press (African Studies Series, 11).

———. 1977. Gyinna-Gyinna: Making the djinn manifest. *African Arts* 10, no. 3:46-52, 87.

Breuil, Henri. 1914. A propos des masques quaternaires. *L'Anthropologie* 25:420-22. See Deonna, Waldemar.

———. 1952. *Quatre cents si-ecles d'art pariétal: les cavernes ornées de l'âge du renne.* Montignac, Dordogne: Centre d'études et de documentation préhistoriques.

Breuil, Henri, and Raymond Lantier. 1959. *Les hommes de la pierre ancienne: paléolithique et mésolithique.* Paris: Payot.

Bühler, Alfred. 1969. *Kunst der Südsee/Art of Oceania.* Catalogue du Musée Rietberg, Zurich. Zurich: Atlantis Verlag.

Bunzel, Ruth L. 1932. Introduction to Zuñi ceremonialism (pp. 467–544); Zuñi origin myths (pp. 545–609); Zuñi ritual poetry (pp. 611–835); Zuñi Katchinas: An analytical study (pp. 837–1086). In *Forty-Seventh Annual Report of the Bureau of American Ethnology, 1929–30.* Washington, D.C.: Government Printing Office.

Buraud, Georges. 1948. *Les masques: essai.* Paris. Editions du Seuil.

Burkert, Walter. 1985. *Greek religion: Archaic and classical.* (Revised edition of the original German version of 1977.) Trans. J. Raffan. Oxford: Basil Blackwell.

Caillois, Roger. 1960. *Méduse et Cie.* Paris: Gallimard.

———. 1962. Préface. In *Masques,* ed. H. Demoulin-Bernard, pp. 3–8. Paris: Olivier Perrin.

———. 1967. *Les jeux et les hommes (Le masque et le vertige).* (Revised and augmented edition of 1958 original.) Paris: Gallimard.

Calame, Claude. 1986. Facing otherness: The tragic mask in Ancient Greece. *History of religions* 26:125–42.

Calame-Griaule, Geneviève. 1965. *Ethnologie et langage: la parole chez les Dogon.* Paris: Gallimard.

———. 1968. s.v. "Dogon." In *Dictionnaire des civilisations africaines,* ed. G. Balandier and J. Maquet. Paris: Fernand Hazan.

Campbell, Joseph. 1960. *The masks of God: Primitive mythology.* London: Secker and Warburg.

Camps, Gabriel, 1974. *Les civilisations préhistoriques de l'Afrique du Nord et du Sahara.* Paris: Doin.

———. Symboles religieux dans l'art rupestre du Nord de l'Afrique. In *Les religions de la préhistoire:* Actes du Valcamonica Symposium '72, ed. Emmanuel Anati, pp. 323–33. Capo di Ponte: Edizioni del Centro Camuno di Studi Preistorici.

Cartailhac, Emile, and Henri Breuil. 1906. *La caverne d'altamira à Santillane près Santander (Espagne).* Monaco: Imprimerie de Monaco.

Cauvin, Jacques. 1985. La révolution idéologique: l'art néolithique au Proche-Orient. In *Le grand atlas de l'archéologie,* ed. Christine Flon, pp. 172–73. Paris: Encyclopaedia Universalis.

Cazeneuve, Jean. 1957a. *Les dieux dansent à Cibola: le shalako des Indiens Zuñis.* Second ed. Paris: Gallimard.

———. 1957b. *Les rites et la condition humaine d'areès des documents ethnographiques.* Paris: Presses Universitaires de France.

———. 1967. *L'ethnologie.* Paris: Larousse.

Chappaz-Wirthner, Suzanne. 1974. Les masques du Lötschental. *Annales valaisannes* 2, 49:3–95.

Christinger, Raymond, and Willy Borgeaud. 1963. *Mythologie de la Suisse ancienne.* Vol. 1. Geneva: Georg.

Clark, J. G. D. 1954. *Excavations at Star Carr: An early mesolithic site at Seamer near Scarborough, Yorkshire.* Cambridge: University Press.

Codrington, Robert Henry. 1891. *The Melanesians: Studies in their anthropology and folk-lore.* Oxford: Clarendon Press.

Cole, Herbert M. 1975. The history of Ibo *mbari* houses: Facts and theories. In *African images*, ed. D. F. McCall and E. G. Bay, pp. 104–32. New York: Africana Publishing Co.

———, ed. 1985. *I am not myself: The art of African masquerade.* Los Angeles: Museum of Cultural History, University of California.

Contenson, H. de. 1967. Troisième campagne à Tell Ramad, 1966: rapport préliminaire. *Annales archéologiques arabes syriennes* 17:17–24.

Coquet, Agnès. 1983. Une société de Papouasie et ses masques: les Orokolo. In *Oceanie, le masque au long cours*, ed. F. Lupu, pp. 143–55. Rennes: Ouest-France.

Cornevin, Robert. 1960. *Histoire des peuples de l'Afrique noire.* Paris: Editions Berger-Levrault.

Cranstone, B. A. L. 1961. *Melanesia: a short ethnography.* London: Trustees of the British Museum.

Crowley, Daniel J. 1972. Chokwe: Political art in a plebian society. In *African art and leadership*, ed. D. Fraser and H. M. Cole, pp. 21–39. Madison: University of Wisconsin Press.

Dall, William Healey. 1884. On masks, labrets, and certain aboriginal customs, with an inquiry into the bearing of their geographical distribution. In *Third Annual Report of the Bureau of Ethnology to the Secretary of the Smithsonian Institution, 1881–82.* Washington, D.C.

Damm, Hans. 1969. Bermerkungen zu den Schädelmasken aus Neubritannien (Südsee). *Jahrbuch des Museums für Völkerkunde zu Leipzig* 26:85–116.

Dark, Philip. 1973. Kilenge big man art. In *Primitive art and society*, ed. A. Forge, pp. 49–69. London: Oxford University Press.

Deacon, Arthur Bernard. 1934a. Geometrical drawings from Malekula and other islands of the New Hebrides. *Journal of the Royal Anthropological Institute of Great Britain and Ireland* 64:129–75.

———. 1934b. *Malekula: A vanishing people in the New Hebrides.* Edited by C. H. Wedgwood. London: George Routledge and Sons.

De Bilde, Marguerite. 1979. Masques d'Afrique et pouvoir mâle: essai de sémiotique esthétique. M.A. Thesis, Université Laval, Québec.

Delafosse, Maurice. 1922. *Les Noirs de l'Afrique.* Paris: Payot.

DeMott, Barbara. 1982. *Dogon Masks: A structural study of form and meaning.* Ann Arbor, Michigan: UMI Research Press.

Denich, Bette. 1976. Toward a feminist paradigm in anthropology. *Reviews in Anthropology* 3:443–52.

Deonna, Waldemar. 1914. Les masques quaternaires. *L'anthropologie*

25:107–113. Followed by a critical commentary by H. Breul, pp. 420–22, and a response by W. Deonna, pp. 597–98.

Dieterlen, Germaine. 1941. *Les âmes des Dogons*. Paris: Institut d'ethnologie.

———. 1956. Parenté et mariage chez les Dogon (Soudan français). *Africa* 26:107–48.

———. 1960. Symbolisme du masque en Afrique occidentale In *Le masque*. Catalogue de l'exposition tenue au Musée Guimet à Paris, pp. 49–55. Paris: Musées nationaux.

———. 1965. La réincarnation chez les Dogon. In *Réincarnation et vie mystique en Afrique noire*, ed. D. Zahan, pp. 53–68. Paris: Presses Universitaires de France.

———. 1971. Les cérémonies soixantenaires du Sigui chez les Dogon. *Africa* 41:1–11.

———. 1978. La cosmologie des Dogon et les cérémonies soixantenaires du Sigui (Mali). *Cahiers internationaux de symbolisme* 35–36:175–85.

Dieterlen, Germaine, and Youssouf Cissé. *Les fondements de la société d'initiation du Komo*. Cahiers de l'homme, n.s., 10. Paris: Mouton.

Dietschy, Hans. 1960. Note à propos des danses des Caraja: "pas de deux," amitié formelle et prohibition de l'inceste. *Bulletin de la Société suisse des américanistes*, 11, no. 19:1–5.

———. 1970–71. Die Tanzmasken der Karaja-Indianer Zentralbrasiliens und der Aruanï-Fisch. *Bulletin der Schweizerischen Gesellschaft für Anthropologie und Ethnologie* 47:48–53.

Disselhoff, H.-Dietrich. 1936. Bemerkungen zu Fingermasken der Beringmeer-Eskimo. *Baessler-Archiv* 19:181–87.

Dohrenwend, Doris J. 1975. Jade demonic images from Early China. *Ars Orientalis* 10:55–78.

Douglas, Mary. 1970. *Purity and danger: An analysis of concepts of pollution and taboo*. London: Routledge and Kegan Paul.

———. 1975. *Implicit meanings: Essays in anthropology*. London: Routledge and Kegan Paul.

Drewal, Henry John. 1974a. Efe: Voiced power and pageantry. *African Arts* 7, no. 2:26–29, 58–66, 82–83.

———. 1974b. Gelede masquerade: Imagery and motif. *African Arts* 7, no. 4:8–19, 62–63, 95–96.

Drewal, Henry John, and Margaret Thompson Drewal. 1983. *Gelede: Art and female power among the Yoruba*. Bloomington: Indiana University Press.

Drewal, Margaret Thompson, and Henry John Drewal. 1975. Gelede Dance of the Western Yoruba. *African Arts* 8, no. 2:36–45, 78–79.

———. 1978. More powerful than each other: An Egbado classification of Egugun. *African Arts* 11, no. 3:28–39, 98–99.

Dupré, Marie-Claude. 1968. A propos d'un masque des Téké de l'ouest (Congo-Brazzaville). *Objets et mondes* 8, no. 4:295–310.

Duvignaud, Jean. 1980. Préface. In *Les masques et leurs fonctions*, ed. Cherif Khaznadar, pp. 8–9. Rennes: Maison de la culture.

Ebeling, Ingelore. 1984. *Masken und Maskierung: Kult, Kunst und Kosmetik; von den Naturvölkern bis zur Gegenwart*. Cologne: DuMont.

Eliade, Mircea. 1949. *Le mythe de l'éternel retour: archétypes et répétition*. Paris: Gallimard.

———. 1957. *Mythes, rêves et mystères*. Paris: Gallimard

———. 1958–67. Le origini mitico-rituali. In *Enciclopedia universale dell'arte*, 15 vols. (s.v. Maschera), col. 877–82. Venice: Istituto per la collaborazione culturale, 1958–1967.

———. 1959a. *Naissances mystiques: essai sur quelques types d'initiation*. Paris: Gallimard.

———. 1959b. *Traité d'histoire des religions*. Paris: Payot.

———. 1963. The history of religions in retrospect: 1912–1962. *Journal of Bible and Religion* 31:98–109.

———. 1967. On understanding primitive religions. In *Glaube, Geist, Geschichte: Festschrift für Ernst Benz zum 60. Geburtstage am 17. November 1967*, ed. G. Müller and W. Zeller, pp. 498–505. Leiden: E. J. Brill.

———. 1968. *Le chamanisme et les techniques archaïques de l'extase*. Second ed. Paris: Payot.

———. 1971. *La nostalgie des origines: méthodologie et histoire des religions*. Paris: Gallimard.

———. 1976–83. *Histoire des croyances et des idées religieuses*. 4 vols. Paris: Payot. 1:1976; 2:1978; 3:1983; 4:forthcoming.

———. 1978. *Occultisme, sorcellerie et modes culturelles*. Trans. Jean Malaquais. Paris: Gallimard.

Elisofon, Eliot, and William Fagg. 1978. *The sculpture of Africa*. 1958. New York: Hacker Art Books.

Errington, Frederick Karl. 1974. *Karavar: Masks and power in a Melanesian ritual*. Ithaca: Cornell University Press.

Evans-Pritchard, Edward E. 1965. *Theories of primitive religion*. Oxford: Clarendon Press.

Eyo, Ikpo. 1974. Abua masquerades. *African Arts* 7, no. 2:52–55.

Fagg, William, and John Pemberton III. 1982. *Yoruba: Sculpture of West Africa*, ed. Bryce Holcombe. New York: Alfred A. Knopf.

Faure, Henri. 1965. *Les appartenances du délirant: les investissements d'objet dans le vécu psychotique*. Thesis, Université de Paris. Paris: R. Foulon & Cie.

Fenton, William N. 1937. The Seneca society of faces. *The Scientific Monthly* 44:215–38.

———. 1941. Masked medicine societies of the Iroquois. *Annual Report of the Board of Regents of the Smithsonian Institution* 1940, pp. 397–429. Washington, D.C.

Fischer, Eberhard. 1978. Dan forest spirits: Masks in Dan villages. *African Arts* 11, no. 2:16–23, 94.

———. 1980. Masks in a non-poro area: the Dan. *Ethnologische Zeitschrift Zürich* 1980, no. 1:81–88.

Fischer, Eberhard, and Hans Himmelheber. 1976. *Die Kunst der Dan.* Zurich: Museum Rietberg.

Fischer, Eberhard, and Lorenz Homberger. 1986. *Masks in Guro Culture, Ivory Coast.* Zürich: Museum Rietberg.

Fitzhugh, William W., and Susan A. Kaplan, eds. 1982. *Inua: Spirit world of the Bering Sea Eskimo.* Washington, D.C.: The Smithsonian Institution Press.

Forge, Anthony. 1966. Art and environment in the Sepik. In *Proceedings of the Royal Anthropological Institute of Great Britain and Ireland for 1965,* pp. 23–31. London.

Fortes, Meyer. 1965. Some reflections on ancestor worship in Africa. In *African systems of thought,* ed. M. Fortes and G. Dieterlen, pp. 122–44. London: Oxford University Press.

Fortes, Meyer, and Germaine Dieterlen, eds. 1965. *African Systems of Thought.* London: Oxford University Press.

Foss, Perkins. 1973. Festival of Ohworu at Evwreni. *African Arts* 6, no. 4:20–27, 94.

Fraser, Douglas. 1966. The heraldic woman: A study in diffusion. In *The many faces of primitive art,* ed. D. Fraser, pp. 36–99. Englewood Cliffs, N.J.: Prentice-Hall.

Frazer, Sir James George. 1933–36. *The fear of the dead in primitive religion.* 3 vols. London: Macmillan and Co.

Freud, Sigmund. 1950. *Totem and taboo: Some points of agreement between the mental lives of savages and neurotics.* Trans. James Strachey. New York: W. W. Norton & Co.

———. 1952. *Métapsychologie.* Trans. M. Bonaparte and A. Berman. Paris: Gallimard.

Frobenius, Leo. 1897–98. Über Oceanische Masken. (Six communications) *Internationales Archiv für Ethnographie* 10 (1897):69–70, 206–9; 11(1898):82–85, 130–32, 162–64.

———. 1898. Die Masken und Geheimbünde Afrikas. *Nova Acta: Abhandlungen der Kaiserlichen Leopoldinisch-Carolinischen Deutschen Akademie der Naturforscher* 74, no. 1:1–278.

———. 1932. Mensch und Maske. *Der Erdball* 6, no. 2:41–45.

Ganay, Solange de. 1937. Notes sur le culte du Lebe chez les Dogon du Soudan français. *Journale de la Société des américanistes* 7:203–11.

Gardi, René, and Alfred Bühler. 1958. *Sepik: Land der sterbenden Geister.* Zurich: Büchergilde Gutenberg.

Gilbert, S., D. Guillemaut, and A. Bourges. 1980. *Les masques.* Internal working document. Rennes: Maison de la culture. My pagination.

Gill, Sam D. 1982. *Native American religions: An introduction.* Belmont, CA: Wadsworth Publishing Co.
Gimbutas, Marija. 1982. *The goddesses and gods of Old Europe, 6500–3500 BC: Myths and cult images.* Revised ed. London: Thames and Hudson.
Girard, Jean. 1965. L'importance sociale et religieuse des cérémonies exécutés pour les malanggan sculptés de Nouvelle-Irlande. *L'anthropologie* 58:241–67.
Glotz, Samuël. 1975. Les origines de la tradition du masque en Europe. In *Le masque dans la tradition européenne,* ed. S. Glotz, pp. 1–43. Paris: La Roue à livres diffusion.
———. 1978. Le carnaval vu par un folkloriste. *Volkskunde* 79:30–43.
———. 1980. Le masque en Europe. In *Les masques et leurs fonctions,* ed. Cherif Khaznadar, pp. 87–90. Rennes: Maison de la culture.
Goldman, Irving. 1979. *The Cubeo: Indians of the Northwest Amazon.* Second ed. Urbana: University of Illinois Press.
Goonatilleka, M. H. 1976. *Masks of Sri Lanka.* Colombo: Department of Cultural Affairs.
Gow-Smith, Francis. 1925. The arawana, or fish dance, of the Caraja Indians of Matto Grosso, Brazil. *Indian Notes* 2, no. 2:96–99.
Graziosi, Paolo. 1970. Recenti missioni per lo studio dell'arte rupestre nel Fezzan. In *Valcamonica symposium,* ed. Emmanuel Anati, pp. 329–43. Capo di Ponte: Edizioni del Centro.
Green, Kathryn L. 1987. Shared masking traditions in Northeastern Ivory Coast. *African Arts* 20, no. 4:62–69, 92.
Gregor, Joseph. 1936. *Die Masken der Erde.* Munich: R. Piper & Co.
Gregory, C. A. 1980. Gifts to men and gifts to god: Gift exchange and capital accumulation in contemporary Paua. *Man* 15:626–52.
Griaule, Marcel. 1933. [Mission Dakar-Djibouti, 1931–33:] Introduction méthodologique. *Minotaure* 2:7–12.
———. 1952. Le savoir des Dogon. *Journal de la Société des africanistes* 22:27–42.
———. 1954. Remarques sur l'oncle utérin au Soudan. *Cahiers internationaux de sociologie,* n.s., 16:35–49.
———. 1963 [1938]. *Masques dogons.* Second ed. Paris: Institut d'ethnologie.
———. 1966. *Dieu d'eau: entretiens avec Ogotemmêli.* 1948. Paris: Librarie Arthème Fayard.
Griaule, Marcel, and Germaine Dieterlen. 1965. *Le renard pâle.* Vol. 1: *Le mythe cosmogonique.* Fasc. 1: *La création du monde.* Paris: Institut d'ethnologie.
Grimes, Ronald L. 1975. Masking: Toward a phenomenology of exteriorization. *Journal of the American Academy of Religion* 43:508–16.
Groves, William C. 1936. Secret beliefs and practices in New Ireland. *Oceania* 7:220–45.

Gründ, François, and Chérif Khaznadar, eds. 1982. *Le long voyage des masques: relations entre les masques d'Orient et d'Occident*. Rennes: Maison de la culture.

Gruyter, W. Jos. de. 1941. *Het masker: Ontstaan, beteekenis, schoonheid*. 's Graveland: De Driehoek.

Guiart, Jean. 1949. Les effigies religieuses des Nouvelles-Hébrides. *Journal de la Société des océanistes* 5, no. 5:51–86.

―――. 1960. Le dieu porteur de masque en Nouvelle-Calédonie (pp. 30–32); Sociologie du prestige aux Nouvelles-Hébrides (pp. 33–34); Mannequins funéraires et crânes surmoulés (pp. 35–37). In *Le masque*. Catalogue from the exposition held at the Musée Guimet in Paris. Paris: Musées nationaux.

―――. 1962. *Les religions de l'Océanie*. Paris: Presses Universitaires de France.

―――. 1963. *Océanie*. Paris: Gallimard.

―――. 1966. *Mythologie du masque en Nouvelle-Calédonie*. Publications de la Société des océanistes, 18. Paris: Musée de l'homme.

―――. 1983. Préface; Les masques en Mélanésie orientale. In *Océanie, le masque au long cours*, ed. F. Lupu, pp. 11–12, 55–65. Rennes: Ouest-France.

Guidieri, Remo. 1975. Note sur le rapport mâle/femelle en Mélanésie. *L'homme* 15, no. 2:103–19.

―――. 1981. Statue et masque: présence et représentation dans la croyance. Paper presented at Convegno Internazionale *Nel senso della maschera/Au sens du masque*. Montecatini Terme, 15–17 octobre 1981. Ronéotypée.

Guilaine, Jean. 1985. [L'Europe préhistorique, le néolithique:] Cultes et concepts religieux. In *Le grand atlas de l'archéologie*, ed. Christine Flon, pp. 48–49. Paris: Encyclopaedia Universalis.

Haddon, Alfred Cort. 1893. The secular and ceremonial dances of Torres Straits. *Internationales Archiv für Ethnographie* 6:131–62.

Halpin, Marjorie. 1979. Confronting looking-glass men: A preliminary examination of the mask. In *Ritual symbolism and ceremonialism in the Americas: Studies in symbolic anthropology*, ed. N. R. Crumrine, pp. 41–61. Greenley, CO: University of Northern Colorado, Museum of Anthropology.

―――. 1983. The mask of tradition. In *The power of symbols: Masks and masquerade in the Americas*, ed. N. Ross Crumrine and Marjorie Halpin, pp. 219–26. Vancouver: University of British Columbia Press.

Halverson, John. 1987. Art for art's sake in the Paleolithic. *Current Anthropology* 28:63–89.

Hampaté Ba, Amadou, and Germaine Dieterlen. 1966. Les fresques d'époque bovidienne du Tassili n'Ajjer et les traditions des Peul: hypothèses d'interprétation. *Journal de la Société des africanistes* 36:141–57.

Harley, George W. 1950. *Masks as agents of social control in Northwest Liberia*. Papers of the Peabody Museum of American archaeology and ethnology, Harvard University, vol. 32, no. 2. Cambridge, Mass.

Harper, Peggy. 1970. The role of dance in the Gèlèdé ceremonies of the village of Ijìó. *Odù*, n.s., 4:67-94.

Hart, Keith. 1985. The social anthropology of West Africa. *Annual Review of Anthropology* 14:243-72.

Hartmann, Günther. 1967. *Masken südamerikanischer Naturvölker*. Berlin: Museum für Völkerkunde (my pagination).

———. 1968. Mais- und Baum-Masken der Tukuna (Westbrasilien). *Tribus* 17:121-28.

———. 1973. *Litjoko: Puppen der Karaja (Brasilien)*. Berlin: Museum für Völkerkunde.

———. 1977. Masken der Pau d'Arco-Kayapo, Brasilien. *Tribus* 26:103-8.

Hauser-Schäublin, Brigitta. 1976-77. *mai*-Masken der Iatmul, Papua New Guinea: Stil, Schnitzvorgang, Auftritt und Funktion. *Verhandlungen der Naturforschenden Gesellschaft in Basel* 87-88:119-45.

Heine-Geldern, Robert. 1964. One hundred years of ethnological theory in the German-speaking countries: Some milestones. *Current Anthropology* 5:407-18.

Helfrich, Klaus. 1973. *Malanggan -1: Bildwerke von Neuirland*. Berlin: Museum für Völkerkunde.

———. 1985. Zeremonialschädel aus Mittel-Neuirland. *Baessler-Archiv*, n.f., 33:123-88.

Hendry, Jean. 1964. Iroquois masks and maskmaking at Onondaga. *Smithsonian Institution, Bureau of American Ethnology, Bulletin 191* (Anthropological Papers, no. 74):349-425.

Hertz, Robert. 1907. Contribution à une étude sur la représentation collective de la mort. *L'année sociologique* 10 (1905-1906, published in 1907):48-137.

Hesse, Karl, and Theo Aerts. 1979. *Baining Dances*. Institute of Papua New Guinea Studies.

Heyden, Marsha Vander. 1977. The Epa mask and ceremony. *African Arts* 10, no. 2:14-21, 91.

Himmelheber, Hans. 1938. Art et artistes Batshiok. *Brousse* (my pagination).

———. 1960. *Les masques africains*. Trans. S. Wallon. Paris: Presses Universitaires de France.

———. 1965. Le système de la religion des Dan. In *Les religions africaines traditionnelles*, edited by le Centre du monastère bénédictin de Bouaké, Côte d'Ivoire. Paris: Editions du Seuil.

———. 1966. Masken der Guéré II. *Zeitschrift für Ethnologie* 91:100-108.

Hinckley, Priscilla. 1980. *The Sowo mask: Symbol of sisterhood*. Boston: Boston University, African Studies Center (Working papers, 40).

Hipszer, Hermine. 1966. Masques à la recherche d'un danseur. *Bulletin annuel du Musée et Institut d'ethnographie de la Ville de Genève* 9:53–63.
———. 1967. Quelques masques de hiboux et de corbeaux. *Anthropos* 62:68–88.
Höfler, Otto. 1934. *Kultische Geheimbünde der Germanen*. 1. Frankfurt am Main: Verlag Moritz Diesterweg.
Holas, Bohumil. 1947. Danses masquées de la Basse-Côte. *Etudes guinéennes* 1:61–67.
———. 1952. *Les masques kono (Haute-Guinée française): leur rôle dans la vie religieuse et politique*. Paris: Librarie orientaliste Paul Geuthner.
———. 1962. *Les toura: esquisse d'une civilisation montagnarde de Côte d'Ivoire*. Paris: Presses Universitaires de France.
———. 1964. *Sculpture sénoufo*. Abidjan: Centre des sciences humaines.
———. 1965. Le bois, matière première des accessoires cérémoniels en Côte d'Ivoire. In *African systems of thought*, ed. M. Fortes and G. Dieterlen, pp. 351–65. London: Oxford University Press.
Hole, Frank. 1982. Symbols of religion and social organization at Susa. In *The hilly flanks and beyond: Essays on the prehistory of southwestern Asia*, ed. T. Cuyler Young, Jr., et al., pp. 315–31. Chicago: The Oriental Institute of the University of Chicago.
Holm, Bill. 1972. *Crooked beak of heaven: Masks and other ceremonial art of the Northwest Coast*. Seattle: University of Washington Press.
Honigmann, John H. 1977. The masked face. *Ethnos* 5:263–80.
Horton, Robin. 1965. *Kalabari sculpture*. Lagos: Department of Antiquities.
Hubert, Henri, and Marcel Mauss. 1904. Esquisse d'une théorie générale de la magie. *L'année sociologique* 1902–1903:1–146.
Hudson, A. B. 1966. Death ceremonies of the Padju Epat Ma'anyan Dayaks. *Sarawak Museum Journal* 13, no. 27:341–416.
Huizinga, Johan. 1955. *Homo ludens: A study of the play-element in culture*. Boston: Beacon Press.
———. 1968. New physical anthropological evidence bearing on the relationship between Dogon, Kurumba and the extinct West African Tellem populations. *Proceedings of the Koninklijke Nederlandse Akademie van Wetenshappen*, Series C, 71:16–30.
Hultkrantz, Åke. 1976. Les religions des Indiens d'Amérique. In *Histoire des religions*, 3 vols., ed. H.-C. Peuch, 3:711–802. Paris: Gallimard, Encyclopédie de la Pléiade, 1970–76.
Hummel, Siegbert. 1961. Boy dances at the New Year's festival in Lhasa. *East and West* 12:40–44.
Ingold, Tim. 1985. Khazanov on nomads. *Current Anthropology* 26: 384–87.
Jacobs, Sue-Ellen. 1977. Toward an anthropology of women's liberation. *Reviews in anthropology* 4:229–36.

Jeanmaire, Henri. 1951. *Dionysos: histoire du culte de Bacchus*. Paris: Payot.
Jedrej, M. C. 1980. A comparison of some masks from North America, Africa, and Melanesia. *Journal of Anthropological Research* 36:220–30.
———. C. 1986. Dan and Mende masks: A structural comparison. *Africa* 56:71–80.
Jensen, Adolf Ellegard. 1933. *Beschneidung und Reifezeremonien bei Naturvölkern*. Stuttgart: Strecker und Schröder/Verlag.
———. 1963. *Myth and cult among primitive peoples*. Trans. Marianna Tax Cholding and Wolfgang Weissleder. Chicago: University of Chicago Press.
Jeudy-Ballini, Monique. 1984. A propos d'une femme remarquable: le statut de la *kheng* chez les Sulka de Nouvelle-Bretagne (Papouasie-Nouvelle-Guinée). *Journal de la Société des océanistes* 78 (tome XL):17–34.
Joseph, Marietta B. 1974. Dance masks of the Tikar. *African Arts* 7, no. 3:46–52, 92.
Joshi, O. P. 1976. Tattooing and tattooers: A socio-cultural analysis. *Bulletin of the International Committee on Urgent Anthropological and Ethnological Research* 18:45–66.
Juàrez Frias, Fernando, and Bernardo Pérez Rodríguez. 1981. *Maschere del Messico*. Milan: Edizioni di Comunità.
Karutz, Richard. 1901. Zur westafrikanischen Maskenkunde. *Globus* 79:361–68.
Kaufmann, Christian. 1968. Über Kunst und Kult bei den Kwoma und Nukuma (Nord-Neuginea). *Verhandlungen der Naturforschenden Gesellschaft in Basel* 79:63–112.
———. 1979. Art and artists in the context of Kwoma society. In *Exploring the visual art of Oceania*, ed. S. M. Mead, pp. 310–34. Honolulu: The University Press of Hawaii.
Kenyon, Kathleen M. 1972 (1954). Ancient Jericho. In *Old World Archaeology: Foundations of Civilization*, ed. C. C. Lamberg-Karlovsky, pp. 89–94. San Francisco: W. H. Freeman and Co.
———. 1979. *Archaeology in the Holy Land*. Fourth ed. London: Ernest Benn Ltd.
———. 1981. *Excavations at Jericho*. Vol. 3: *The architecture and stratigraphy of the tell*. Ed. Thomas A. Holland. 2 vols. (text and plates). London: British School of Archaeology in Jerusalem.
Kenyon, W. A. 1961. Kwakiutl masks. *Le théâtre dans le monde/World Theatre* 10:41–45.
Keppler, Joseph. 1941. *Comments on certain Iroquois masks*. Contributions from the Museum of the American Indian, Heye Foundation, vol. 12, no. 4. New York.
Kiki, Albert Maori. 1968. *Kiki: Ten thousand years in a lifetime. A New Guinea autobiography*. Melbourne: F. W. Cheshire.

Kirby, Ernest-Théodore. 1985. Masques d'Amérique du Sud: la transformation homme/animal. In *Le masque du rite au théâtre*, ed. O. Aslan and D. Bablet, pp. 41–48. Paris: Editions du C.N.R.S.

Kleinschmidt, Peter. 1966. *Die Masken der Gigaku. Der ältesten Theaterform Japans*. Wiesbaden: Verlag Otto Harrassowitz.

Klingbeil, Waldemar. 1935. *Kopf-, Masken- und Maskierungszauber in den antiken Hochkulturen, insbesondere des Alten Orients*. Berlin: Verlag Arthur Collignon.

Koehler, H. K. L. 1833. *Masken: Ihr Ursprung und neue Auslegung einiger der merkwürdigsten auf alten Denkmälern die bis jetzt unerkannt und unerkläsrt geblieben waren*. St. Petersburg: Druckerei der Kaiserlichen academie der Wissenschaften.

Koppers, Wilhelm. 1930. Die Frage eventueller alter Kulturbeziehungen zwischen dem südlichsten Südamerika und Südostaustralien. In *Proceedings of the Twenty-Third International Congress of Americanists, 1928*, pp. 678–86. New York.

Krantz, Catherine. 1983. La Papouasie; Données sur les masques Baining. In *Océanie, le masque au long cours*, ed. F. Lupu, pp. 135–42, 207–11. Rennes: Ouest-France.

Krause, Fritz. 1910. Tanzmaskennachbildungen vom mittleren Araguaya (Zentralbrasilien). *Jahrbuch des städtischen Museums für Völkerkunde zu Leipzig* 3 (1908/9, published in 1910):97–122.

Krickeberg, Walter. 1932. Nordamerikanische Masken. *Der Erdball* 6: 56–59.

Krieger, Kurt, and Gerdt Kutscher. 1960. *Westafrikanische Masken*. Berlin: Museum für Völkerkunde.

Kroeber, Alfred L., and Catherine Holt. 1920. Masks and moieties as a culture complex. *Journal of the Royal Anthropological Institute of Great Britain and Ireland* 50:452–60.

Krusche, Rolf. 1975. Zur Genese des Maskenwesens im östlichen Waldland Nordamerikas. *Jahrbuch des Museums für Völkerkunde zu Leipzig* 30:137–90.

Kuhn, Roland. 1954. *Maskendeutungen im Rorschachschen Versuch*. Second ed. Basel: S. Karger.

———. 1957. *Phénoménologie du masque à travers le test de Rorschach*. Trans. J. Verdeaux. Preface by G. Bachelard. Paris: Desclée de Brouwer.

Lafargue, Fernand. 1971. L'Amwi Goli. *Cahiers des religions africaines* 9 (vol. 5, 1971): 113–42.

———. 1973. Le *goli*: contribution à l'étude des masques baoulé. *Annales de l'Université d'Abidjan, série F (Ethnosociologie)* 5:69–98.

La Fontaine, Jean. 1977. The power of rights. *Man*, n.s., 12:421–37.

Laguna, Frederica de. 1936. Indian masks from the Lower Yukon. *American Anthropologist*, n.s., 38:569–85.

Lajoux, Jean-Dominique. 1977. *Tassili n'Ajjer: art rupestre du Sahara préhistorique.* Second ed. Paris: Editions du Chêne.

Lalande, André, ed. 1960. *Vocabulaire technique et critique de la philosophie.* Eighth ed. Paris: Presses Universitaires de France.

Lamberg-Karlovsky, C. C., and Martha Lamberg-Karlovsky. 1972. An early city in Iran. In *Old World archaeology: Foundations of civilization,* ed. C. C. Lamberg-Karlovsky, pp. 174–83. San Francisco: W. H. Freeman and Co.

Laming-Emperaire, Annette. 1962. *La signification de l'art rupestre paléologique des techniques,* 2 vols., s.v. Masque, 2:590. Paris: Editions de l'Accueil.

Lamp, Frederick. 1985. Cosmos, cosmetics, and the spirit of Bondo. *African Arts* 18, 3:28–43, 98.

Landman, Gunnar. 1927. *The Kiwai Papuans of British New Guinea: A nature-born instance of Rousseau's ideal community.* London: Macmillan & Co., 1927; reprinted, New York: Johnson Reprint Corp., 1970.

Lantier, Raymond. 1961. *L'Art préhistorique.* Paris: Editions Charles Massin.

Laplanche, Jean and J.-B.Pontalis. 1971 *Vocabulaire de la psychanalyse.* Paris: Presses Universitaires de France.

Laufer, Carl. 1959. Jugendinitiation und Sakraltänze der Baining. *Anthropos* 54:905–38.

———. 1970. Die Mandas-Maskenfeier der Mali-Baining (Neubritannien, Melanesien). *Jahrbuch des Museums für Völkerkunde zu Leipzig* 27:160–84.

Lawal, Babatunde. 1975. Yoruba-Sango ram symbolism: From Ancient Sahara or Dynastic Egypt? In *African images,* ed. D. F. McCall and E. G. Bay, pp. 225–51. New York: Africana Publishing Co.

Layard, John. 1934. The journey of the dead from the small islands of North-Eastern Malekula. In *Essays presented to C. G. Seligman,* ed. E. E. Evans Pritchard, R. Firth, B. Malinowski, and I. Schapera, pp. 113–42. London: Kegan Paul, Trench, Trubner and Co.

———. 1936. Maze-dances and the ritual of the labyrinth in Malekula. *Folklore* 47:123–70.

———. 1942. *Stone men of Malekula: Vao.* London: Chatto & Windus.

Leach, Edmund Ronald. 1954. A Trobriand Medusa? *Man* 54:103–5.

———. 1967. Virgin Birth. In *Proceedings of the Royal Anthropological Institute of Great Britain and Ireland for 1966,* pp. 39–49. London.

Lechevallier, Monique, and J. Perot. 1973. Eynan and Beisamoun. *Israel Exploration Journal* 23, no. 2:107–8.

Leenhardt, Maurice. 1933. Le masque calédonien. *Bulletin du Musée d'ethnographie du Trocadéro* 6:3–21.

———. 1947. *Arts de l'Océanie.* Paris Editions du Chêne.

———. 1954. Le masque et le mythe en Nouvelle-Calédonie. *Etudes mélanésiennes,* n.s., 8:9–20.

———. 1971a. *Do Kamo: la personne et le mythe dans le monde mélanésien.* New edition. Paris: Gallimard.

———. 1971b. *La structure de la personne en Mélanésie.* Milan: S.T.O.A. Edizionei.

Lehuard, Raoul. 1972. De l'origine du masque "tsaye". *Arts d'Afrique noire* 4:12–37.

Leiris, Michel. 1933. Masques dogon. *Minotaure* 2:45–51.

———. 1941. La notion d'awa chez les Dogon. *Journal de la Société des africanistes* 11:229–30.

Leiris, Michel, and Jacqueline Delange. 1967. *Afrique noire: la création plastique.* Paris: Gallimard.

Leleur, Annette. 1979–80. Sexes or chaos? *Folk* 21–22:161–94.

Le Moal, Guy. 1980. *Les Bobo: nature et fonction des masques.* Paris: Office de la recherche scientifique et technique outre-mer ORSTOM.

Le Quellec, Jean-Loïc. 1985. Les gravures rupestres du Fezzan (Libye). *L'anthropologie* 89, no. 3:365–83.

Leroi-Gourhan, André. 1964. *Les religions de la préhistoire (paléolithique).* Paris: Presses Universitaires de France.

———. 1975a. Iconographie et interprétation. In *Les Religions de la préhistoire.* Actes du Valcomonica Symposium '72, ed. Emmanuel Anati, pp. 49–55. Capo di Ponte: Edizioni del Centro Camuno di Studi Preistorici.

———. 1975b. *Préhistoire de l'art occidental.* Fourth ed. Paris: Editions d'Art Lucien Mazenod.

———. 1977. Le préhistorien et le chamane. *L'ethnographie* nos. 74–75 (118th year, volume 73):19–25.

———. 1982. *The dawn of European art: An introduction to palaeolithic cave painting.* Trans. S. Champion. Cambridge: Cambridge University Press.

Lévi-Strauss, Claude. 1960a. Amérique du Nord et Amérique du Sud. In *Le masque.* Catalogue de l'exposition tenue au Musée Guimet à Paris, pp. 21–27. Paris: Musées nationaux.

———. 1960b. Introduction à l'œuvre de Marcel Mauss. In *Sociologie et anthropologie.* By M. Mauss, pp. IX-LII. 1950. Paris: Presses Universitaires de France.

———. 1961. Les nombreux visages de l'homme. *Le théâtre dans le monde/World Theatre* 10:11–20.

———. 1962. *Tristes tropiques.* Paris: Union générale d'éditions, "Le monde en 10/18."

———. 1973–74. *Anthropologie structurale.* 2 vols. Second ed. Paris: Librairie Plon. 1974 (1958) and 1973.

———. 1979 [1975]. *La voie des masques.* Revised and expanded by "Trois excursions." Paris: Plon.

Lévy-Bruhl, Lucien. 1949. *Les carnets de Lucien Lévy-Bruhl.* Paris: Presses Universitaires de France.

———. 1963a. *Le surnaturel et la nature dans la mentalité primitive*. 1931. New edition. Paris: Presses Universitaires de France.
———. 1963b. *La mythologie primitive: le monde mythique des Australiens et des Papous*. 1935. New edition. Paris: Presses Universitaires de France.
Lewis, Albert B. 1922. *New Guinea masks*. Chicago: Field Museum of Natural History, Department of Anthropology (Leaflet no. 4).
Lewis, Gilbert. 1980. *Day of shining red: An essay on understanding ritual*. Cambridge: Cambridge University Press.
———. 1983. *The rock art of southern Africa*. Cambridge: Cambridge University Press.
———. 1985. Testing the trance explanation of southern African rock art: Depictions of felines. *Bollettino del Centro Camuno di Studi Preistorici* 22:47–62.
———. 1986. Cognitive and optical illusions in San rock art research. *Current anthropology* 27:171–78.
Lhote, Henri. 1958. *A la découverte des fresques du Tassili*. Paris: Arthaud.
———. 1976. *Vers d'autres Tassilis: nouvelles découvertes au Sahara*. Paris: Arthaud.
Lips, Eva. 1959. Zum geistigen Gehalt einiger Masken aus Melanesien und Westafrika. In *Opuscula ethnogica memoriae Ludovici Biro sacra*, pp. 225–63. Budapest: Ungarische Akademie der Wissenschaften.
Little, Kenneth L. 1960. The role of the secret society in cultural specialization. In *Cultures and societies of Africa*, ed. S. and Ph. Ottenberg, pp. 199–213. New York: Random House.
———. 1967. *The Mende of Sierra Leone: A West African people in transition*. 1951. Revised edition. London: Routledge and Kegan Paul.
Lomas, Peter W. 1979. Malanggans and manipulators: Land and politics in Northern New Ireland. *Oceania* 50:53–66.
Lommel, Andreas. 1970. *Masken: Gesichter der Menschheit*. Zürich: Atlantis Verlag.
Long, Charles H. 1980. Primitive/civilized. The locus of a problem. *History of religions* 20:43–61.
Lot-Falck, Eveline. 1957. Les masques eskimo et aléoutes de la collection Pinart. *Journal de la Société des américanistes* 46:5–43.
———. 1960. Les masques eskimo (pp. 9–11); Les masques d'Angmassalik (p.12); Les masques sibériens (pp. 13–14); Les masques de chamans sibériens (pp. 15–16); Les masques funéraires du Tachtyk (Kyrgyz du Ienisseï) (pp. 17–18); Les masques funéraires aléoutes et eskimo (pp. 19–20). In *Le masque*. Catalog of the exposition held at Musée Guimet à Paris. Paris: Musées nationaux.
Lowie, Robert H. 1966 [1937]. *The history of ethnological theory*. Reprint, New York: Holt, Rinehart and Winston.
Lucas, Heinz. 1962. *Lamaistische Masken: Der Tanz der Schreckensgötter*. Kassel: Erich Röth-Verlag.

Lumley, Henry de. 1985. Le masque chez l'homme préhistorique In *Le carnaval, la fête et la communication*. Actes des premières recontres internationales, pp. 175–80. Nice: Editions Serre.

Lupu, François, ed. 1983. *Océanie: le masque au long cours*. Rennes: Ouest-France.

MacGowan, Kenneth, and Herman Rosse. 1924. *Masks and demons*. London: Martin Hopkinson and Co.

McIntosh, Susan Keech, and Roderick James McIntosh. 1983. Current directions in West African prehistory. *Annual Review of Anthropology* 12:215–58.

———. 1985. [L'Afrique:]Archéologie et histoire de l'art. In *Le grand atlas de l'archéologie*, ed. Christine Flon, pp. 312–13. Paris: Encyclopaedia Universalis.

McNaughton, Patrick R. 1979. *Secret sculptures of Komo: Art and power in Bamana (Bambara) initiation associations*. Philadelphia: Institute for the Study of Human Issues.

———. 1987. African borderland sculpture. *African Arts* 20, no. 4:76–77, 91–92.

Maertens, Jean-Thierry. 1978. *Le dessein sure la peau: essai d'anthropologie des inscriptions tégumentaires*. Paris: Aubier Montaigne.

Maesen, Albert. 1961. Masques d'Afrique. *Le théâtre dans le monde/World Theatre* 10:31–40.

Mamiya, Christin J., and Eugenia C. Sumnik. 1982. *Hevehe: Art, economics and status in the Papuan Gulf*. Los Angeles: University of California, Museum of Cultural History.

Maquet, Jacques. 1968. Masques. In *Dictionnaire des civilizations africaines*, ed. G. Balandier and J. Maquet, pp. 265–69. Paris: Fernand Hazan.

Maringer, Johannes. 1960. *The gods of prehistoric man*. Ed. and trans. Mary Ilford. New York: Alfred A. Knopf.

———. 1982. Der menchlich Kopf/Schädel in Riten und Kult der vorgeschichtlichen Zeit. *Anthropos* 77:703–40.

Mark, Petre. 1983. Diola masking traditions and the history of the Casamance (Senegal). *Paideuma* 29:3–22.

Marschack, Alexander. 1972. *The roots of civilization: The cognitive beginnings of man's first art, symbol and notation*. London: Weidenfeld and Nicholson.

Mauss, Marcel. 1938. Une catégorie de l'esprit humain: la notion de personne, celle de "moi." *Journal of the Royal Anthropological Institute of Great Britain and Ireland* 68:263–81.

———. 1967. *Manuel d'ethnographie*. 1947. Paris: Payot.

———. 1971 [1921]. L'expression obligatoire des sentiments (rituels oraux funéraires australiens). Reproduced in *Essais de sociologie*, pp. 81–88. Paris: Editions de Minuit.

Mead, Margaret. 1946. Masks and men. *Natural History*, June: 280–85.
Meigs, Anna S. 1984. *Food, sex, and pollution: A New Guinea religion*. New Brunswick, NJ: Rutgers University Press.
Mellaart, James. 1971. *Çatal Hüyük: une des premières cités du monde*. s.1: Librairie Jules Tallandier, Jardin des Arts.
Merriam, Alan P. 1978. Kifwebe and other masked and unmasked societies among the Basongye. *Africa-Tervuren* 24:57–73, 89–101.
Métraux, Alfred. 1964. A myth of the Chamacoco Indians and its social significance. *Journal of American Folklore* 56:113–19.
Meuli, Karl. 1932–33. Maske, Maskereien. In *Handwürterbuch des Deutschen Aberglaubens*, vol. 5, ed. E. Hoffmann-Krayer and Hanns Bächtold-Stäubli. Berlin: Walter de Gruyter & Co.
———. 1943. *Schweizer Masken*. Zurich: Atlantis-Verlag.
———. 1946. Vom Ursprung der Maskenfeste [1939]. In *D'Basler Fasnacht*, edited by the Basler Fasnachts-Comité, pp. 9–18. Basel: Editions-Comité.
———. 1967. Les origines du carnaval. In *Annuaire XV: 1961–62*, edited by La Commission royale belge de folklore, pp. 63–85. Brussels: Ministère de l'éducation nationale et de la culture.
———. 1975. *Gesammelte Schriften*. Ed. Th. Gelzer. 2 vols. Basel/Stuttgart: Schwabe & Co.
Meyer, Adolf Bernard, and Richard Parkinson. 1895. *Schnitzereien und Masken vom Bismarck-Archipel und Neu-Guinea*. Dresden: Abhandlungen aus dem Königlichen ethnographischen Museum zu Dresden, 10.
Michel-Jones, Françoise. 1978. *Retour aux Dogon: figure du double et ambivalence*. Paris: Le Sycomore.
Millot, Jacques 1963. Masques peints du théâtre chinois. *Objets et mondes* 3, no. 3:233–36.
Montandon, George. 1934. *L'ologénèse culturelle: traité d'ethnologie cycloculturelle et d'ergologie systématique*. Paris: Payot.
Monts, Lester P. 1984. Conflict, accommodation, and transformation: The effect of Islam on music of the Vai secret societies. *Cahiers d'études africaines* 95 (vol. 24), no. 3:321–42.
Mori, Fabrizio. 1965. *Tadrart Acacus: Arte rupestre e culture del Sahara preistorico*. Turin: Giulio Einaudi.
———. 1974. The earliest Saharan rock-engravings. *Antiquity* 48:87–92.
Mulamba, Mutatayi. 1982. Regard sur la statuaire kuba. *Cahiers des religions africaines* 16, nos. 31–32:113–33.
Müller, Werner. 1962. Les religions des Indiens d'Amérique du Nord. In *Les religions amérindiennes*, ed. W. Krickeberg, H. Trimborn, W. Müller and O. Zerries, pp. 213–326. Trans. L. Jospin. Paris: Payot.
Museum für Völkerkunde Basel, ed. 1970. *Ethnographische Kostbarkeiten aus den Sammlungen von Alfred Bühler im Basler Museum für Völkerkunde*. Basel.

Muzzolini, Alfred. 1984. *L'art rupestre du Sahara central: Classification et chronologie. Le boeuf dans la préhistoire africaine*. Thèse de 3e cycle, Université de Provence, Aix et Marseille 1983. 2 vols., third edition.

Mylonas, George E. 1966. *Mycenae and the Mycenaean Age*. Princeton: Princeton University Press.

Narr, Karl J. 1961. *Urgeschichte der Kultur*. Stuttgart: Alfred Kröner Verlag.

Nebesky-Wojkowitz, René de. 1976. *Tibetan religious dances: Tibetan text and annotated translation of the 'chams yig*. La Haye: Mouton.

Nelson, Edward William. 1899. The Eskimo about Bering Strait. In *Eighteenth Annual report of the Bureau of American Ethnology, 1896–97*. Washington, D.C.

Nevermann, Hans. 1933. *Masken und Geheimbünde in Melanesien*. Berlin: Verlag von Reimar Hobbing.

———. 1972. Les religions du Pacifique. In *Les religions du Pacifique et d'Australie*, by H. Nevermann, E. A. Worms, and H. Petri, pp. 7–151. Trans. L. Jospin. Paris: Payot.

Newcomb, Franc Johnson. 1956. Navajo symbols in sand paintings and ritual objects. In *A study of Navajo symbolism*, by F. J. Newcomb, S. Fishler, and M. C. Wheelwright. Papers of the Peabody Museum of Archaeology and Ethnology, Harvard University, vol. 32, no. 3. Cambridge, Massachusetts.

Nicklin, Keith. 1974. Nigerian skin-covered masks. *African Arts* 7, no. 3:8–15, 67–68, 92.

Niessen, Carl. 1960. Vorformen der Maske: Daunen und kleine Federn als Maskierungszutat. *Ethnologica* 2:274–84.

Noma, Seiroku. 1957. *Masks*. Trans. M. Weatherby. Rutland, Vt.: Charles E. Tuttle Co.

Offiong, Daniel A. 1982. The process of making and the importance of the Ekpo mask. *Anthropologica* 24:193–206.

Ogibenin, Boris L. 1975. Masks in the light of semiotics: A functional approach. *Semiotica* 13:1–9.

Opler, Morris E. 1936. An interpretation of ambivalence of two American Indian tribes. *Journal of Social Psychology* 7:82–116.

Ortoli, Henri. 1941. Le décès d'une femme enceinte chez les Dogon de Bandiagara. *Bulletin de l'Institut français d'Afrique noire* 3:64–73.

Ottenberg, Simon. 1973. Afikpo masquerades: Audience and performers. *African Arts* 6, no. 4:32–35, 94–95, 97.

———. 1975. *Masked rituals of Afikpo: The context of an African art*. Seattle: The University of Washington Press.

Ottenberg, Simon, and Linda Knudsen. 1985. Leopard society masquerades: Symbolism and diffusion. *African Arts* 18, no. 2:37–44, 93–95, 103–4.

Palavecino, Enrique. 1954. *La màscara y la cultura*. Buenos Aires: Ediciones de la Municipalidad.

Panoff, Michel, and Michel Perrin. 1973. *Dictionnaire de l'ethnologie*. Paris: Payot (Petite bibliothèque Payot, 224).
Pâques, Viviana. 1964. *L'arbre cosmique dans la pensée populaire et dans la vie quotidienne du Nord-Ouest africaine*. Paris: Institut d'ethnologie.
Parker, Arthur C. 1909. Secret medicine societies of the Seneca. *American anthropologist*, n.s., 11:161–85.
Parsons, Elsie Clews. 1929. Masks in the Southwest of the United States. *Mexican Folkways* 5, no. 3: 152–56.
Paulme, Denise. 1940. *Organisation sociale des Dogon (Soudan français)*. Paris: Editions Domat-Montcrestien.
———. 1956. *Les sculptures de l'Afrique noire*. Paris: Presses Universitaires de France (L'oeil du connaisseur).
Peek, Philip M. 1983. The celebration of Oworu among the Isoko. *African Arts* 16, no. 2:34–41, 98.
Peekel, Gerhard. 1937–38. Über das Wesen der Tubuanmaske von Neupommern. *Archiv für Anthropologie und Völkerforschung*, n.s., 24:64–76, 103–39, 247–74.
Penner, Hans H. 1986. Rationality and Religion: Problems in the comparison of modes of thought. *Journal of the American Academy of Religion* 54:645–71.
Pernet, Henry. 1969. Mascarade et cosmologie: essai sur l'interprétation des masques rituels primitifs. *Revue de théologie et de philosophie*, pp. 145–63.
———. 1979. "Primitive" ritual masks in the history of religions: A methodological assessment. Ph.D. diss., University of Chicago.
———. 1981. La diffusion du masque rituel: notes sur un problème négligé. *Bulletin de la Société suisse pour la science des religions* 3:18–26.
———. 1982a. Masks and women: Toward a reappraisal. *History of Religions* 22:45–59.
———. 1982b. Le mort et son modèle: note sur quelques rituels mélanésien. *Numen* 29:161–83.
———. 1985. Masque, psychanalyse et ambivalence à l'égard des morts. In *Le carnaval, la fête et la communication*. Actes des premières rencontres internationales, pp. 475–85. Nice: Editions Serre.
———. 1987. Masks: Theoretical perspectives; Ritual masks in nonliterate cultures. In *The Encyclopedia of Religion*, 16 vols., ed. Mircea Eliade, vol. 9:259–69. New York: Macmillan.
Perret, Robert. 1936. Recherches archéologiques et ethnographiques au Tassili des Ajjers (Sahara central): les gravures rupestres de l'Oued Djaret, la population et les ruines d'Iherir. *Journal de la Société des africanistes* 6:41–64.
Phillips, Ruth B. 1978. Masking in Mende Sande society initiation rituals. *Africa* 48:265–77.

———. 1980. The iconography of the Mende Sowei mask. *Ethnologische Zeitschrift Zürich* 1980, no. 1:113–32.
Picard, Charles. 1948. *Les religions préhelléniques (Crète et Mycènes)*. Paris: Presses Universitaires de France.
Pollaczek, Penelope Pearl, and Harold D. Homefield. 1954. The use of masks as an adjunct to rôle-playing. *Mental Hygiene* 38:299–304.
Poole, Fitz John Porter. 1986. Metaphors and maps: Towards comparison in the anthropology of religion. *Journal of the American Academy of Religion* 54:411–57.
Poole, Jean. 1943. Still further notes on a snake dance of the Baining. *Oceania* 13:224–27. See also Read, W. J., and Bateson, G.
Pouwer, J. 1956. A masquerade in Mimika. Antiquity and Survival 5: 373–86.
Poynor, Robin. 1978. The Egungun of Owo. *African Arts* 11, no. 3:65–76, 100.
———. 1987. Naturalism and abstraction in Owo masks. *African Arts* 20, no. 4:56–61, 91.
Ptak, Wolfgang. 1977. Die Tanzfeste der Macuna-Indianer (Süd-Kolumbien). *Jahrbuch des Museums für Völkerkunde zu Leipzig* 31:185–99.
Rabaté, Marie-Rose. 1967. La mascarade de l'Aïd el Débir à Ouirgane (Haut Atlas). *Objets et mondes* 7, no. 3:165–84.
Ray, Dorothy Jean. 1975. *Eskimo masks: Art and ceremony*. 1967. Vancouver: J.J. Douglas Ltd.
Read, W. J. 1931–32. A snake dance of the Baining. *Oceania* 2:232–36. *See also* Bateson, G. and Poole, J.
Redinha, José. 1956. *Màscaras de madeira da Lunda e Alto Zambeze*. Lisbonne: Companhia de diamantes de Angola (Diamang), Serviços culturais, Dundo, Lunda, Angola. Museu do Dundo: Subsídios para a história, arqueologia e etnografia dos povos da Lunda.
Reed, Robert C. 1976. An interpretation of some "anthropomorphic" representations from the Upper Palaeolithic. *Current Anthropology* 17: 136–38.
Reinbacher, Erwin. 1956. Eine vorgeschichtliche Hirschmaske aus Berlin-Biesdorf. *Ausgrabungen und Funde. Nachrichtenblatt für Vor-und Frühgeschichte* 1:147–51.
Reinhardt, Loretta R. 1979. Mende secret societies and their costumed spirits. In *The fabrics of culture*, ed. J. M. Cordwell and R. A. Schwarz, pp. 231–66. La Haye: Mouton.
Richards, J. V. Olufemi. 1973. The *Sande* and some of the forces that inspired its creation or adoption with some references to the Poro. *Journal of Asian and African Studies* 8:69–77.
———. 1974. The Sande mask. *African Arts* 7, no. 2:48–51.
Riesenfeld, Alfons. 1950. *The megalithic culture of Melanesia*. Leiden: E.J. Brill

Riley, Olive L. 1955. *Masks and Magic*. London: Thames & Hudson.
Ritzenthaler, Robert E., ed. 1953. *Handbook of West African art*. Milwaukee: Milwaukee Public Museum.
Rivers, William Halse R. 1914. *The history of Melanesian society*. 2 vols. Cambridge: University Press
Rohrlich-Leavitt, Ruby, ed. 1975. *Women cross-culturally: Change and challenge*. La Haye: Mouton.
Röllin, Werner. 1987. Le carnaval et les mascarades en Suisse. *Schweizerisches Archiv für Volkskunde* 83:60–74.
Rønneseth, Ottar. 1986. Felszeichnungen in Tibesti (Tschad) und Klimaänderungen in der Ost-Sahara. *Praehistorische Zeitschrift* 61:64–83.
Roy, Christopher D. 1987. The spread of mask styles in the Black Volta Basin. *African Arts* 20, no. 4:40–47, 89–90.
Rütimeyer, Ludwig. 1917. Über Fell- und Kindermasken aus Ceylon. *Verhandlungen der Naturforschenden Gesellschaft in Basel* 28, no. 2:354–62.
———. 1924. *Ur-Ethnographie der Schweiz*. Basel: Helbing und Lichtenhahn.
Sainte-Fare Garnot, Jean. 1960. Egype antique. In *Le masque*. Catalogue of the exposition held at the Musée Guimet à Paris, pp. 61–63. Paris: Musées nationaux.
Sanday, Peggy Reeves. 1981. *Female power and male dominance: On the origins of sexual inequality*. Cambridge: Cambridge University Press.
Schaeffer, Claude F. A. 1939. *The cuneiform texts of Ras Shamra-Ugarit*. London: Oxford University Press.
Schieffelin, Edward L. 1976. *The sorrow of the lonely and the burning of the dancers*. New York: St. Martin's Press.
Schmidt, Wilhelm. 1919–20. Die kulturhistorische Methode und die nordamerikanische Ethnologie. *Anthropos* 14–15:546–63.
Schneider-Lengyel, Ilse. 1934. *Die Welt der Maske*. Munich: R. Piper & Co. Verlag
Schultz, H. 1963–65. Umutina - Brasilien (Oberer Paraguay): Totenkulttänze. Publikationen zu wissenschaftlichen Filmen (Göttingen) 1, B:113–24.
Schweeger-Hefel, Annemarie. 1970. Erdherrin und Masken in Sarma. *Paideuma* 16:96–130.
———. 1976. Mythe und historisches Geschehen? *Paideuma* 22:169–77.
Schwimmer, Erik. 1981. Power and secrecy: The semiotics of manipulation and detection. *Recherches sémiotiques/Semiotic Inquiry* I:214–43.
Segy, Ladislas. 1953. The mask in African dance. *The Negro History Bulletin* 14, no. 5:99–101, 116.
Serpenti, Laurent M. 1976. Ndambu, the feast of competitive giving (Frederik-Hendrik island, Irian-Barat). *Tropical Man* 5 (1972–73, published in 1976):162–87.
Shalleck, Jamie. 1973. *Masks*. New York: Viking Press.

Sieber, Roy. 1962. Masks as agents of social control. *African Studies Bulletin* 5, no. 11:8–13.
Siegmann, William C. 1980. Spirit manifestation and the Poro society. *Ethnologische Zeitschrift Zürich* 1980, no. 1:89–95.
Simmons, A. H., and G. O. Rollefson. 1985. Fouilles de site néolithique ancien de 'Ain Ghazal (Jordanie). *L'Anthropologie (Paris) 89*, no. 2:255–56.
Speck, Frank G. 1949. *Midwinter rites of the Cayuga long house*. Philadelphia: University of Pennsylvania Press.
———. 1950. Concerning iconology and the masking complex in Eastern North America. *University Museum Bulletin* (University of Pennsylvania, Philadelphia) 15, no. 1.
———. 1955. *The Iroquois: A study in cultural evolution*. 1945. Second edition. Bloomfield Hills, MI: Cranbrook Institute of Science.
Speiser, Felix. 1923. *Ethnographische Materialien aus den Neuen Hebriden und den Banks-Inseln*. Berlin: C. W. Kreidel's Verlag.
———. 1934. Versuch einer Kulturanalyse der zentralen Neuen Hebriden. *Zeitschrift für Ethnologie* 66:128–86.
———. 1937. Über Kunststile in Melanesien. *Zeitschrift für Ethnologie* 68 (1936, published in 1937):304–69.
———. 1941. *Kunststile in der Südsee*. Basel: Museum für Völkerkunde.
———. 1944. Die Frau als Erfinderin von Kultgeräten in Melanesien. *Schweizerische Zeitschrift für Psychologie und ihre Anwendungen* 3:46–54.
———. 1945. *Neu-Britannien*. Basel: Museum für Völkerkunde.
———. 1946. Versuch einer Siedlungsgeschichte der Südsee. *Denkschriften der Schweizerischen Naturforschenden Gesellschaft* 77:1–82.
Spiro, Melford E. 1952. Ghosts, Ifaluk, and teleological functionalism. *American Anthropologist* 54:497–503.
———. 1966. Religion: problems of definition and explanation. In *Anthropological approaches to the study of religion*, ed. Michael Banton, pp. 85–126. London: Tavistock Publications.
Stanek, Milan. 1983. Les Iatmul; Les travestis rituels des Iatmul. In *Océanie, le masque au long cours*, ed. F. Lupu, pp. 157–62, 163–86. Rennes: Ouest-France.
Stevens, Phillips, Jr. 1973. The Nupe Elo masquerade. *African Arts* 6, no. 4:40–43, 94.
Stöhr, Waldemar. 1968. Les religions archaïques d'Indonésie et des Philippines. In *Les religions d'Indonésie*. By W. Stöhr and P. Zoetmulder, pp. 7–225. Trans. L. Jospin. Paris: Payot.
Striedter, Karl Heinz. 1983. *Felsbilder Nordafrikas und der Sahara: Ein Verfahren zu ihrer systematischen Erfassung und Auswertung*. Wiesbaden: Franz Steiner Verlag.
Sturtevant, William C. 1983. Seneca masks. In *The power of symbols: Masks and Masquerade in the Americas*, ed. N. Ross Crumrine and Marjorie Halpin, pp. 39–47. Vancouver: University of British Columbia Press.

Tait, D. 1950. An analytical commentary on the social structure of the Dogon. *Africa* 20:175-99.
Tedlock, Dennis. 1979. Zuni religion and world view. In *Handbook of North American Indians*. Vol. 9: *Southwest*, ed. Alfonso Ortiz, pp. 499-513. Washington, D.C.: Smithsonian Institution.
Teilhet, Jehanne H. 1979. The equivocal nature of a masking tradition in Polynesia. In *Exploring the visual art of Oceania*, ed. S. M. Mead, pp. 192-201. Honolulu: The University Press of Hawaii.
Thiam, Bodiel. 1966. "Kouroubla," masque des cérémonies du Poro sénoufo. *Notes africaines* 109:25-27.
Thiele, Peter. 1985. Koreanische Tanzmasken in der Abteilung Ostasien des Berliner Museums für Völkerkunde. *Baessler-Archiv*, n.f., 33:453-95.
Thomas, Louis-Vincent, and René Luneau. 1969. *Les religions d'Afrique noire: Textes et traditions sacrés*. Paris: Fayard/Denoël.
Thompson, Robert Farris. 1974. *African art in motion: Icon and art*. Berkeley: University of California Press.
Tischner, Herbert and Friedrich Hewicker. 1954. *L'art de l'Océanie*. Paris: Editions Braun et Cie.
Tonkin, Elizabeth. 1979. Masks and powers. *Man*, n.s., 14:237-48.
Tooker, Elisabeth. 1970. *The Iroquois ceremonial of Midwinter*. Syracuse, N.Y.: Syracuse University Press.
Turner, Lucy W. 1983. Naskapi trance: Counterbalance to the mask, In *The power of symbols: Masks and masquerade in the Americas*, ed. N. Ross Crumrine and Marjorie Halpin, pp. 30-38. Vancouver: University of British Columbia Press.
Turner, Victor w. 1967. *The Forest of Symbols: Aspects of Ndembu ritual*. Ithaca, N.Y.: Cornell University Press.
Tuzin, Donald. 1975. The breath of a ghost: Dreams and the fear of the dead. *Ethos* 3:555-78.
Tylor, Edward Burnett. 1958. *Religion in primitive culture*. 1903. New York: Harper and Row.
Ucko, Peter J. and Andrée Rosenfeld. 1967. *Felsbildkunst im Paläolithikum*. Trans. W. Wagmuth. Munich: Kindler Verlag GmbH.
Underwood, Leon. 1948. *Masks of West Africa*. London: Alec Tiranti.
Unrug, K. 1983. Eku masks of the Igbirra. *African Arts* 16, no. 4:54-59, 87-88.
Valentine, C.A. 1961. *Masks and men in a Melanesian society: The* Valuku or Tubuan *of the Lakalai of New Britain*. Lawrence, Kansas: University of Kansas Publications.
Vallois, H. V. 1971. Le crâne-trophée capsien de Faïd Souar II, Algérie (fouilles Laplace, 1954). *L'Anthropologie* 75:191-220, 397-414.
Van Baal, J. 1966. *Dema: Description and analysis of Marind-Anim Culture (South New Guinea)*. La Haye: Martinus Nijhoff.

Van Baaren, Theodorus Petrus. 1968. *Korwars and korwar style: Art and ancestor worship in North-West New Guinea*. Paris: Mouton.
Vandenhoute, P. J. L. 1948. *Classification stylistique du masque dan et guéré de la Côte d'Ivoire occidentale (A.O.F.)*. Mededelingen van het Rijkmuseum voor volkenkunde, 4. Leiden: E. J. Brill.
Van Renselaar, H. C., and R. L. Mellema. 1956. *Asmat: Art from Southwest New Guinea*. Amsterdam: Royal Tropical Institute no. 121; Department of Cultural and Physical Anthropology no. 55 (my pagination).
Vansina, Jan. 1961. *De la tradition orale: essai de méthode historique*. Tervuren, Belgique: Musée Royal de l'Afrique centrale.
———. 1984. *Art history in Africa: An introduction to method*. London: Longman.
VanStone, James W. 1968–69. Masks of the Point Hope Eskimo. *Anthropos* 63–64:828–40.
Vercoutter, J. 1964. Egypte. In *Dictionnaire archéologique des techniques*, 2. vols., s.v. Masque, 2:593–94. Paris: Editions de l'Accueil.
Villeminot, Jacques, and Paule Villeminot. 1966. *La Nouvelle-Guinée: 700 000 Papous, survivants de la préhistoire*. Verviers: Marabout Université.
Vlček, Emanuel, and Jiří Kukla. 1959. Halstatské kultovní masky z lid'skych lebek z Hraskovy jeskyne z Kilenc-fa v jihoslovenském krasu. *Pamàtky archeologické* 2:507–56.
Vormann, Franz. 1911. Tänze und Tanzfestlichkeiten der Monumbo-Papua (Deutsch-Neuguinea). *Anthropos* 6:411–27.
Vrydagh, P. André. 1968. Trois masques tonga. *Objets et mondes* 8, no. 3:227–32.
Wagner, Roy. 1984. Ritual as communication: Order, meaning, and secrecy in Melanesian initiation rites. *Annual review of anthropology* 13:143–55.
Waite, Deborah. 1966. Kwakiutl transformation masks. In *The many faces of primitive art: A critical anthology*, ed. D. Fraser, pp. 266–300. Englewood Cliffs, N.J.: Prentice Hall.
Walden E. 1940. Totenfeiern und Malagane von Nord-Neumecklenburg (Nach Aufzeichnungen von E. Walden, bearbeitet von Hans Nevermann). *Zeitschrift für Ethnologie* 72:11–38.
Wassing, René S. 1977. *Asmat, een verdwijnende koppensnellerskultuur in Irian Jaya*. Delft: Volkenkundig Museum Nusantara.
Webster, Hutton. 1968 [1932]. *Primitive secret societies: A study in early politics and religion*. New York: Octagon Books, Inc.
Weil, Peter M. 1971. The masked figure and social control: The Mandinka case. *Africa* 41:279–93.
Wells, Louis T., Jr. 1977. The harley masks of Northeast Liberia. *African Arts* 10, no. 2:22–27, 91–92.
Westermark, Edward. 1906–1908. *The origin and development of the moral ideas*. 2 vols. London: Macmillan and Co.

Whyte, Susan Reynolds. 1977–78. What difference does the difference make? *Folk* 19–20:5–13.
Wiebe, Donald. 1987. The prelogical mentality revisited. *Religion* 17: 29–61.
Williams, Francis Edgar. 1940. *Drama of Orokolo: The social and ceremonial life of the Elema.* Oxford: Clarendon Press.
Williams, Martin A. J., and Hugues Faure, eds. 1980. *The Sahara and the Nile: Quaternary environments and prehistoric occupation in northern Africa.* Rotterdam: A. A. Balkema.
Wilson, Edmund. 1956. *Red, black, blond and olive. Studies in four civilizations: Zuñi, Haiti, Soviet Russia, Israel.* London: W.H. Allen.
Winzinger, Franz. 1964. Die Steinmaske aus dem Heiligen Land. *Pantheon* 22:151–54.
Wissler, Clark. 1946. *Masks.* Science Guide No. 96. New York: American Museum of Natural History.
Zahan, Dominique. 1960. *Sociétés d'initiation bambara: le n'domo, le korè.* Paris: Mouton.
Zelenietz, Martin, and Jill Grant. 1980. Kilenge *Narogo*: Ceremonies, resources and prestige in a West New Britain society. *Oceania* 51:98–117.
Zemp, Hugo. 1965. Eine esoterishce Überlieferung über den Ursprung der maskierten Stelzentänzer bei den Dan (Elfenbeinküste). In *Festschrift Alfred Bühler,* ed. C. A. Schmitz and R. Wildhaber, pp. 451–66. Basel: Pharos-Verlag.
Zerries, Otto. 1962. Les religions des peuples archaïques de l'Amérique du Sud et des Antilles. In *Les religions amérindiennes.* By W. Krickeberg, H. Trimborn, W. Müller and O. Zerries, pp. 327–465. Trans. L. Jospin: Paris: Payot.
Zimoń, Henryk. 1986. Wilhelm Schmidt's theory of primitive monotheism and its critique within the Vienna school of ethnology. *Anthropos* 81:243–60.
Züchner, Christian. 1972. Die Menschendarstellungen des französischen Jungpaläolithikums: Ein Beitrag zur Geschichte der eiszeitlichen Kunst in Westeuropa. Inaugural-Dissertation der Philosophischen Fakultät der Friedrich-Alexander-Universität Erlangen-Nürnberg.
Zwernemann, Jürgen. 1978. Masken der Bobo-Ule und Nuna im Hamburgischen Museum für Völkerkunde. *Mitteilungen aus dem Museum für Völkerkunde in Hamburg* 8:45–83.

Index of Authors and of Principal Peoples and Regions Cited

Abdel-Rasoul, K., 99
Abua, 126
Adams, M., 12, 99, 121, 126, 128, 143, 145
Adande, A., 13
Adelman, K., 121
Aerts, Th., 68
Africa, 5, 9, 16, 19–20, 21–22, 27, 30, 31–32, 35, 37, 41, 42, 45, 64–66, 71, 72, 77, 79, 81, 85, 105, 110, 119–21, 125, 127–28, 130–31, 137, 143, 147, 151, 153, 161
Alaska, 71
Algeria, 36
Alon, D., 38
America, 5, 9, 16, 19–20, 26–27, 41, 45, 71–77, 81, 101, 105, 110, 121, 125, 127, 132, 143, 147, 151, 153–54, 161
Amiet, P., 40
Anati, E., 30
Angola, 149, 151
Andree, R., 2
Aniakor, Ch. C., 64–65
Ankermann, B., 146
Antiquity, 26, 106–107
Apaches, 107
Arawak, 76
Asia, 6, 9, 16, 27, 106, 165
Asmat, 87–90, 100, 110
Augé, M., 48, 155
Australia, 27
Avdeev, A., 147
D'Azevedo, W., 137, 149
Aztecs, 81

Bachelard, G., 125
Baer, G., 146
Baining, 68, 78, 83, 97, 126, 145, 151
Bambara (Bamana), 46, 62–63, 78, 126, 133, 145
Banks Islands, 96

Barguet, P., 38
Barnett, R. D., 23, 40
Bartels, M., 82
Bar-Yosef, O., 37–39
Bastian, A., 2, 13, 18
Bastin, M., 64, 93, 145, 147, 149, 151
Bateson, G., 128
Beaudoin, G., 46, 50
Bedaux, R. M. A., 51
Bédouin, J.-L., 17, 22, 24, 41–42, 74, 87, 125
Beeman, W., 71
Bégouën, H., 25, 26, 28
Beier, U., 122, 153
Benin, 19
Bensa, A., 66
Bering Straits, 71, 147
Bernolles, J., 31–32, 60
Binford, L. R., 81
Birket-Smith, K., 23
Bismarck Archipelago, 68
Bleakley, P., 9
Boas, F., 73, 147, 151
Bobo, 12, 21, 63, 127–30, 132
Bochet, G., 13, 132, 164
Boggiani, G., 149
Bolens, J., 151
Borgatti, J. M., 19, 47, 93
Borgeaud, Ph., 19
Borgeaud, W., 13
Bororo, 156
Boston, J. S., 64, 126, 146, 149, 151, 156
Bourges, A., 17
Bozo, 63
Bradbury, R. E., 111
Bravmann, R. A., 16
Brazil, 91, 98, 101, 143
Breuil, H., 23–28, 81
Brown, H. A., 70
Bühler, A., 14, 37, 82, 84, 86–87, 91
Bunzel, R. L., 76, 129

Buraud, G., 13, 125, 127
Burkert, W., 17
Burkina Faso, 12, 16, 19, 46, 63–64
Bushmen, 27

Caillois, R., 123–24
Calame, C., 131
Calame-Griaule, G., 46–48, 51, 53, 59, 109, 152
Cameroon, 146
Campbell, J., 26
Camps, G., 29–31, 35, 36–37
Capitan, J. L., 24
Cartailhac, E., 23–24, 27
Cauvin, J., 37
Cazeneuve, J., 6, 74, 76, 118
Chappaz-Wirthner, S., 4, 17, 105
China, 19, 101
Chokwe, 149
Christinger, R., 13
Cissé, Y., 62, 123, 145
Clark, J. G. D., 23, 36
Codrington, R. H., 69, 96, 110
Cole, H. M., 21–22, 32, 64, 93, 119, 124, 136, 143
Congo-Brazzaville, 64
Contenson, H. de, 37
Coquet, A., 70–71
Cornevin, R., 51
Cranstone, B. A. L., 9
Crowley, D. J., 149
Cubeo, 76–77, 78

Dall, W. H., 18, 147
Damm, H., 82–84
Dan, 12, 19, 62–63, 129, 151
Dark, Ph., 96
Deacon, A. B., 91, 95–96, 150–51
De Bilde, M., 53
Delafosse, M., 51
Delange, J., 32, 54, 121, 125
DeMott, B., 46
Denich, B., 155
Deonna, W., 24
Dieterlen, G., 31, 46–56, 59–63, 108, 111, 123, 145, 153
Dietschy, H. J., 77, 150, 153
Disselhoff, H.-D., 72, 147
Dogon, 46–63, 66, 107–09, 121, 126–27, 129, 132, 137, 139–40, 143–45, 147, 149, 151–52, 164
Dohrenwend, D., 19
Douglas, M., 18, 48
Drewal, H. J., 19, 64, 131–32, 146, 149
Drewal, M. Th., 19, 64, 132, 146
Dumézil, G., 165
Dupré, M.-C., 64
Duvignaud, J., 17, 22

Ebeling, I., 13
Edo, 19
Egypt, 12, 26–27, 29, 34, 38, 42, 101–02
Elema, 70, 89–92, 145
Eliade, M., 13, 41, 80, 90, 96, 119–20, 122, 133–34, 137–38
Elisofon, E., 48
Errington, F. K., 19
Eskimo (see Inuit)
Etruria, 101
Eurasia, 146
Europe, 1, 3, 6, 9, 20, 23–29, 34, 38, 42, 81, 106, 136–37, 165
Evans-Pritchard, E. E., 125, 157, 159
Eyo, E., 126

Fagg, W., 48, 64
Faure, Henri, 125
Faure, Hugues, 35
Fenton, W. N., 17, 26, 128–29, 153
Fischer, E., 12, 63, 129, 137, 146
Fitzhugh, W. W., 71
Forge, A., 149
Fortes, M., 48, 111–12
Foss, P., 146
Fraser, D., 19, 107
Frazer, J. G., 103
Freud, S., 103–04, 107, 109, 112
Frobenius, L., 2, 26–27, 69, 81–82, 145

Gambia, 153
Ganay, S. de, 55
Gardi, R., 14
Gilbert, S., 17
Gill, S., 124
Gimbutas, M., 38–40
Girard, J., 16
Girard, M. F., 82, 85–86, 93

Glotz, S., 16, 17, 41
Gola, 149
Goldman, I., 77, 93
Goonatilleka, M. H., 12
Gow-Smith, F., 143, 150
Gran Chaco, 147
Grant, J., 86, 96
Graziosi, P., 30, 34
Green, K. L., 16, 19
Gregor, J., 17–18
Gregory, C. A., 85
Griaule, M., 46–62, 79, 108–09, 121–22, 126–28, 130, 137, 139, 144–45, 149, 153, 164
Grimes, R. L., 13
Grimm, J. and W., 1
Groves, W. C., 101
Gründ, F., 71
Gruyter, W. J. de, 119
Guiart, J., 37, 66–68, 82–87, 110, 146, 149, 155
Guidieri, R., 141, 160
Guilaine, J., 39
Guillemaut, D., 17
Guinea, 143, 147

Haddon, A. C., 143, 151
Halpin, M., 119
Halverson, J., 28
Hampaté Ba, A., 31
Harley, G. W., 129, 149
Harper, P., 64, 146
Hart, K., 48
Hartmann, G., 13, 91, 98, 146–47
Hauser-Schäublin, B., 70
Hebron, 37
Heine-Geldern, R., 138
Helfrich, K., 82, 84, 86
Hendry, J., 17, 129
Hertz, R., 99, 108
Hesse, K., 68
Hewicker, F., 123
Heyden, M. V., 145–46
Himmelheber, H., 63, 123, 129–30, 138, 146, 149
Hinckley, P., 147–48
Hipszer, H., 79, 123
Ho, Ch. K., 81
Höfler, O., 26

Holas, B., 64, 128, 132, 143, 145–47, 151, 153
Hole, F., 40
Holm, B., 74
Holt, C., 138
Homefield, H. D., 125
Honigmann, J. H., 125
Hopi, 74
Horton, R., 12
Hua, 146
Hubert, H., 125
Hudson, A. B., 99
Huizinga, J., 51, 160
Hultkrantz, Å., 110
Hummel, S., 146

Ibo (Igbo), 64, 126
Igbirra, 130, 151
Ingold, T., 18, 35
Inuit, 21, 27, 41, 71–73, 79, 147
Irian Jaya, 97–99
Iroquois, 17, 128–29, 137, 144
Ivory Coast, 12–13, 62, 64, 145, 151

Jacobs, S., 155
Japan, 41–42
Jeanmaire, H., 107
Jędrej, M. C., 11, 18, 19
Jensen, A. E., 111, 149, 155, 157
Jericho, 36–38
Jeudy-Ballini, M., 145–46, 150
Joseph, M. B., 146
Joshi, O. P., 15
Juárez Frías, F., 36

Kalabari, 11
Kaplan, S. A., 71
Karaja, 77, 143, 146, 150
Karutz, R., 17
Kaufmann, Ch., 70, 149, 154
Kenyon, K. M., 36–37
Kenyon, W. A., 72
Keppler, J., 129
Khaznadar, Ch., 71
Kiki, A., 70, 91
Kilenge, 96
Kirby, E.-T., 136
Kiwai, 89, 93
Kleinschmidt, P., 42
Klingbeil, W., 17
Knudsen, L., 137

Koehler, H. K. L., 13
Kono, 143, 145, 147
Koppers, W., 18
Krantz, C., 68, 70
Krause, F., 143, 146, 154
Krickeberg, W., 9
Krieger, K., 54, 60
Kroeber, A. L., 18, 138
Krusche, R., 138
Kuba, 64
Kuhn, R., 17, 125
Kukla, J., 36, 81
Kutscher, C., 54, 60
Kwakiutl, 72–74
Kwoma, 154

Labrador, 21
Lafargue, F., 128, 151
La Fontaine, J., 157
Laguna, F. de, 147
Lajoux, J.-D., 31–33
Lakalai, 121
Lalande, A., 121
Lamberg-Karlovsky, C. C. and M., 41
Laming-Emperaire, A., 27–28
Lamp, F., 147
Landtman, G., 90, 93–94, 146, 155
Lantier, R., 24, 81
Laplanche, J., 112
Laufer, C., 17, 68, 97, 126, 137, 147, 149
Lawal, B., 31
Layard, J., 90–91, 95–96, 99
Leach, E., 107, 137
Lechevallier, M., 37
Leenhardt, M., 66, 68, 85, 132, 137
Lehuard, R., 64
Leiris, M., 16, 32, 46, 54, 121, 125
Leleur, A., 137, 141
Le Moal, G., 12, 21, 64, 127–30, 132
Lengua, 147
Le Quellec, J.-L., 24, 30–31, 35
Leroi-Gourhan, A., 24, 26–28, 34, 120
Lévi-Strauss, C., 9, 13, 15, 18, 20–21, 72, 74, 77, 132, 135, 156
Lévy-Bruhl, L., 26, 94, 117–20, 123–24
Lewis, A. B., 90
Lewis, G., 19, 162

Lewis-Williams, J. D., 30
Lhote, H., 30–32
Liberia, 12, 62, 147–49
Lips, E., 82
Little, K. L., 123, 145
Lomas, P. W., 85
Lommel, A., 9, 13, 32, 37
Long, Ch. H., 134
Lot-Falck, E., 13, 72
Lowie, R. H., 138
Lucas, H., 28
Lumley, H. de, 26, 81
Lunda-Batshioko, 151
Luneau, R., 110
Lupu, F., 164

MacGowan, K., 13
McIntosh, S. K. and R. J., 21, 31, 35
McNaughton, P. R., 20, 128
Maertens, J.-Th., 15
Maesen, A., 41
Malekula, 82, 90, 94–97, 151
Mali, 13, 46, 62, 64, 107
Mamiya, Ch. J., 70
Mandinka, 153
Mannhardt, W., 1
Maquet, J., 60, 124
Marind-Anim, 89
Maringer, J., 24, 26, 28, 81
Mark, P., 16, 133, 149
Marka, 63
Marshack, A., 26
Mauss, M., 13, 15, 72, 125, 131, 157
Mead, M., 17
Meigs, A. S., 146
Melanesia, 5, 9, 19, 37, 45, 66–71, 77, 82–99, 102, 105, 107, 110, 121, 125, 127, 130–31, 137, 143, 147, 151, 153–54, 161
Mellaart, J., 35, 40
Mellema, R. L., 87
Mende, 19, 129, 145, 148, 152
Merriam, A. P., 32, 149
Métraux, A., 154
Meuli, K., 3, 5, 16–17, 104–07, 109, 113, 122, 155
Meyer, A. B., 11
Michel-Jones, F., 46–48
Millot, J., 13

Mitchell, J. C., 111–12
Montandon, G., 6, 10, 13, 17, 41, 66, 72
Monts, L. P., 16
Moore, F., 149
Mori, F., 29, 30, 35
Mossi, 46
Mulamba, M., 64
Müller, W., 72–74, 146
Museum für Völkerkunde Basel, 70, 84
Muzzolini, A., 31–32, 35
Mycenae, 40, 42, 101
Mylonas, G. E., 40, 42

Nahal Hemar, 37–38
Narr, K. J., 26
Naskapi, 21
Navaho, 145
Ndembu, 151
Near East, 35, 37, 42
Nebesky-Wojkowitz, R. de, 126
Nelson, E. W., 71, 73, 117
Nevermann, H., 13, 69, 81, 89, 91, 94, 96, 110, 122, 146, 153
New Britain, 68, 83–84, 96–97, 121, 126, 128, 132, 145, 150, 151
New Caledonia, 66–67, 132
Newcomb, F. J., 145
New Guinea, 5, 14, 69–70, 82, 87–94, 110, 146, 151, 154
New Ireland, 84, 101
New Mexico, 74, 126
New Quebec, 21
Nicklin, K., 107, 147
Niessen, C., 13
Nigeria, 19, 64, 126, 130, 144, 151
Noma, S., 42
Nukuma, 154
Nuna, 132
Nyonyosi, 49

Oceania, 9, 19, 37, 41, 82, 107, 110
Offiong, D. A., 93, 126
Ogibenin, B. L., 131
Opler, M. E., 107–108
Orokolo, 70, 89, 145
Ortoli, H., 107
Ottenberg, S., 137, 157

Palavecino, E., 9
Panoff, M., 138
Pâques, V., 62
Parker, A. C., 138
Parkinson, A., 11
Parsons, E. C., 76
Paulme, D., 13, 47, 54, 126, 145, 149, 153
Peek, Ph. M., 12, 151
Peekel, G., 69
Pemberton, J., 64
Penner, H. H., 118, 134, 162
Pérez Rodriguez, B., 36
Pernet, H., 5
Perret, R., 34
Perrin, M., 138
Perrot, J., 37
Peul, 31, 46, 62
Phillips, R. B., 147
Picard, Ch., 42
Piette, E., 24
Pollaczek, P. P., 125
Polynesia, 9
Pontalis, J.-B., 112
Poole, F. J. P., 18
Poole, J., 90, 151
Pouwer, J., 91, 97–99, 149, 151
Poynor, R., 19, 144
Ptak, W., 146
Pueblo, 74

Rabaté, M., 16
Ray, D., 79
Redinha, J., 151
Reed, R. C., 24
Reinbacher, E., 23
Reinhardt, L. R., 145, 147, 153
Richards, J. V., 129, 147
Riesenfeld, A., 66
Riley, O. L., 58
Ritzenthaler, R. E., 149
Rivers, W. H. R., 69, 143, 146
Rohrlich-Leavitt, R., 155
Rollefson, G. O., 37
Röllin, W., 17, 105
Rome, 101
Rønneseth, O., 35
Rosenfeld, A., 24
Rosse, H., 13

Roy, Ch. D., 19
Rütimeyer, L., 131, 146

Sahara, 29–35
Sainte-Fare Garnot, J., 12
Sanday, P. R., 137, 140
Schaeffer, C. F. A., 41
Schieffelin, E. L., 91
Schmidt, W., 136, 138
Schneider-Lengyel, I., 15–17
Schultz, H., 101
Schweeger-Hefel, A., 19, 49
Schwimmer, E., 48, 150
Segy, L., 13
Senoufo, 13, 32, 64, 151, 164
Sepik, 5, 69, 82
Serpenti, L. M., 85
Shalleck, J., 13
Siberia, 101
Sieber, R., 11
Siegmann, W., 22, 137
Sierra Leone, 129, 147
Simmons, A. H., 37
Songye, 32
Speck, F. G., 21, 128–29, 132, 144, 146
Speiser, F., 16, 19, 82, 84, 107, 131–32, 136
Spiro, M. E., 6, 80, 111
Stanek, M., 69–70
Stevens, Ph. Jr., 16
Stöhr, W., 111
Striedter, K. H., 31, 34
Sturtevant, W. C., 129
Sulka, 145, 150
Sumnik, E. C., 70
Susa, 40
Swiss, 4

Tait, D., 46
Tassili n'Ajjer, 29–32
Tedlock, D., 74, 76, 126, 153
Teilhet, J. H., 9, 15
Teke, 64
Tellem, 49–51
Thiam, B., 151
Thiele, P., 27
Thomas, L.-V., 110
Thompson, R. F., 133
Tibet, 101, 126

Tikar, 146
Tischner, H., 123
Tonkin, E., 157
Tooker, E., 144
Torres Straits, 151
Toura, 145
Tukano, 76
Tukuna, 98
Turner, L. W., 21
Turner, V. W., 146, 151
Tuzin, D., 111
Tylor, E. B., 2, 103, 110

Ucko, P. J., 24
Ugarit, 40
Underwood, L., 107
Unrug, K., 130, 151

Valentine, C. A., 68, 119, 121, 139, 149
Vallois, H. V., 36, 81
Van Baal, J., 89, 91, 96
Van Baaren, Th., 37
Vandenhoute, P. J. L., 16, 63
Van Renselaar, H. C., 87, 90–91
Vansina, J., 31, 34, 138, 155
VanStone, J. W., 72
Vanuatu, 16, 42, 80, 94
Vercoutter, J., 38
Villeminot, J. and P., 18, 124
Vlček, E., 36, 81
Vormann, P., 145, 151
Vrydagh, P. A., 146

Wagner, R., 48
Waite, D., 73
Walden, E., 87
Wassing, R. S., 87–88
Wè, 121, 145
Webster, H., 137
Weil, P. M., 128, 153
Wells, L. T., Jr., 63
Westermarck, E., 103, 110
Whyte, S. R., 142
Wiebe, D., 118
Williams, F. E., 70–71, 89–92, 145
Williams, M., 35
Wilson, E., 126, 128
Winzinger, F., 37
Wissler, C., 9

Yorkshire, 35
Yoruba, 19, 31, 64, 122, 131–32, 145
Zahan, D., 62, 63, 127, 133, 146
Zaire, 32, 64
Zambia, 151
Zara, 16
Zelenietz, M., 86, 96
Zemp, H., 151, 153
Zerries, O., 76–77, 80, 147, 149
Zimoń, H., 138
Zorzi, R., 36
Züchner, Ch., 26
Zuñi, 74, 76, 126, 129, 146
Zwernemann, J., 132

www.ingramcontent.com/pod-product-compliance
Lightning Source LLC
Chambersburg PA
CBHW062028220426
43662CB00010B/1514